Three Years in Afghanistan

An American Family's Story of Faith, Endurance, and Love

MATTHEW COLLINS

Endorsements for Three Years in Afghanistan

Riveting! Heartrending! Challenging! I haven't read a more compelling story in years. This book is a story of compassion, courage, faithfulness, and grace in the most difficult of circumstances. It stimulated my faith to grow as I was reminded what God can do if you totally surrender to Him. I devoured this book. You have to read it!

David Stevens, MD
Chief Executive Officer
Christian Medical & Dental Associations

Anyone who earnestly seeks to imitate God by sacrificially loving others will eventually arrive at the crossroads of faith and fear. Through masterful storytelling, Matthew Collins discloses his struggle to fully trust God with his wife and children in post-Taliban Afghanistan. Many of my Memphis co-workers and I had the good fortune of working with Matthew and his team, seeing firsthand how they struggled to acquire language and cultural skills as a foundation for their wide-ranging humanitarian service to the Afghan people. There was plenty to be afraid of, including kidnapping threats, spontaneous anti-Western riots, and pitched street battles between rival warlords. Over the years, more than a few committed Western aid workers violently lost their lives.

Three Years in Afghanistan is the story of imperfect men and women who repeatedly opted for faith rather than fear, perseverance rather than retreat. By holding fast to their conviction that God had led them to Afghanistan, Matthew and his team provided food to starving villages, cured thousands of patients (mostly women and children) with tuberculosis, and provided job skills and computer training in one of the remotest corners of the country. All the while they sought to love Afghans and understand the wild idiosyncrasies of Afghan culture. Anyone who has ever dreamed of living a God-glorifying, world-defying, risk-taking life will enjoy learning from Matthew Collins.

Rick Donlon, MD
Co-founder and CEO
Resurrection Health

This true tale of one American family, helping lead humanitarian relief in shattered Afghanistan, is both inspiring and instructive. It is a story of innovation and creativity in the harshest and most dangerous of circumstances. But it is also an account of extraordinary cross-cultural cooperation: Christians genuinely loving Muslims in pursuit of a vision to make the world better. A must read.

Rod D. Martin
CEO of The Martin Organization
part of the startup team at PayPal,
dubbed a "tech guru" by Fox Business

Matthew Collins is a vivid storyteller who weaves candidness and truths into his life experiences and then openly shares them with us. *Three Years in Afghanistan* is his and his family's journey and presents a great read for anyone contemplating cross-cultural service. It strips away the romanticism and idealism of working overseas, looks at the struggles and joys in an objective way, and challenges the reader to look beyond the surface and count the cost to follow Christ to the ends of the earth.

Jeff Palmer
Executive Director
Baptist Global Response

As a military veteran of multiple tours in Afghanistan, I wholeheartedly recommend *Three Years in Afghanistan*. In 2003, the coalition presence provided Matt Collins and his team of aid workers a window of relative stability in Afghanistan to help those impoverished by years of war and Taliban oppression. Not one to sit by the side and just offer ideas, Matt leveraged his years of experience serving in difficult places to move his family to a remote region of Afghanistan so that they could live amongst the Afghan people to provide desperately needed humanitarian aid and community health development. I encourage everyone to read this true story of an American family making a difference and standing in the gap that many of us held open so that they could meet the personal needs of the Afghan people.

For those considering such a mission as Matt's, this book marks the trail for you to follow. Matt and Christine are people of action who demonstrate how to exhibit cultural sensitivity and humility enabling them to live among and serve a people the outside world knows very little about. I also lived amongst the Afghan people, but did so with guns, helicopters, and HESCO barriers...with my family safely back in the USA. Matt, Christine, and their young daughter and son did it with nothing more than faith and a desire to serve others more than self. This book will inspire you to action.

Brig. General Robert Armfield
United States Air Force

For Christine.
I love you with all my heart.

Table of Contents

Part IV: Adapt

Part V: Overcome

Part VI: Love

Prologue

September 12, 2004, midday

The sound of a nearby explosion interrupted my thoughts. Everyone had said that Iskandar[1] was the safest city in Afghanistan, a place where reasonable minds prevail over hysteria and violence. Not today.

The sky was full of acrid smoke from nearby burning compounds, while the noise of automatic gunfire—punctuated by grenade blasts—slightly obfuscated the shouts of the mob outside:

"Down with Karzai! Death to America!"

Staying low, I glanced out the window from the second story of our downtown office. American military helicopters buzzed the city at a hundred feet, flying around the plumes of smoke and competing with dozens of kites for airspace.

Don't cut down the kids' kites, I thought for a fleeting second.

I needed to get back to the safer basement area where the women—and my one-year-old daughter Ellie—were taking cover. I paused for a moment to collect my thoughts. *What am I doing here?*

That wasn't the real question that was tormenting me. I was asking myself why I had brought my family to Afghanistan.

---

1   Name changed due to security

Part I

Call

Wanted. Men for hazardous journey. Low wages. Bitter cold.
Long hours of complete darkness. Safe return doubtful.
Honor and recognition in the event of success.
—Ernest Shackleton, in his 1907 recruitment ad in
the London Times for his *Endurance* expedition to the South Pole

I shall be telling this with a sigh, somewhere ages and ages hence:
Two roads diverged in a wood, and I—I took the one less traveled by,
And that has made all the difference.
—Robert Frost

Chapter 1

Welcome to Afghanistan!

Could I bring my family here? The wheels of my mind dwarfed the drone of our small, twin-engine plane as it cut through the mountains of northern Afghanistan. Squinting my eyes, I made out the shape of a small village jammed underneath a mountain crag in a valley two miles below. *Could Christine and I raise kids in a place like this?*

Wade craned his neck and got my attention, snapping me back to our present situation. "We are off course!" he shouted above the noise of the props. "Should have passed the Nuristani Mountains by now and be looking into the Wahan Corridor to the east. We're heading in the wrong direction!" That meant we were now headed right for Taliban-occupied territory.

It was July 2001 and my first day in Afghanistan. Wade had served as an aid worker for many years in Central Asia and had

3

convinced my good friend, James, and me to accompany him on a humanitarian mission to Faizabad, capital of Badakhshan Province, the last stronghold of the Northern Alliance. The Taliban had seized control of nearly 90 percent of Afghanistan, but a rag-tag army composed of a shaky alliance between Uzbek and Tajik commanders was holding them off from this last piece of terra firma in northeast Afghanistan under the command of the indomitable Ahmed Shah Massoud. Revered as the "Lion of Panshir," Massoud had fought the Russians two decades before and was now the last man standing between the Taliban and this more moderate corner of the country. The small town of Faizabad was filled with refugee camps, the educated elite who had fled from the Taliban, and the administration of Rabbani, the rightful President of Afghanistan as recognized by most countries.

Several hours earlier, Wade, James, and I had boarded a United Nations King Air plane in Islamabad, Pakistan, bound direct for Faizabad. But now we were headed toward the northern city of Mazar-i-Sharif, which had recently fallen to the Taliban. The mountains gave way to a more lunar landscape as we approached Mazar. I swallowed hard as we landed.

At the airport in Mazar, I came face-to-face with the Taliban for the first time. Grizzly bearded men wearing black turbans, traditional *shalwar kamis* (baggy trousers and tunics), and Ray-Ban aviator sunglasses surrounded our plane. Each had a well-used AK-47, and none looked thrilled to see us. The carcasses of several Russian fighter jets and rusting tanks littered the airfield. An old Mercedes with several more Talibs waited at a distance next to the dust-covered runway. We wondered if we were going to be spending the next few months in Mazar-i-Sharif as involuntary guests. *This trip might be over before it started!* I thought to myself. This wasn't what I had in mind when I'd kissed my wife goodbye a few days earlier. I silently prayed: *God, please get us through this. I want to see Christine again!*

"I'm going to take a quick picture. That all right?" James asked from the seat behind me. He was the one who had actually roped me into this trip. James was the best networker I knew, constantly meeting new people and knowing immediately where they should plug in. He'd met Wade at a conference somewhere the year before, and now here we were in Afghanistan! James was full of sports analogies and new ideas, most of them good. He exuded energy, drank a lot of coffee, and made split-second decisions. I loved the fact that James always spoke his mind; he had a big heart, and you always knew where you stood with him. He was an effective leader, working in the area of vocational rehabilitation. But this was his first trip outside the United States (except for a honeymoon in Cancun). He'd resembled a kid in a candy shop in Pakistan, talking with everyone and taking pictures. Wade killed his idea with a look and calmly instructed us to stay in our seats.

Our hotshot pilot jumped out of his seat and helped unload some cargo from the back of the plane. Several Talibs approached the plane and looked us over suspiciously, but much to our relief, no one looked in our bags or checked our American passports with Northern-Alliance issued visas, which were illegal and unwelcome in Taliban country. Ten minutes later we were again airborne, both relieved and perplexed at why our pilot hadn't informed us about his unscheduled detour. I shook my head. *OK, this is outside my comfort zone. I don't know anything about this place!* I leaned back to James and yelled, "We are no longer in Kansas!"

Less than an hour later we landed on the perforated metal airstrip of Faizabad, now safe in Northern Alliance territory. I locked out the window to see several Russian jeeps and a small crowd of armed men—all dusty and wearing earth-colored shalwar kamis. I tried to pick out the several Americans I knew would be in the crowd, but with beards and local clothing, they blended right in. My eye was drawn to a fair-skinned girl holding a sign written in large English letters: "WELCOME TO AFGHANISTAN!" I thought: *That little girl looks like an American! Living in the middle of Afghanistan!* We got off the plane and met Grace: eight years old, light brown hair, blue eyes, and with a demeanor as comfortable in her town of Faizabad as in a city park. She stood next to her daddy, an American aid worker and one of our hosts. Grace greeted us warmly, with a promise to show us her house and toys. "And you can even meet my pet bird!" *Wow. These guys have created an oasis for their families in Afghanistan. It's possible!*

Our American hosts were eager to show us around Faizabad, but we stood out in our Western clothes. They took us to their mud-walled compound where we quickly changed into the shalwar kamis that we had purchased in Pakistan. These traditional Afghan clothes start with a pair of very baggy trousers—with a waistline large enough to encompass several grown men—pulled together by a string. A knee-length tunic is then worn on top. Blending in a little better, we proceeded on a walking tour.

The town of Faizabad had been just a small provincial capital before the onslaught of refugees fleeing the Taliban. Marco Polo had traveled through here in 1273 AD, and apparently not much had changed since his visit. The town once had limited electricity due to a small hydro generator on the river, but twenty years of fighting had blown Faizabad back to the dark ages. Several dozen vehicles plied the town's dirt roads, but transportation for the majority of the population was by foot or by animal. Homes and shops were constructed from mud, straw, and rock. Men used the wind to separate wheat from chaff on threshing floors and then ground it into flour using millstones that were powered by diverted water, just as they had done centuries ago. Despite the fact that we were in an area outside Taliban control, women still wore the all-encompassing burqa, even in the oppressive heat of the day.

Faizabad is ringed by rugged hills, most of which were crowned by pieces of artillery. The raging Kokcha River, fed by melting snow from the Hindu Kush, bisects the town, bringing life to this

6

otherwise dry part of the world. A ribbon of green poplar and fruit trees lined the river and grew in some courtyards. Otherwise, the color of the town was shades of brown. "This is a dry and weary land, where there is little water," James whispered.

We ended up in the heart of Faizabad: the bazaar. Taking advantage of their position on the Silk Road between Europe and the East, the inhabitants of Afghanistan survived the centuries as raiders and traders. Afghans are natural businessmen and dearly love the bazaar. Around us, ancient-looking men sold potatoes, rice, apricots, cherries, chickens, nails, and hand grenades. I approached a small stand where two weathered gray beards were selling AK-47s, rocket-propelled grenades (RPGs), and Russian Makarov pistols. Fifty dollars could buy you a dodgy-looking RPG; for a hundred you could be the proud owner of a Chinese-made AK-47. One man put it this way: "You foreigners love your cameras, but we Afghans love our guns." Indeed, it was a fashion statement for a man to have an AK-47 slung over his shoulder, and many did. This was a land at war, and these men were preparing to make a last stand.

Rudyard Kipling wrote the following in his 1892 poem "The Young British Soldier:"

When you're wounded and left on Afghanistan's plains
And the women come out to cut up what remains
Jest roll on your rifle an' blow out your brains
An' go to your Gawd like a soldier.

But looking around on that afternoon in late July 2001, that is not what I saw. I didn't see bloodthirsty men who hated Americans ... I saw people who were doing their best to protect and provide for their families and who were determined to maintain their way of life. They disliked the Taliban more than I did. The Afghans in Faizabad were friendly, hospitable, and hopeful that we would see something deeper in their country than just tragedy and devastation. Refugees who were slowly starving asked us if we were having a good experience in their country.

Looking around at faces that afternoon in the bazaar—just several hours after arriving in Afghanistan—many of my preconceived notions about Afghans were challenged. This was a land of extremes and paradoxes: while most of the men knew how to fight, there was a more gentle side that few outsiders had seen. I saw one man proudly bearing his weapon and another lovingly cradling his young child. Society treated women as second class yet honored their guests with a level of hospitality unknown in the Western world. I found their resoluteness and lack of self-pity in the face of extreme hardship to be encouraging—these people were humans just like me, they loved their families like I love mine, and they were worthy of respect. "These are a noble-minded people," James whispered in my ear.

As we walked, Wade explained that most of these Afghans we were meeting had kind feelings toward the US for our country's aid in the *mujahedeen's* fight against the Soviets in the '80s. They hoped that America would eventually give them a hand in their existential fight against the Taliban.

Over the next few days, we saw the dire humanitarian situation in Faizabad up close. Refugees were living in squalid camps next to the river; entire households were dwelling in small tents supplied by the United Nations. We were told that many of the women were not able to leave the tent to go to the public latrine because the family was too poor to afford appropriate head coverings. There were few education facilities for the refugees. Most were hungry. We watched children with swollen bellies playing on scrapped Russian tanks.

"That little girl…she could be my daughter," James observed, choking back tears. He and his wife had adopted a little girl three years prior.

"I wish there was something we could do for her…right now!" I responded.

We met former physicians and university professors who had fled the Taliban when Kabul fell. They were now working as tailors and carpenters in town, trying to cobble together enough of a living to keep their families alive. There was no indication things would get any better... the resistance was short on funds and the Taliban was advancing. Everyone thought that when the Taliban did finally overrun Faizabad, it would be a wholesale slaughter.

Despite the risk, the aid workers in Faizabad were doing all they could to meet human needs. They were feeding thousands of refugees each day, building and supplying schools, and providing basic health services and education. They assisted villagers with maintaining their livestock, trained widows in small, home-based business (like sewing), and tried to introduce sustainable technology into the communities, such as simple solar ovens. They lived in simple mud houses with little electricity and worked in dangerous conditions, but I never heard them complain. These people were making a difference. They inspired me.

As a teenager, I had a drive to succeed, but it was self-centered. I grew up in a military family and thought that I would be a success if I could become a fighter pilot. My goal in life was to go to the Air Force Academy and to fly F-16s. Then, at the age of fifteen, I had a near-death experience (or at least it seemed like it at the time). I was alone in a canoe out in the bay, trying to paddle home against a strong current, when the dorsal fin of a large shark popped up only a few feet away. The shark was tracking me! As I paddled as hard as I could toward shore, I promised God that I would serve Him with my life if He would save me.

I quickly forgot about that promise, but then I experienced God personally my senior year of high school. I went on a missions trip where I was exposed to the needs of the world. More importantly, I met God on that trip. He opened the eyes of my heart to understand the wonder of knowing Him through faith in Jesus Christ. The promise of Psalm 37:4 became my heartbeat: "Delight yourself also

9

in the Lord, and He will give you the desires of your heart." I discovered that nothing compares to a real, personal relationship with the Creator of the cosmos. Not even flying jets! God changed the desires of my heart—now I wanted to honor Him by making a difference in the lives of other people, particularly those in greatest need.

I changed my trajectory from the Air Force Academy to a different course. Initially my family and friends thought I was crazy. I learned that walking by faith and not by sight can be a lonely road. After university I served overseas for three years, helping with an orphanage in the Philippines and assisting with a project to build a surgical hospital in Mozambique, Africa. Jesus wasn't kidding when He said that it is better to give than to receive: I experienced that joy!

God also created within me a thirst for adventure, and I found plenty of that along the way. Discovering hidden waterfalls in the jungles of Mindanao (and evading would-be abductors on the same island), scuba diving with sharks in South Africa, sailing a native dhow along an archipelago of mysterious islands off the remote northern coast of Mozambique—these were fringe benefits that came from delighting in God. My friends had nicknamed me Indiana Jones, but now I felt junior varsity compared to these new heroes I'd met in Faizabad.

Commander Jon, a young aid worker from Alabama, was something of a local celebrity. His bread kitchens fed hundreds of people every day and he was coordinating the construction of schools for refugee children. But what endeared him to the people of Faizabad was that he had learned their language in less than a year, he sported his turban like a real Afghan, and he clearly loved them. An engineer by training, Jon built an effective water filtration system using rocks, sand, hose, and locally available metal tanks, and then turned it into a project benefiting local communities. "Before I came here I lived with my Mama," he told me one day. "But now I have found my new home."

Commander Jon was famous for playing *buzkashi* ("goat pulling") with the locals. This traditional Afghan version of polo embodies the Afghan spirit and utilizes a decapitated goat, sewn up at the neck, as the "ball." Dozens of men on horseback violently jostle for possession of the ball; the individual who gets it around the field and into a ring scores a point. Whips are used on animals and fellow competitors. The annual buzkashi games in Badakhshan were quite the event. The big man of each village rode his horse into town like a rock star. Some of them never rode home. On the second day of the buzkashi tournament, Jon jumped on a horse and rode into the fray. It didn't take long for him to win the hearts of the entire region, an event that led to his being dubbed "Commander Jon" by President Rabbani. As I got to know Jon, I wondered if I could make a difference in people's lives in Afghanistan like this man had done.

I was impressed with the aid workers I met in Faizabad but also the hospitality of the Afghans. My new aid worker friends explained that one of the most difficult parts of their jobs was conducting village surveys. In every village they visited, hungry people insisted on feeding them a meal before they left. They knew that they were eating food that belonged in the mouths of pregnant women and children. They would try to beg off, but the village leaders would insist to the point of physically preventing them from leaving until they had enjoyed a meal made up of the very best of their food stock. "Perhaps you will reach the next village, and they will hear that we didn't feed you a proper meal," they would explain. "If this happens, our village will have no honor left."

We learned firsthand the famous Afghan saying: "A guest is more valuable than a father." One of the first Afghans I got to know in Faizabad was a friendly doctor named Shafi. Several days after we arrived, Dr. Shafi invited us to his home for dinner.

"*Salaam Aleykum!*" ("Peace be unto you!") I exclaimed, crossing his threshold after leaving my shoes at the door.

11

"*Waleykum a Salaam*," ("And unto you peace") Shafi responded with a smile, grasping my extended hand with both of his.

"*Chitor Asten? Khub Asten? Famil Etan Chitoras? Sehat Shuma Khubas?*" I had been studying a list of greetings that Wade had written out for me on a scrap of paper, and I was pretty sure that Shafi was impressed. He rattled off the same Dari greetings while I was still greeting him, which meant: "How are you? Are you good? How is your family? Is your health good?"

Shafi showed us into a room lit by kerosene lanterns with a large Persian carpet covering the floor. We were escorted to the end of the room farthest from the door—the places of honor—and sat down on the floor on top of cushions and pillows called *toshaks*. (These cushions were the only furniture in almost all the homes of Faizabad and in the rest of Afghanistan.) A boy brought a silver pitcher of warmed water and went from person to person, pouring water over our hands into a basin. A young man unfolded a large, plastic tablecloth called a *dastarkhan*, and the floor was transformed into our table. Several young male relatives entered with large platters full of steaming *kabuli palau* (rice with raisins and diced carrots), *kofte* (minced beef cooked in oil), and *mantu* (a pastry filled with vegetables and meat). The barefoot young men labored to arrange the dozens of platters in front of us on the dastarkhan in decorous fashion.

Once the spread was complete, our host commanded: "*bukhoren!*" (Eat!) No conversation transpired during the meal. I noticed that the Afghans considered the process of eating food to be most important, and they went right at it. Every couple of men shared a large platter of rice, and it was proper manners to serve yourself from the smaller platters and to eat with your right hand. The Afghans were skilled at balling up rice with their right hand and feeding themselves in a neat and dignified manner. I made quite a mess of myself. I tried to use pieces of bread as utensils to ball up my rice and meat, but I couldn't keep the oil from dripping down my arm and by the end of the meal had rice scattered everywhere.

The food was delicious, but we couldn't come close to finishing what was set before us. Our host begged us to eat more three times, and when he was convinced that we were indeed stuffed, the young men brought out a generous assortment of fruit. At least half of the meal still sat before us uneaten, and the young men gathered up the leftovers and took them to the room next door for the women of the house to eat. We leaned back against the tosnaks, and Dr. Shafi began to regale us with stories of Massoud's battles against the Taliban, the plight of refugees in Badakhshan, and exploits of Afghans long ago.

I whispered in Wade's ear: "I think we could do this! My family, I mean. I think I could bring Christine here."

"Then you are certifiably nuts!" he responded. Perhaps he was employing reverse psychology or had accurately surmised that I was trying to impress. Either way, the wheels in my mind were turning.

Dr. Shafi was the former director of the medical school in Kabul. When the Taliban took over Kabul, he fled with his family to Mazar-i-Sharif. When the Taliban finally took Mazar, he made his way to Faizabad. Refusing to give up his profession for other occupations that might have provided a better income, he practiced medicine in a small, one-room mud building in the bazaar. His private clinic consisted of a few instruments that he had carried with him on exodus: an old desk, several medical books, a bed for examinations, and a curtain for privacy. On the side, he trained and consulted with the local doctors at the hospital in town. Dr. Shafi was an intelligent and gentle soul. When I left, he gave me a small box containing lapis, a deep blue semi-precious stone mined from the mountains of Badakhshan. "Please do not ever forget us here in Afghanistan," he asked.

After a week in Faizabad, Wade had to return to London. Tim, an engineer from Florida and Commander Jon's roommate, invited us to accompany him out to some far-flung villages to the west in the direction of Rostaq to visit his organization's projects that helped thousands of refugees. We set off in a sweatbox of a Russian jeep over some remarkable terrain. I was amazed at how quickly the topography and features of the land changed. We drove through mountain passes, traversed rolling hills, passed fascinating rock pinnacles punctuated by hundreds of caves, and traveled through flat desert all within a couple of hours. Much of our drive was on a narrow, dirt track right along the edge of a steep gorge dropping down into a raging river. I spotted numerous white-water rapids and wondered if anyone had ever tried to run that river in a raft or kayak. Our Tajik driver looked about fifteen years old and barreled over this rutty track with no fear. Our jeep had no air conditioning, and its windows didn't roll down. I wasn't sure if the heat was going to kill us or if we were going to die more mercifully by simply flying off one of the hairpin curves and tumbling down into the river below. Of one thing I was certain: we were heading in the direction of Taliban positions.

We approached a bridge that spanned the gorge. It consisted of two thin metal tracks, similar in width to those used for oil changes back home. Before we had a chance to object, our nut-case of a driver began the crossing, a hundred feet above the wild river. We held our breath for a long, existential minute, knowing that the smallest error in steering would result in freefall, followed by imminent death on impact or by drowning.

"That was crazy!" I shouted up to Tim from the backseat. Squished between James and another guy, my Afghan clothes were drenched in sweat. Suddenly, any previous notion of bringing my family to this country seemed clearly insane. "Are we taking a different route back?"

"Negative. Only one way back," Tim responded, coolly. "Par for the course."

We were greeted at the other side by several friendly Northern Alliance soldiers who engaged Tim in spirited conversation. On the side of the road sat one of their tanks and a pile of tank shells.

"What is he saying?" I interrupted the flow of Dari.

"He says that if the Taliban takes Rostaq, they are going to blow the bridge, and we'd better be on the other side first. It will delay them from reaching Faizabad by several months while they build another."

"How are they going to blow it?"

"They have it wired with dynamite." Our driver hit the accelerator as I tried to digest this last statement.

We saw only a handful of vehicles that day but passed many Afghans traveling by donkey, camel, and on foot. Most were heading in the opposite direction, away from the Taliban. Hundreds of villagers worked with shovels and axes, widening and strengthening the road on which we were traveling. This was part of a large "food for work" road construction project being run by the two young men we were on our way to meet. This project was vital for getting food and supplies out to tens of thousands of villagers and refugees.

We arrived in Rostaq that evening and met Kevin and Sam. Kevin, a strapping young man from the hills of North Carolina, had been working in Afghanistan for the past year and a half. Sam, his younger apprentice, was an engineering student in the States but was volunteering for the summer. Both were wearing the local shalwar kamis and sporting impressive beards and baseball caps. Sam's beard was growing out sideways, with very little gravitational effect. I was immediately struck by their obvious love for the Afghan people—and by their strong body odor. Neither had bathed for weeks.

"One of the greatest things about living in Afghanistan is that no one tells you to take a bath. No mother or wife here to harass you!" explained Kevin over dinner. "That's right!" piped up his admiring disciple.

Later that night, one of their Afghan staff approached me and sheepishly asked me to tell them to clean up. "Please tell Mr. Kevin and Mr. Sam that they really need to take a bath and trim their beards," he pleaded.

Kevin and Sam were doing excellent work. In addition to their road construction projects, they were helping to feed and educate throngs of refugees who had fled the Taliban. The next day we drove out to several squalid camps on an oppressive desert landscape. Water and bread had to be trucked in to keep the people alive. These camps made the refugee camps in Faizabad look luxurious.

"If the Taliban overruns Massoud's front line positions, most of these people are dead," Kevin explained to me.

"How far away is the Taliban from us right now?" I asked, thinking about my wife at home and the bridge from yesterday.

"About fifteen kilometers," he responded. "Did you hear the whistling of artillery shells last night? Several of them flew over our heads."

We were within range of the Taliban's big guns, and all around us were signs of war. I noticed more than a few refugees missing limbs. The ground was littered with spent shell casings. The line between the Taliban and Northern Alliance positions was constantly shifting; it hadn't been long since the Taliban held the ground we were standing on.

James picked up an anti-aircraft shell and tossed it to me. "Take that home as a souvenir to Christine!" Examining it more closely, I realized that I was holding a piece of unexploded ordnance. I gently placed it back on the ground.

We visited several of the schools that Kevin had constructed for refugee children. A building less than a hundred feet away from one school had been leveled several nights before by an artillery shell fired by the Taliban. We arrived in the morning while the girls were in session. The school principal invited us into some of the classrooms. There we were given a privilege not normally afforded to foreigners in Afghanistan at the time ... to actually see the faces of older girls and young women. Dozens of schoolgirls sat on the floor in each small classroom—this school had no desks— taking notes on old notebooks or scraps of paper. They clearly considered it a great privilege to attend school. Looking into their eyes and seeing the haunting expressions of tragedy burned a powerful impression on my heart ... one that would help bring me back to Afghanistan.

I wondered what kind of person believed it against the will of God for girls like these to learn to read and write. What kind of person beat a woman for accidentally showing her ankles when the wind blew her burqa in the wrong direction? What kind of a person thought that it was virtuous to publicly stone women accused of adultery, while they privately molested young boys? I prayed that God would intervene and rescue this country from the Taliban. Seeing the devastation all around, the heroic efforts of these aid workers seemed like a drop in the bucket. *Could I make a difference in a place like this?*

One week later, as James and I flew across the Atlantic toward home, I wondered if I would ever see Afghanistan again. We'd made it back across the bridge, holding our breath while our barely pubescent driver navigated the thin metal tracks at speeds that tested my bladder control. We'd spent a few more days getting to know the people of Faizabad. The prognosis for their future was dire. The Taliban was amassing its strength to wrest the last 10 percent of Afghanistan from the weaker Northern Alliance. Had it not been for Massoud's strategic brilliance and resolve, Faizabad would have fallen to the Taliban years earlier. I looked out the window and prayed for the safety of my new friends and all the people I was leaving behind who had nowhere left to run.

At that time, I had no idea that in exactly one month, September 9, 2001, Tunisian suicide bombers posing as journalists would assassinate Massoud. I had no idea that the Twin Towers would fall two days later, or that the American military would commence Operation Enduring Freedom on October 7. I had no idea that on November 13, the Northern Alliance, aided by American Special Forces on the ground and incredible aerial firepower, would victoriously ride into Kabul, freeing the country from the scourge of Taliban rule. At the time, the plight of the resistant Afghans in northeastern Afghanistan was unknown by most people in the world.

I pulled out a letter from the airplane's backseat pocket. On our last evening in Faizabad, a solemn Afghan named Waheed had given it to me.

"I have written a letter to George Bush," he stated. "I have asked him to please send the American army to come and help us defeat the Taliban. When you go back to America, please deliver it to him."

"I'm afraid to say that I don't know President Bush personally," I tried to explain. "I could mail your letter to him."

Waheed looked at me with disappointment all over his face. What did I mean, I didn't know the President? I must be a small man, after all. Misjudged this *kharedji* (foreigner).

"Will he read it if you mail it to him?" he asked.

"Waheed, I can't guarantee it. America is a big country, and I'm sure the President gets a lot of mail," I answered truthfully.

"There is no way that you can just go to his office and give it to him?" he persisted.

"Could you just drop by Rabbani's office, have a conversation with him, and hand-deliver a letter?" I tried to help him see reality.

"Sure, his house is just down the road!" Waheed gestured with his face. "It would be no problem!"

"I'll do my best," I promised.

I tapped the letter (which Waheed believes saved Afghanistan) and asked God if this was really what He was calling me to do. I sensed a still, small voice telling me in my soul, "This is your calling; I have prepared you for this." I told God that He was going to have to make this one clear. *I've got two fleeces: if You want my family in Afghanistan, You have got to call Christine there—independently from me. And You have got to open the door wider.*

Northern Alliance fighters near Faizabad, August 2001. This rag-tag tribal army is all that stood between the Taliban and Afghanistan's Northeastern province of Badakhshan.

Your heart and my heart are very, very old friends.
—Hafiz

'Arise, my love, my beautiful one, and come away ...'
—Solomon

Chapter 2

A Silver Pendant

Christine wore a silver pendant of Africa around her neck. She grew up in southern Chad, where her dad trained local pastors in a small seminary and made long treks with them into the bush. He built a tennis court behind their house, using chicken wire for the net, where he taught his children important life skills through sports. Christine—along with her younger sister and two younger brothers—helped him plant a garden, where they each grew their own row of vegetables. They learned individual responsibility but were a team. It was a simple and peaceful life, punctuated by drama.

One day, Islamic extremists from Sudan attacked their town, destroying foreign houses and killing several French citizens. The mob moved toward the house where Christine's family lived. The extremists broke through the gates and rushed the house. Christine's dad huddled over his family in the kitchen, asking Jesus to save their lives, while tribesmen waved machetes over their heads and destroyed almost all of their earthly possessions. Christine's younger sister looked up in the mayhem and noticed a man dressed in green Islamic robes—the only one without a club or machete. He gave her a look that assured her that she would be all right and deftly directed the mob's violent wrath toward objects instead of people. They beat on the refrigerator with machetes, tore up Christine's prized stamp collection, and smashed her mother's wedding china, but the family was not harmed.

During her first year of boarding school on the edge of the magnificent Rift Valley of Kenya, fourteen-year-old Christine flew back home to Chad for Christmas with three American high school seniors as her escorts. At the airport in Addis, Ricky picked up a newspaper and noticed a story on page seventeen as they were beginning their descent into Ndjamena. A coup d'état was underway in Chad, with rebels fighting for Ndjamena's airport. Upon landing, the captain announced that they were quickly refueling the plane and would be taking off for Nigeria within minutes. The three guys convinced the Ethiopian flight crew to let them off—they lived there, after all—and Christine was dropped off with them on the edge of the flight line.

French Special Forces soldiers, who were fighting to defend the airport, drove up in a jeep and begin to chew out these American teenagers. "What are you doing here?! Don't you know there is a battle going on? The rebels are only a kilometer away!" They took the teens to a hangar where a crowd of expats was waiting for evacuation. Next thing she knew, Christine was on an Air France 747 bound for Paris in December in her sundress, along with her three teenage escorts.

Her dad spent the day at the wheel of his truck with a gun to his head, being forced to drive Chadian soldiers and their families out of town ahead of the rebel invasion. He finally convinced them to take the truck but let him go: "I respect the way you are trying to take care of your families. Please allow me to take care of mine." He arrived home out of breath asking frantically, "Where is Christine?!" Don't worry, he was told, she is safe...on her way to France. "With Ricky and his buddies?!" Her dad knew Ricky and his motto: "*Let the good times roll!*" Now he was really worried. The dust settled, and a week later Christine was headed back to Chad to join her family for a late Christmas.

The airline ticket agent in Paris looked at her in disbelief. "But you were just evacuated from there a week ago! And now you want to go back?"

"That is where my family is. I am going home!" Christine responded.

The next year, tragedy struck during Christine's sophomore year of high school. One day she was pulled out of class at Rift Valley Academy to find that her parents had made the trip to bring some devastating news. Through tears they explained that her six-year-old brother David was now with Jesus. A few days earlier he had complained of stomach pain. It got so bad that he was rushed to a bush hospital. Doctors performed an appendectomy, but infection quickly set in. He died as medical workers frantically tried to save his life.

Christine's faith was tested at a young age. The family persevered in their mission, but things got harder. Back in the States, Christine's maternal grandmother was dying of cancer, and her mother traveled back to her childhood home in Pennsylvania to say goodbye. Her dad, struggling with grief over the death of his youngest son and discouragement that he didn't have the money to fly the entire family back to the US, tried to continue the mission work and care for Christine's younger sister and brother. But his son fell sick with malaria. Fifteen-year-old Christine came home to Chad and kept the family going.

I met Christine in the fall of 1998, and it was love at first sight (for me). I had noticed her picture in an old college yearbook; her stunning blue eyes and innocent smile had jumped off the page and pierced my heart. I was starting a master's degree at the same university where she had just completed her education degree. Alas, we would never meet, or so it seemed. But several months later, Christine's best friend (who happened to go to my church) took it upon herself to introduce us, based upon the common love she knew we shared for Jesus, and for Africa.

"Christine is the most beautiful person I know, on the inside and outside!" she had gushed. Initially I'd blown her off, having heard this spiel before and having no clue that this spiritual giant was the same beauty I'd noticed in her college yearbook. When I walked into a dining room and saw Christine standing there for the first time, my pulse quickened and my brain froze. My vocal chords would not form coherent sentences. I had recently come back from two years of working in Mozambique, where I'd dealt with bandits, land mines, mambas, and thieves of every stripe, and I thought I was scared of nothing. But I was terrified of Christine.

A few days later, I played with my phone for an hour and then finally summoned the courage to dial the last digit of her number and invite her on an innocuous (in retrospect: loser) date. She was busy that evening. I came up with a second idea, but struck out a second time. *I'm being rejected!* the horror slowly sunk in. "OK. Gotta run...great talking with you!" I stammered, moving into abort mode. Click. I sat there in stunned silence, ready to plunge into excuses and self-pity, when I sensed God's Spirit whispering: "You are supposed to be with her. Call her again!" I did some push-ups, and then completely uncharacteristically, picked up the phone and dialed Christine's number.

"Hey, Christine. This is Matthew, the guy who just called you before." *Idiot.* Silence on the other end.

"A group of friends is coming over to my place after church on Sunday." Pause, and then more silence.

"Well, uh, I was wondering if you would like to come over to my place and join us for lunch? I'd love to hear more about your growing up in Africa and everything—maybe you could bring some pictures?" I winced and waited. Silence for what felt like an eternity.

"I might be able to come for lunch with your friends," Christine answered, without much enthusiasm. "Where do you live?"

I got off the phone, exhaled, performed a celebratory fist pump, then called my sister, who lived down the street: "Tammy, you and Douglas need to come over for lunch on Sunday! I'm grilling up!"

On Sunday my attempts to impress were falling flat, much to Douglas' amusement. The stories over lunch sounded less dashing than when I had rehearsed them in my mind. I had even managed to burn the chicken. After lunch we sat on the couch and I showed her my prized photo album of worldwide exploits, turning to pictures of a recent summit of Mt. Baker in Washington State.

"That looks really dangerous!" Christine pointed to a photo of me standing next to a large crevasse on Mt. Baker.

"Well it is…better not fall in one of those: if you survive the impact, you don't have long until you freeze to death!" I was preparing a dramatic explanation for why we climb mountains, such as "because it is there!" when Christine pre-empted:

"Why would somebody voluntarily do something so dangerous, just for fun? We only have one life to live, which is a gift." Douglas choked back laughter from across the room.

"Uh, can you show me some of your photos from Africa?" I tried to change the subject. Christine pulled a Ziploc bag out of her purse containing ten prints—a camel, a mud hut, a Chadian village called Kutu, etc. Nothing of her and her family growing up in Africa, as I had hoped.

It wasn't just my lack of suave; Christine was guarding her heart. She had made a commitment to two American families living in northern Chad to come and teach their children for two years. They lived in an oasis village called Bardai, a six-day drive across the Sahara from civilization. I came to realize the importance of this calling and commitment; if I tried to distract Christine from this, could I expect God's blessing on our relationship? We pursued a friendship, and I imagined trekking across the Sahara with a camel caravan to surprise Christine midway through her deployment, with a diamond ring in my pack. None of that came to be. Several months before Christine was due to leave, a war broke out between tribes in the north; both families were forced to evacuate. Normally, I'm not happy to hear about new wars, but now I was free to marry Christine.

After a surprise dinner in a French restaurant that my family created within the confines of their master bathroom (it was a finer affair than you might imagine—a five-course dinner on bone china with silver, tuxedo-clad waiters, and a transformed room with many candles and flowers), I asked Christine to marry me. We walked outside through a series of torches and down to the dock. My brother Tim, complete in a tuxedo under his wetsuit bottoms, stood in the water with a torch in one hand and the rope to a rowboat in the other. Christine sat on blankets garnished with roses, and we paddled out into the bay. I told Christine that she was the one I had waited for, and something about two being better than one (the context speaks of keeping each other warm, which proved more prophetic than I realized), and asked her if she would be my wife. She said yes! It was just a few minutes before Y2K.

When I returned home from Afghanistan in August 2001, Christine wanted to hear all about the trip. I was vague. As I processed over the next few days, I told some stories but preferred to try to focus on our life together in America. To be honest, I foresaw life in Afghanistan for a family to be unbearably difficult. Christine was about as tough as they come and had quite a background of international travel, but she had never lived in this part of the world. It wasn't just the security situation; I couldn't imagine asking Christine to live in a country where she would have to cover her head and divert her eyes downward anytime she was in the presence of a man. I couldn't bear the thought of uneducated Afghan men looking down on my wife simply because she is a woman.

As much as I tried to forget about Afghanistan, Christine wanted to know more. She pored over my photos, especially of the girls in the mud schoolhouses. We wept together on 9/11 and sat glued to the evening news as we watched the Taliban regime fall and a new door open to the country. A few months later, Christine told me that she thought she was being called to Afghanistan and would be disappointed if we didn't end up serving there together. I told her that she had to spend a little time on the ground there before she could make that determination. Surely a trip to Afghanistan would give her a strong dose of reality!

We visited Mazar-i-Sharif in November 2002 along with three friends from home: Clay, Susan, and Catherine. Clay and Susan were a married couple, ten years older than Christine and me. Their daughter, Lucy, was the flower girl in our wedding. Both were involved in higher education: Susan taught college-level math while Clay served as a university administrator.

I'd first met Clay when he granted me admission to my master's program. Tall, athletic, genuine and winsome, I liked him from the start. He had a gift for bringing people into the group. James and I had shown them pictures of Afghanistan, talking about the difficult plight of the Afghan people and how brown everything was. Hardly inspiring, but something had stirred in Susan's heart—if no one wanted to go demonstrate God's love in a hard place like this, she would! She told Clay they were going to Afghanistan.

Catherine was familiar with human needs; she had grown up among the Quechua people in the mountains of Peru. The daughter of a mission doctor, she had pursued nursing with quiet intensity. Fancy clothes and material possessions mattered little to Catherine: she was in love with Jesus and her heart was with the poor and unreached. She was to become the Mother Teresa of Afghanistan.

We traveled into northern Afghanistan by land via Uzbekistan. Night and day different from Afghanistan, Uzbekistan's capital city, Tashkent, was highly Russified, with many ugly Soviet-built apartment buildings and a more nominal practice of Islam in society. The weather was cold and gray, and the border guards in the town of Termez especially grumpy. They seemed to suspect anyone traveling to Afghanistan and searched every item inside our luggage microscopically.

We drove across the "Friendship Bridge," which the Russians had built in the early '80s, several years after their Fortieth Army had crossed the *Amu Darya* River on floating pontoon bridges to invade Afghanistan. We were actually relieved to be on the Afghan side of the border.

A customs officer walked out to our vehicle, slapped his hand across his heart, and boomed in a loud voice: "Welcome to Afghanistan!" Within five minutes, our passports were stamped, tea had been offered, and we were cruising through the sand dunes of northern Afghanistan. An hour-and-a-half drive across the desert later, we arrived in Mazar-i-Sharif.

Compared to Faizabad, Mazar seemed like a metropolis but still retained an "edge of the frontier" feel about it. All roads lead to a shrine in the middle of town, so the city was easy to navigate on foot. Most roads were composed of dirt as were most buildings Toward the middle of town, some buildings were made of concrete and the locals were proud of the fact that they had electricity several hours a day while Kabul still had none. Little yellow Russian-built taxis competed with herds of sheep, goats, and camels for dominance of the streets, and we found it fascinating to watch life pass by from the roof of the office building where we were staying. Early in the morning, before the day's dust was stirred up, we could make out the jagged shape of the mountains south of Mazar.

Afghanistan is a country of climatic extremes; in most of the cities the summer gets scorching hot, but the temperatures drop during winter. Up in the mountainous areas temperatures drop thirty degrees below zero and snow accumulation is measured in meters. Mazar is known for milder winters, although it normally will snow a few times in January. During our first week the weather was glorious. It was chilly at night, but during the days the temperatures rose to 60 degrees F with sunshine. We had packed light but were thankful for our light jackets in the evenings.

Then the blizzard of the decade hit. Winds blew dark clouds in from the mountains south and east of Mazar, and the snows began to fall. It didn't stop for days. The combination of wind, sub-freezing temperatures, and snow shocked the population of Mazar and propelled us even further outside our comfort zone. We were staying at a nongovernmental organization's (NGO) office building that had just been rented the week before. It had yet to be winterized. The drafts in our room brought in cold air and snow through the window cracks. We learned quickly that winter is a more difficult time to survive in Afghanistan than summer because there is no such thing as central heat. The air temperature in the room was below freezing even during the daytime; the snow that had blown inside didn't melt and our shampoo bottle froze inside our duffle bag.

Our Afghan hosts set up small propane heaters—made locally from tin—in the rooms for us. Even when cranked to full capacity, the sides of these heaters were barely warm to the touch. We tried not to think too much about the rusty propane cylinder in the room with us, sharing our airspace as we slept. One evening we were desperate to get warmer, so I asked Christine to help me light the propane heater in our room. She was a little nervous.

"These things are not safe, Matthew. I can't believe we have a gas tank inside the room with us. What if I blow you up?"

"There is nowhere else to put it, sweetheart." I had moved the tank as far away from the heater as possible, stretching the hose taut to the other end of the room. "Just turn the valve counter-clockwise when I say, and I'll see if I can light this bad boy." I was about to light one of my precious few matches.

"Is that right or left?"

"Well, first right all the way, then left. We better be sure it is off before I light my match." I was too stuffed up to smell the propane gas that had filled the heater and was starting to replace the air in my section of the room.

I lit the match. Whoosh!! The air around me lit on fire, creating a fiery silhouette effect and singeing off my arm hair and some of my eyebrows. I jumped backwards, yelping strange noises. Thankfully, no permanent damage... nothing burned that wouldn't grow back.

Christine was four months pregnant with our first child, and I was anxious to keep her warm. Our primary method for warmth was simply huddling under blankets, a strategy that isn't conducive toward productivity. Just when we were beginning to feel sorry for ourselves, we would step outside and see the Afghans coping with the cold with far fewer resources. Many men and children had no socks and would trudge through snow with just a cheap pair of plastic shoes. People at the bazaar burned egg crates and anything else they could find to try to stay warm. One man sat in the snow, huddling under a piece of plastic. He was completely still, and his skin looked blue. "Clay, I think that guy is dead!" I started but then he moved just a twitch. Surely, I thought, Christine would not want to live in this place.

Then we visited the schools. We accompanied a group of Afghan educators on a tour of the various educational facilities of Mazar, from Balkh University to local elementary schools. The president of the university pleaded for professors from the West, and teachers begged for desks and more books. We visited elementary schools where classes were crammed into the hallways and high schools where hundreds of girls squatted for hours in unheated tents. They had no desks or chairs and couldn't sit on the ground because it was frozen. The girls didn't complain about the conditions; they were thrilled to be in school. One school girl stood and addressed us in perfect English:

"Welcome, dear guests. My name is Nezakat, the daughter of Abdul Rakhman. When the Taliban came to our beautiful city in 1998 and defeated our leader, Commander Abdul Rashid Dostum, these evil men were going to kill my father. We left our house and fled to Badakhshan. We lived in tents and were always moving around. We lost everything. My father was an important man, but we had nothing. We were so hungry that sometimes we boiled weeds to make tea. We came back to Mazar six months ago. The Taliban destroyed our house, but I don't mind because I am back in school. My sisters and I were not able to go to school for four years! I want to study medicine and become a doctor. We love America. Thanks to you from our hearts for sending your soldiers to help us get rid of the Taliban!"

Susan began a friendship with the Afghan women next door through hand signals. She noticed them peeking through the curtains of their second-story windows watching us eat breakfast each morning. Soon Susan, Catherine, and Christine were regularly waving back and forth with them, and eventually the neighbor women invited them over for tea (all by hand signal). Walking into the house next door, they entered a shrouded world. These women had been through civil war, famine, the oppression of the Taliban, and still lived in a society that did not grant them equal rights with men. They had suffered so much but were dignified, friendly, and hospitable to their guests. Christine perceived that they found it therapeutic to be able to recount their stories to Western women. They found merciful hearts in Christine, Catherine, and Susan. They were still navigating through the fog of post-traumatic stress syndrome. Curiously, most of these Afghan ladies were still wearing the burqa, but it was as if they could live vicariously through their new American friends. "Enjoy your freedom," they told them. "Enjoy it for us."

I was ready to get back to the freedom of America, but Afghanistan did not let us go easily. During the blizzard, strong winds had swept sand dunes across much of the road north to the border, more than doubling our travel time.

We were in danger of missing our flights. We drove to Termez airport and began running the gauntlet of paperwork, numerous stamps, and security checks. We made it to the holding room just a minute before they opened the doors, and then it became a race across an icy tarmac to the airplane. All of the contenders knew that there were fewer seats on the plane than people in the crowd, and some attempted a full sprint across the ice. So here was Christine, four months pregnant, running and sliding with me across an ice field of a tarmac in frozen Uzbekistan! *This is crazy! When we get home, we are finished with Central Asia! Never coming back!* I did my best to hold her arm and not wipe out myself. We made it to the plane, claimed two seats, and let out sighs of relief. I looked out the window ... they were using blowtorches to melt the ice off our Russian airplane's ugly propellers. I shook my head. *Crazy!*

As we flew home, Christine was looking back to Afghanistan. There was something about her experience with Afghan women that took hold of her heart and would not let go. I glanced down at the silver pendant hanging from Christine's neck. It was of Afghanistan. A new friend in Mazar had given it to her with no knowledge of the African pendant that she had worn from childhood. *There is no way this is a coincidence.* I looked into Christine's eyes and saw peace and resolve. I knew that she was going to make a difference in the lives of Afghan women. God had called us to this.

Top, school girls crouching in the cold in their classroom in Mazar. Bottom, the Shrine of Hazrat Ali in the center of Mazar.

And without faith it is impossible to please him, for whoever would draw
near to God must believe that he exists and that
he rewards those who seek him.
Hebrews 11:6 (ESV)

There is no fear in love. But perfect love drives out fear...
1 John 4:18 (ESV)

Chapter 3

My Treasure

April 3, 2003, early morning

I held little Ellie for the first time and felt a love I hadn't experienced before. She'd been born three minutes before with meconium in her lungs. She was rudely pushed out of her cocoon, cut into a bright, cruel world where a doctor and nurse swiftly sucked fluid out of her lungs with a loud machine. When they had finished, she'd registered her displeasure with mighty cries.

The doctor had looked at me, standing there white-faced. "It's OK now. You can go to her."

I'd approached the little table where seven-pound Ellie lay screaming under a bright light. "Hey, little Ellie. Daddy loves you."

I had said it to her hundreds of times before, in utero. Immediately she'd stopped crying, turning her head toward my voice.

I stood there, holding my child, pondering wondrous things.

She knew my voice! Do I know my Father's voice? I love her with everything in me. I'd give my life for her in a second. Does God really feel the same about me?

October 6, 2003, 7:30 p.m.

I sat in the wicker rocking chair that I'd spent many hours refurbishing for this very purpose, rocking my six-month old Ellie. We read our favorite book together, *Guess How Much I Love You,*[2] for the hundredth time. Big Nutbrown Hare was trying to outdo Little Nutbrown Hare in showing how much he loved her, and I spread my arms as wide as I could. Ellie giggled, but I felt conflicted as I read. *My Little Nutbrown Hare is my treasure, and I would do anything to protect her. How can I take her to Afghanistan?!*

October 7, 2003, 2:35 a.m.

I woke up in a cold sweat, my sleep interrupted by a nightmare. The unthinkable had happened to my family in Afghanistan. I slapped my face a couple times until I was sure that I was awake. *It wasn't real... just a bad dream!* I looked over at Christine, who was sleeping soundly, and exhaled deeply. *Everyone is OK!* Just to be sure, I peeked into little Ellie's room. She was sleeping peacefully in her crib. Now wide awake, I walked to the kitchen, poured myself a glass of orange juice, and sat down at the kitchen table. I opened my Bible and read:

> Whoever loves father or mother more than me is not worthy of me, and whoever loves son or daughter more than me is not worthy of me. And whoever does not take his cross and follow me is

---

2   Sam McBratney, *Guess How Much I Love You?* (Cambridge, MA: Candlewick Press, Brdbk edition, 2008).

not worthy of me. Whoever finds his life will lose it, and whoever loses his life for my sake will find it. (Matthew 10:37–39, ESV)

This was heavy stuff. I prayed: *Jesus, I want to love you more. You are worthy of my worship; not just my words, but my life. I know Mary poured out her treasure on your feet ... her alabaster flask of costly perfume ... maybe even her dowry, her future. Ellie is my treasure ... I don't want her to get hurt! I know Abraham was able to offer his only son, believing you would raise him from the dead. This is hard for me ... help me to love you more!*

I believed that God loved us and was sovereign. People said that the safest place to be was in the center of His will. But I also knew that sometimes bad things happened to children, especially in places like Afghanistan. I told myself that much of the risk factor was over-stated. Common sense security protocols, and positioning ourselves to receive local protection, should help mitigate that risk. *After all, we are all scared of the unfamiliar,* I reminded myself. *We overlook real dangers that have become too familiar to us, like driving on the highways of America.* Still, I couldn't be sure that Ellie would be OK. Christine and I had a choice in the matter, but little Ellie didn't. She just went with her Mommy and Daddy. I flipped a couple pages in my Bible:

Then children were brought to him that he might lay his hands on them and pray. The disciples rebuked the people, but Jesus said: "Let the little children come to me and do not hinder them, for to such belongs the kingdom of heaven." And he laid his hands on them and went away. (Matthew 19:13–15, ESV)

I believed that Jesus loved Ellie even more than I did, and that if God was calling us to Afghanistan, I needed to place her in His sovereign hands. I'd experienced God's hand of protection before. He'd healed me from typhoid fever in the Philippines, malaria in Mozambique, and saved me from an abduction attempt by terrorists on the island of Mindanao.

Still, I'm afraid. Father, please give me the faith I need to overcome my fear. Help me trust you. Like Ellie trusts me. Completely.

I turned to a passage that I'd memorized years ago. It felt better reading it from the page:

> Do not be anxious about anything, but in everything by prayer and supplication with thanksgiving let your requests be made known to God. And the peace of God, which surpasses all understanding, will guard your hearts and your minds in Christ Jesus. (Philippians 4:6–7, ESV)

I am anxious, Father. I'm worried that if something happens to Ellie I might lose my faith. Please guard and strengthen my faith! Help me obey and trust you completely. Please give my heart your peace! And please protect my family!

With these words on my lips and in my heart, I shuffled back to my bedroom. I laid down quietly next to Christine and eventually fell back asleep.

But doubts returned, and they were hard to shake. So much was at risk, so much that couldn't be recaptured if lost.

February 3, 2004, noon

It was getting real. We had been offered a position with an NGO to lead a team and direct humanitarian operations in Iskandar, the capital of an important Afghan province. The new Afghan government was asking for assistance with medical, education, and community development projects in their country. The clock was ticking: if we were going to really do this, we needed to pack up a crate, liquidate our assets, and sell our house within the next few months. It was decision time.

James was a trustworthy friend and a man of faith. He came to know God as a university student while partially funding his education through a small side business: selling pot. Jesus changed his heart and life and he had been sold-out ever since. "Matt, we are going to Afghanistan!" James would say with a laugh every time we met up. "Can you believe that!?"

I felt conflicted. It was as if the left side of my brain was primed for action and excited to go, but the other side wanted none of it. It wasn't too late to back out. Sure, it would take a lot of explaining and re-establishing our lives in America, but I could still pull the plug. It would be a relief. But what about pursuing God's call on my life? Did I really believe that He could protect my family?

Right now I needed James' help. I felt like I was having a crisis of faith, and I couldn't think of a better guy with whom to talk things through. We met at our favorite lunch spot, a place with amazing Greek salads.

I took a bite and then explained what was going on in my head: "Last night Christine and I saw this movie about a guy who was a math professor at MIT. He ended up being recruited by a government agent to secretly crack Russian codes. Then it turned out that he was really a paranoid schizophrenic. Half of his life was just in his head— a delusion. I didn't sleep much last night, James. I kept wondering: What if this whole Christian worldview that I believe in, that would lead me to go serve in a place like Afghanistan, is just a delusion?"

James locked his blue eyes on mine. "That," he said, "is a wicked thought!"

I pondered his statement for a moment.

He is right! I believe in Jesus with all of my heart! He gave His life for me on the cross, the righteous for the unrighteous, so that I might have eternal life! This is the base-line truth of my life, and I have no cause to doubt Him! My decision needs to be anchored on what I know is true, not on fears about what the future might hold.

It was a boxing match between faith vs. fear for the allegiance of my heart.

April 2, 2004, 7:00 p.m.

Tomorrow would be busy. We were scheduled to close on our house in the morning, then spend the rest of the day moving out with the help of friends. Sometime in the middle of all that we would celebrate Ellie's first birthday.

She'd fallen asleep in my arms in the rocking chair, as she often did. I studied her long eyelashes, downy blonde hair, and the perfect curve of her lips. She slept peacefully, trustingly, in my arms. The weight of fatherly responsibility far outweighed her few pounds.

At that moment, I chose, once again, to trust my Heavenly Father to care for her and to always love her far more than I ever could.

She is yours, God. I offer my treasure up to You. Please take care of my Little Nutbrown Hare!

This place where you are right now, God circled on a map for you.
—Hafiz

"I drank what?!!"
—Socrates

Chapter 4

Welcome to the

Ancient City!

July 28, 2004

Dear Family and Friends,

Throughout our trip I have thought of you often with thankfulness for your friendship and prayers. We are in Kabul, tired and recovering from jet lag, but so thankful to be here in Afghanistan...with all our luggage! Really we have no

exciting stories to tell (which is a good thing), and our travels have been very smooth.

It is beginning to dawn on me that this is our new home.
Trying to keep on my head scarf with Ellie on my back in her
carrier tugging at it, sweaty bodies pushing and shoving to
get at the luggage on the broken conveyer belt (my husband
gallantly getting all 10 bags after what seemed like hours),
walking out of the airport realizing afresh what I already
knew … no one understood me and I didn't understand
them! Being crammed in the back of an old Land Cruiser
with luggage piled behind and beside me (one arm around
Ellie and one hand on the luggage), bouncing up and down
potholed roads with the sandy mountains looming in the
distance shrouded by the brown haze of dust, and seeing
everything in pretty much one color … brown. What a different world! But I have such a peace and a happiness that we
are finally here.

We have not finished our journey, so please pray
that the final leg of our trip to our new home would go
smoothly. We leave on Saturday. We are hoping that Ellie
will be able to adjust quickly. Last night she was up and
ready to go at 2 a.m. Pray for her health as any microbes
in unfiltered water can cause sickness, and I am especially aware of the germs that are on those little fingers
she loves to suck.

We are looking forward to joining our new team. Our goal
is to learn the language and much about the culture of this
fascinating country as soon as possible. We would appreciate your prayers for the peace of the country as we have had
news of more unrest.

We can't thank you enough for your encouraging emails.
We love you! For those of you that saw us off at the airport,
the images of your faces, your hugs, and seeing you waving

until we were out of sight, bring and will continue to bring smiles and joy to our hearts.

With Gratitude,
Christine

July 31, 2004

Dear Friends,
Greetings from Kabul!

This morning from a second-story balcony I looked out over a dry and dusty city. The early morning provides a welcome but short-lived respite from the heat, and I watched as the sky turned brown as billows of dust headed my way. Water is a precious and rare commodity in this country, and it represents life. We hope to help bring water to this parched land.

Yesterday we were having a look around Kabul with some friends we know from home, and I noticed a young boy whose face had been completely burned off. I have seen a lot of injured and deformed children in my years overseas, but I have never seen anything quite like this. It is my prayer that he will have a new face in heaven. How incredibly blessed our children (and all of us are) in America, and most of the time we don't even realize it.

Thanks for remembering us over here. Right now we are really hoping that Ellie will be able to finish getting over jet lag. It takes its toll on everyone, but when the little one can't sleep at night, no one sleeps. We really are doing well and grateful to be here.

I had better run ... we leave in a few minutes to get on our last flight to Iskandar!

Miss all of you,
Matthew for the three of us

Afghanistan is a country with an ancient culture and history, and nowhere is this more evident than in Iskandar. Strategically located on the historic trade routes between China, India, the Middle East, and Europe, many figures of history—including Alexander the Great and Genghis Khan—spent time in this city. Locals claim their city is more than 3,000 years old.

An aid worker named Cheryl flew with us to Iskandar. We'd rendezvoused at Dubai International Airport, and she was of tremendous help with Ellie and all our luggage. We'd eaten at Chili's at a mall in Dubai the night before we flew into Kabul, talking with a mixture of excitement and nervousness about what lay ahead. Cheryl had an interest in mother/child health work and nutritional gardening and was ready to make a long-term commitment to the Afghan people. Little did we know that six years later she would be gunned down along with her fellow Nuristan Eye Camp Team in Badakhshan on their way back to Kabul in 2010. She was a friend and an inspiration.

We flew over part of the *Hindu Kush* ("Killer of Hindus") mountain range, looking down on jagged peaks and high plains filled with mesas and canyons, until we approached Iskandar's dusty airport. It was surrounded by an impromptu military town of tents, prefabricated buildings, sand bags, and razor wire. Stepping off the plane, we were blasted by the hot, dry air blowing in from the west. But so glad to have arrived at our new home!

Our new team met us on the flight line, along with a beaming James, who had made the trip two months earlier with his family. "Welcome to the Ancient City!" Christine and I exchanged a knowing glance. *These are the people we will live and work with for this next chapter in our lives. They will be our new family.* Two gray-bearded men labored to pull a large wooden cart with half of the plane's luggage stacked on top. It was soon surrounded by a mob of passengers. "That trunk is ours ... and that suitcase under the big crate!" I pointed, and many helping hands—Afghan and American—grabbed bags and carried them over to the Big Land Cruiser (affectionately known as the BLC) and the Little Land Cruiser (LLC).

"Matt, you are going to love this place!" James gushed as he drove my family in his van north into the city. Compared to Kabul, we were impressed with Iskandar's relative sense of order and cleanliness. Old pine trees lined the street into the city, along with houses made from mud, straw, and rock, with crumbling courtyards revealing irrigated green fields. We passed a small bazaar. James continued the introduction: "Paved streets, we have got electricity most of the time, look at all the girls going to school!" Throngs of schoolgirls in their new uniforms and headscarves competed with auto rickshaws (locally known as *zaranges*), herds of goats, and vehicles like ours for dominance of the streets. We passed a horse and carriage, which caught Ellie's attention.

"The *jeweys* in Kabul were pretty rough," I responded. These uncovered drainage canals lining every street were full of garbage and human waste, contributing to an overall sewage smell of the city and the highest fecal count in the air of any city on the planet.

"No jeweys here!" James replied. Not literally accurate, but the drainage canals here were much cleaner. "Matt, get this. God has really provided for us here. I met a guy on the plane over who had a house for rent that worked out perfect for us. He is now my landlord!" This was remarkable. As we discovered later, it is tricky finding locals who will rent their home to a foreigner. "I bought this van from the same guy!"

We drove by Iskandar's central park. "Look at this park, Matt! People here love it. On Fridays it is full of families on picnics." There was no grass to speak of, but hundreds of century-old pine trees towered over the park, providing shade and a sense of nature. "The Taliban used to hang the bodies of their victims on these trees for a couple days," James said. Now the park was full of young men playing soccer and volleyball. It even had an improvised clay tennis court and a soccer stadium ringed by a cement running track.

We turned into a newer section of town where most of the NGOs and other private businesses were located. A few minutes later we turned right into a green gate. "This is it... welcome to your new home!" A short, barrel-chested man with a flowing white beard—the spitting image of an Afghan Santa Claus—opened the gate. "This is Naseer, your *choakidar*." The Dari word *choakidar* literally means "one who sits," a polite word for guard. "He claims to be thirty years old, but people here don't know their birthdays so it is easy to lose track." Naseer looked at least sixty. Everyone called him *Kaka*, Dari for uncle.

"*Salaam Aleykum*!!!" Kaka roared. "*Khushamaden!!!*" (Welcome!) "He sounds kind of angry," I said. *This is the guy who is going to protect my family while we sleep.* "No worries, brother," James assured me. "He is hard of hearing." I stepped out of the van and saluted Kaka with the Afghan greetings I had been practicing. "*Khubasten, Chitorasten? ChiAldaren? Familetan Chitoras?*" Impressed, Kaka grabbed my hand with an iron grip and pumped my arm, yelling the same Dari greetings back: "Are you good, how are you? How is your health? How is your family? Did your journey pass safely?"

A second guard limped and trotted up to the van, bouncing off his prosthetic and crutch. He was tall and muscular, blind in one eye and missing a leg. "This is Ghulam," James said with a grin. "He was a commander, fought for the Russians, then switched sides a couple of times." It appeared that Ghulam's war injuries didn't slow him down a bit. He made solid eye contact with his good eye, placed his right hand over his chest, showered me with greetings, and then gave a hearty laugh. *Well, we are in great shape. One deaf guard, and a commander minus a leg.* James must have read my mind: "With these guys, what could possibly go wrong? You are plenty safe here!" he said with a smirk.

The BLC and LLC pulled into the office gate with our teammates and worldly possessions. Two Afghan ladies walked out the front door of the office, wearing scarves over their heads, but no burqas. "*Salaam Aleykum!*" Hands over hearts, slight bowing. Christine exited the vehicle, holding Ellie. The women rushed over and warmly greeted her, kissing both cheeks. They fussed over Ellie, pinching her cheeks in greeting. "That is Hassina," James pointed to the woman on the left. She had a kind face, with a nose and forehead that reminded me of Massoud. *Clearly a Tajik.* "She cleans the office and guesthouse. She is sweet. The other one is Pashtun, the cook. She overdoes the oil; can't stand her cooking. Every time I'm here at the office and I smell lunch, I get nauseated. Just can't take her cooking." I never learned Pashtun's real name, but James was right: she was a horrible cook.

We were introduced to Zelme, our office manager, and Aziz, our language teacher and translator. Both spoke excellent English. Zelme was a thirty-five-year-old, handsomely mustached Hazara, tall and dignified, debonair in speech and dress. He had recently married Fatima, a seventeen-year-old with a Pashtun/Tajik pedigree. Their marriage was unique not only for its near-scandalous crossing of tribal lines, but also because Zelme and Fatima really were in love. Aziz was shorter, younger, and more traditional. A Tajik from a Shia minority, he wore a beard and earth-toned shalwar kamis. Polite, humble, and quietly earnest in his Islamic faith, I trusted him immediately. Over the years I grew to appreciate Aziz all the more.

Our baggage was unloaded and we were shown into our NGO's staff house. Rod and Sadie, both in their late sixties, lived in a bedroom downstairs and shared the living room with the rest of the house. Rod had built houses in California in his former life, but he and Sadie had spent the past decade or two serving the poor from Africa to Pakistan. Both were excellent at logistics and had come to Iskandar the year before to lay the foundation for our NGO's work in this part of the country. They had recruited this team and started our initial project work. Their goal was to stick around for at least another year to run operations so that we could focus on language learning. Rod was a man of prayer, getting up at 5:00 a.m. to walk circles inside the courtyard in the cool of the morning while he prayed. Sadie loved her novels, evidenced by five bookcases full of paperbacks lining the living room walls. When she wasn't working on spreadsheets, she was sitting in her recliner, devouring a book.

Catherine, our good friend from the States who traveled with us to Mazar in 2002, had moved to Iskandar with James and his family. She lived in a small room down in the basement. An intense language learner, she had made considerable progress in Dari during her two months in country. As the years went on, she earned her Mother Teresa moniker by fearlessly caring for women with dangerous diseases like tuberculosis (TB) in their mud homes. She also trained village women how to do the same. She would sleep on dirt floors, eat local food, and mercifully touch critically sick women in dark rooms—places our Afghan health workers feared to tread. Petite like Christine, she was tough as nails.

Catherine was excited to see all of us, but especially little Ellie. She'd worked on the labor and delivery ward at the hospital where Ellie was born and let me assist as she washed, weighed, and measured newborn Ellie.

"Look at you, Ellie, you have grown up to be such a big girl!" she exclaimed. Ellie grinned and rushed into "Auntie" Catherine's arms.

Catherine shared the basement with Audrie, a fellow nurse. Before coming to Iskandar, Audrie worked in Kabul for several years with another NGO. She had a good command of the Dari language. A great organizer and manager, she proved to be an invaluable help to our team with logistics and volunteered at the central hospital helping to organize a public health office. She managed life in Afghanistan while dealing with the early stages of multiple sclerosis. I never once heard her complain about her condition.

Audrie and Catherine shared a small kitchen with a two-burner propane stove top, a mini fridge, and an improvised sink.

The satellite Internet communication equipment was piled next to their kitchen, powered by a noisy Chinese stabilizer. They lived in one-hundred-square-foot rooms, each furnished with a single bed, a small metal desk, and a wardrobe that was locally constructed from Russian particleboard. Their living room was furnished with toshaks. Every morning around 5:30 they had to race to shut the small windows near the ceiling of their rooms (which were at ground level outside) before Kaka came along with his whisk broom outside, sweeping dust into their rooms, caking everything. Both of these women had graduated top of their class. I couldn't help but be impressed by their contentment to live in such humble conditions.

We were shown upstairs to our quarters. They were composed of a generous three rooms. A bedroom for Christine and me, one for Ellie, and a connecting room that we used for a private office, living room, and storage. I opened a frosted window in Ellie's room and noted with satisfaction that it faced the back of our compound (safer since it was farthest from the main street). Dr. Jack and Tiffany lived upstairs with us, all of their worldly goods being squeezed into one room. We shared a makeshift kitchen, an upstairs living room, and a bathroom. Dr. Jack gave me an instructional tour of the bathroom, which had a small shower room divided by cement and frosted glass from an even smaller room with toilet and sink. I noticed that the small sink was close enough to the toilet that you could vomit into it while still sitting on the toilet.

"Convenient," I half joked, pointing at the sink.

"More than you might think," Dr. Jack responded. "Everyone gets Giardia (intestinal infection). I realize this might sound kind of weird, but I think we need a policy that when taking a shower, we will all leave the bathroom door unlocked. Just in case of emergency." *Whoa. We are all going to get to know each other really well around here!*

Dr. Jack was a family doc from New England, with a heart for the poor and underserved. He worked for a number of years on an

Indian reservation in Arizona, running the emergency room, then later moved into the hood of Memphis, serving in an inner-city clinic with Christ Community Health Services. Dr. Jack specialized in taking the lower position; instead of absorbing glory for his medical work, he modeled humility and servanthood. He could have commuted to work from the safety and affluence of the suburbs, but Jack and Tiffany fixed up an old crack house and lived among the people they served. They were used to hearing the odd gunshot a block away. "Coming here from inner-city Memphis, Iskandar really doesn't feel too dangerous to me. I love this city." Tiffany was a high school Spanish teacher and brought enthusiasm and fun to the room. She immediately took it upon herself to be sure that Ellie grew up trilingual ... she spoke to her only in Spanish.

Jack did have one flaw, from my perspective ... the guy was always washing dishes. I realized from the start that this habit could have implications for me. Christine was bound to notice. *This is going to put a crimp in my style.*

"Hey man, it seems like you are always doing dishes," I said. "Up and beyond the call of duty, huh? Couldn't you leave them for Hassina in the morning?"

"Actually, I kind of enjoy doing dishes," Jack responded. "Something to do here where you see immediate results." *Oh, boy. The bar has been raised. Going to be doing a lot of dishes.*

That night, around the plastic kitchen table, Jack explained to me the basics of the community health project he was developing. He explained that maternal and infant mortality were the biggest health care problems in Afghanistan. TB was next.

"TB was effectively wiped out decades ago in the West, unfortunately over 75,000 people in this country have active, pulmonary Mycobacterium Tuberculosis, which is contagious. The World Health Organization estimates that in one year each of these patients will infect another fifteen people with TB. The disease is spread through coughing. This year 20,000 Afghans will needlessly die of TB, most of them women."

"I thought TB could be cured with antibiotics," I said.

"It is totally curable, but it takes eight months to treat with a regimen of four to five antibiotics, depending on the category of TB."

The problem was that most Afghans, more than 70 percent, lived out in villages, far from any hospital or clinic. Therefore most babies were born on dirt floors in villages and TB patients did not have regular access to the regimen of medications or the supervision that they needed to achieve treatment success. Drug-resistant TB ensued.

Jack's plan was to take awareness, detection, and treatment to the village level by training community health workers in hundreds of villages. We would help upgrade skills at the clinic level, but our focus would be out in the villages. Dr. Jack was already running a pilot program, working out of one district clinic and training community health workers in thirty villages. He explained that many didn't think our approach of community health would work.

"Right now, we are kind of swimming upstream. But I think it is the solution. I know that you have been thinking about your niche here, Matthew. Think no longer. You could totally run this program. Train community health workers in the village, use Afghan health care professionals in existing clinics, wrap it all within the Ministry of Public Health for long-term sustainability. It's more logistics than medical."

I paused for a moment. "Well, then. Let's do this!"

"Thanks, Matthew. Welcome to Afghanistan! I mean it!" Dr. Jack and Tiffany had been in Iskandar for three months and were planning on spending just six months with our team helping us get this program started. Thankfully, they stayed five years and made a real difference in our part of the country.

The next day, Dr. Jack and most of the team took Christine and me out into the villages to see a district clinic. (Ellie stayed behind with Sadie and a doting Hassina.) We piled into the Big Land Cruiser (BLC) and Little Land Cruiser (LLC), packed like sardines in a can. Once again, I realized that *safety* is an abstract word with differing definitions throughout the roads of Afghanistan, particularly when spoken in context of how many bags of cement, animals, and people one should try to load onto the back of a truck. When it comes to the balance between level of risk and economic benefit, safety always gets thrown out the window. We passed a large, Russian-made truck (a Kamaz) so disproportionately loaded with goods and humanity that it leaned over the BLC for a few seconds. Its tires bulged under the weight, threatening to explode at any second.

We pulled into the clinic, a simple government-run comprehensive health center that Dr. Jack and team had helped upgrade. We walked through a small dispensary into the lab, which looked pretty rudimentary. A sink with four bottles of chemical stains. A slide tray with some dodgy-looking slides. A new microscope. A smiling, bearded Afghan lab tech, with only gloves, boots and surgical mask as protective gear. I put my hand over my heart in greeting, being careful to touch nothing, especially the lab tech's hand. *Should we be wearing some kind of biohazard suits in here?* Dr. Jack was explaining things in his calm, professional manner, effectively communicating to my ADD brain: *Hey, this is important! Focus!*

Jack was explaining the use of direct sputum microscopy in diagnosing TB: "With the Ziehl-Neelson stain applied to three samples of the patient's sputum, we can train a lab tech in a matter of weeks to accurately spot TB on the slides with greater than ninety-nine percent accuracy." I looked into the lab tech's microscope, and sure enough, there was the TB. Lots of little red squiggles. Jack continued: "Dr. Maleki and Mirwais will now follow this patient back to his village and work with the village *shura* (leadership council) to educate them in TB." But the key to the patient's treatment would be a community health worker from the village daily observing him take his medicine for the next eight months until he is cured.

"So how does the community health worker make sure that this guy keeps taking his meds once he starts feeling better?" I asked.

"We have an agreement with the World Food Programme, which will provide a monthly supplement of food, helping keep the patient's body strong enough to resist some of the side effects of the medicines throughout his treatment. This patient should start feeling better in a month, and in two months convert to sputum negative, being no longer contagious. But if he stops taking his medicine, the community health worker will pull his food supplement." *Cool. Food as incentive and quality control mechanism.* "We will test the patient's sputum at two, five, and eight months," Jack explained. "After eight months, if the patient remains sputum negative, and his symptoms are gone, he will graduate from the program. Cured!" *We sure are talking a lot about spit. But glad there is hope for this guy.*

We stepped into a larger room with two desks, an assortment of toshaks in one corner, and about sixty fifty-pound bags of rice, plus a hundred or so containers of oil. I studied a large, hand-drawn map on the wall of the village coverage area. Tiffany had made the wooden frame. *This is a strong, cost-effective project. We need to expand this thing!*

Zelme and Mirwais then drove us to a village called De Khak, where the team had trained several community health workers and had a good relationship with the village *harbob* (leader). The road was an hour on dirt tracks, rolling through hilly countryside layered with dust. We passed several primitive villages that somehow eked out an existence on this barren landscape with herds of camels. We drove through a dust storm, tubular in nature, coming straight at us over the dirt track. The dust completely clogged the air filter, and the BLC ground to a stop. "Just one minute, Mr. Matthew," Zelme calmly stated, then jumped out of the vehicle, popped the hood, and pulled out the air filter for the wind to clean. Minutes later, we were back in business. We crested a hill, looking down on the village of

De Khak. Mud homes, each surrounded by crumbling mud walls, stretched across the valley, dotted by a few thirsty-looking trees. But looking down at the ground, I spotted watermelons growing out of the cracked earth. Thousands of them!

We drove down to the village, where local women quickly ushered Christine, Cheryl, Catherine, Audrie, and Tiffany into their domain for hours of drinking hot tea (on a burning hot day), dancing, and downing a sour yogurt drink. Dr. Jack and I went with the men to the leader's mud house, where in the process of conversation I might have inadvertently introduced a new practice into their culture. While chewing on *nan* (flat bread) and drinking tea, I mentioned that I had read in a book that camel herders have a certain procedure for appeasing an angry camel. Evidently when a camel blows his top, he can get really dangerous. The villagers, camel herders themselves, confirmed this. Dr. Jack shot me a look that asked, "What are you doing?" I shrugged back. "Hey, just trying to make conversation."

I opened my mouth and Zelme translated. "Well, what I read is that the recipient of the camel's anger will take his clothes off and lay them in the sand. The camel will then vent his anger by stomping on and otherwise attacking the articles of clothing. Once the camel has concluded his tirade, the herder will put his clothes back on, and man and beast will be reconciled."

Evidently, this was the first time these villagers had heard of this procedure. They decided it was a brilliant plan.

"You must be a camel expert," they said. "We will try this!"

"Uh, no, I'm not! I just read about it!"

The villagers started chattering excitedly. "Zelme, what are they saying?!" I wanted to know. Zelme looked at me with a smirk. "They say that you are the master of camels! Your wisdom is most appreciated."

Harbob insisted that we take watermelons with us back to Iskandar. Several villagers stuffed the back of the LLC with them.

On the way home, the women shared about their adventure in De Khak. "We each had to dance," Cheryl explained. "Solo performance!" Tiffany chimed in: "Christine also danced. Quite the dancer you have there, Matthew!"

I leaned over and asked Christine, "Did you drink the yogurt?"

She had. "I had no choice! The ladies kept offering it to me...I didn't want to be rude!"

I had played with my yogurt but managed not to drink it. The camel conversation had helped distract. I looked at Christine and said, "You are going to get Giardia!"

We made it back to Iskandar at sunset, the soft glow of light painting the minarets of our ancient city with a certain mystique. We pulled into the office and let our hair down. I sat on the living room floor with my new family...Ellie on my lap, happily eating pizza. After goodnight kisses from her new aunts and uncles, we put Ellie to bed. Tiffany put on the first episode of "24," a show we ended up making a ritual of watching together as a team on many nights. *Not too shabby*, I thought. *Feels kind of like camp, except for the fact that we are in Afghanistan!*

Christine and I had come here to obey God's call on our lives but could already see His hand of blessing in putting us right in the middle of a supportive community. I leaned back on the carpet. *Not a bad start to our new lives in Afghanistan!*

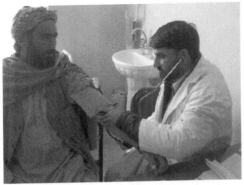

Top, a small lab in a Provincial Health Clinic has played an important role in combating tuberculosis in Afghanistan. The key to health projects was to empower accurate diagnosis and treatment in the district clinics, middle. Matthew with a new friend on a hillside overlooking an Afghan Village.

Part II

Culture Shock

Late Summer, 2004

Dearest Mom and Dad,

I just finished hanging the clothes on the line and dusting (a task done very often here) and Ellie is sleeping, so I am finally able to write a long overdue email to you. We think about you all the time and miss you. I have often started emails to you in my mind, but now I am actually able to write. Mom, thank you for your sweet email. It is always so good to get news from home and most especially from family. I do feel far away and seem to miss everyone so much more.

We really are doing well. Ellie is very healthy and has been getting used to the food ... her stomach bug that she had for so long has cleared up. Her daily diet consists of eggs, tomatoes, a rice cereal in the morning, bananas, bread, squash, rice, and (at times) chicken. There is a lack of green vegetables here so I have been supplementing with some vitamins. She is eating well and even drinking the milk. Her latest words are "no, no" (saying this while shaking her finger), "shoes," "bye-bye," and "Hi." She very seriously babbles and tries so hard to communicate. She definitely has her Daddy's fun personality and someone commented the other day that she has "Collins blood."

Probably the biggest thing that I have struggled with has been feeling the oppression of women here. Being fully veiled when outing, stares from men, not being able to go out when I want, wearing even a small scarf inside the office when the Afghan staff are here (since they are men), and not being sure of the boundaries of even being friendly or nice to men in general has been hard.

That being said, many things have been better than I imagined. For example, since we are living at the guest house at our office, we are here with two other couples, Catherine (the single nurse from home) and another nurse named Audrie. This gives me many opportunities to go out with the other women so I'm not stuck in the office and guest house all day. Matthew has been such a support (of course) and takes me out. We were even able to go on a little "date" to a restaurant here that allows couples to eat together alone. We sat out on a balcony away from the other group of men (I didn't see any other women there) and it was such a pleasant time.

We have been able to spend the majority of our time learning Dari, which is a big advantage to living at our NGO's guesthouse right now. Everyone in the house eats lunch together that is prepared by a local cook, so I'm only responsible for cooking dinner. One of the Afghan ladies who cleans here watches Ellie a few hours each day so that I can attend language class. She is very sweet and I trust her. Ellie does well with her, too, as long as she can go outside in the compound.

Ellie is awake so I'd better close this email. We love you both very much and miss you!

Much Love,
Christine

*Oh, East is East, and West is West, and never the twain shall meet,
Till Earth and Sky stand presently at God's great Judgment Seat...*
—Rudyard Kipling

*It ain't what you don't know that gets you into trouble.
It's what you know for sure that just ain't so.*
—Mark Twain

Chapter 5

When East Meets West

My family went to Afghanistan to try to make a difference in people's lives. There was plenty to stop us. Danger. Xenophobia. Culture shock. The latter almost killed us.

Many travelers confuse country shock with culture shock. Afghanistan is plenty strong to send even the most ardent traveler spiraling into country shock. It may be the sight of dust and guns—the perception that nothing is clean or safe—that switches on the impulse to jump on the first flight out. Or maybe the impression of brokenness—the sight of war-torn buildings and children missing limbs—is what overwhelms the senses. But even if you have a strong tolerance for chaos, the inevitable intestinal bout with Giardia coming soon will likely break the camel's back. The good news about country shock is that it can be overcome in a short amount of time.

Culture shock is an altogether different matter. It is deeper and more long term, running to the core of our personalities and belief systems. Culture shock occurs when we encounter something within another culture that is different from what we expect, bringing on shock, anger, and withdrawal. For me there was an element of fear lurking beneath. It is an inevitable part of crossing culture that often takes years to overcome. The good news is that we can fight through the cycles of culture shock if we are honest in assessing our feelings, adjusting our expectations, and eventually accepting the key differences between our culture and that of our new country.

Unchecked, culture shock leads to withdrawal, darkness, and total failure in our mission. We no longer see the Afghan honor and hospitality; instead, oppression, corruption, and fanaticism overwhelm our consciousness. We withdraw into our cocoons, meet our social needs with other foreigners, and intensely focus on aspects of our job that help us feel that we can do something with competence. Unfortunately, these natural reactions don't help us navigate our way through culture shock; they simply serve to isolate us from the culture we are trying to understand. If we are really going to help Afghanistan develop, we must learn to understand the local culture.

The key to overcoming culture shock is engagement. My family had to fight against the urge to withdraw. We forced ourselves to interact with the local culture. This was challenging in Afghanistan, where both security concerns and historical xenophobia made the distance harder to bridge. But our experience was that the Afghan people open their hearts to foreigners who attempt to learn their language and demonstrate respect for their culture. Afghan and Western cultures mix like oil and water. But as we encountered things that shocked us, we made a concerted effort to adjust our expectations so that we could accept things strange to us. The key to looking past the negative is to seek out and focus on the beautiful aspects of their culture so that we can build meaningful relationships with local people.

I learned from my daughter. She stood out in Afghanistan with her blonde hair and blue eyes. Everywhere she went, Afghans tried to win the affection of little Ellie. She became an unabashed flirt, trying to coax smiles from even the most grumpy strangers. One time she sat on my lap on a flight to Kabul, next to an Iranian mullah. This man had as dour a face as I've ever seen and didn't seem at all happy to be sitting next to a *khafir* (infidel). He refused to respond to Ellie's attempts to win him over. But she was more than up for the challenge. Midway through the flight, she was still smiling and searching for his eyes. Eventually he couldn't take it anymore ... he turned his face to the window and smiled, then glanced across the aisle to make sure none of his other mullah traveling companions noticed. By the time we were approaching Kabul, Ellie was sitting on his lap, pointing out snowcapped mountains with him.

How did she do it? With *faith, endurance, and love.* There were a lot of strange, turbaned men on the plane, but she wasn't afraid of one of them. Because she was with her daddy, whom she trusted. She never gave up. And she modeled a truth written two thousand years ago by a guy named Peter: "Love covers a multitude of sins." (1 Peter 4:8b, ESV)

Afghanistan gave us plenty of bouts with culture shock, but first we had to experience country shock in all of its glory. My first strong dose of country shock came just a few days after landing in Iskandar.

Rodney looked down on me as I lay in bed, sick as a dog: "Well, one thing is for sure," he said. "Giardia is one heck of a weight-loss program!"

I lay halfway in the fetal position, clutching my stomach. As if there was anything left to hold inside. "Oh, man! This is brutal!"

I moaned. "God is punishing me for making fun of Christine for drinking the yogurt!"

Christine had gotten sick, all right. Hers had lasted for three days, and it wasn't pretty. But I had spent much of the past week sitting on that toilet, being so thankful for that little sink that I could throw up into. Country shock, Afghan-style.

It all started two days after we got back from the village, when James had given me the royal tour of Iskandar. I met his new partner, Billy, a sixty-something Texan who had been around the Central Asian block a few times. They were working on starting a vocational rehab project and also considering leadership development. We drove up to the top of a small mountain just outside the city that had a bird's eye view of Iskandar. In the distance we could see the domes and minarets of ancient mosques and an impressive mud fort built by Alexander the Great.

"We often come up here together on Thursday mornings to pray," James explained.

"Join us, Matthew," Billy invited, with his old school Texan drawl. Made me want to unfurl a Texan flag right there and sing "Deep in the Heart of Texas."

Billy loved Jesus and had something of a charismatic stripe. He lifted both arms toward heaven and begun asking the Lord to visit His peace on the city. A few minutes into our prayer time, a military helicopter flew by, noticed three guys doing something on the mountain ridge, and looped around for a closer look. Several Americans with sunglasses and machine guns stared right at us, eye-level. I flashed 'em a thumbs up, and they flew off. Billy hardly missed a beat. It did my heart good to pray with these brothers.

Billy had somewhere to be, so we dropped him off and James wanted to buy me lunch. "Let's find some good Afghan kebabs, Matt!" James was right that there are delicious kebabs in Afghanistan, but he didn't yet know where to find them. We settled at a little sidewalk kebab-stand in the central park.

James tore right into them. "Amazing kebabs, man. Can you believe this? Here we are, in Afghanistan, eating kebabs! This is the daddy."

"I'm just glad for a break from Pashtun's cooking. It's killing me." I took a bite, then winced. "Actually, these are pretty bad."

"They *are* pretty bad. What kind of meat *is* this?"

I took another bite. "Hey, man. I think this is liver!"

For some reason, still unknown to me, we plowed right through those kebabs, wolfing them down with a lot of nan. Maybe we didn't want to offend the bearded kebab guy who stood and watched us from a short distance away, grinning and nodding. Or maybe neither of us wanted to be a pansy.

Now I was paying the price, five days later and fifteen pounds lighter. Not for the last time, I thanked God for the doctor living a few feet away from where I lay, green and groaning. Dr. Jack treated me with Flagyl, not the most pleasant medicine, but effective. "It may leave a metallic taste in your mouth, and could even make you more sick to your stomach for a day or two, but it will get the job done." He kept bringing me filtered water to stay hydrated, and never commented on what a wuss of a patient I was.

Christine and I were not the only ones who got sick. Little Ellie had diarrhea for her first few weeks in country. Dr. Jack continually checked on her and kept us reassured that she was adequately hydrated and was retaining enough nutrients. One evening he handed me a printout of research from the Mayo Clinic corroborating his medical opinion, just to assure us that our little girl was really OK. It wasn't necessary but certainly appreciated. Christine and I realized that we were truly blessed to have a family doctor living with us, eager to serve. Who would have thought?

Once I was back on my feet, Jack took me for a look around at some of Iskandar's sights. I rode on the back of his Chinese-made dirt bike, hardly feeling manly, but glad to be out of bed.

"Lot of speed bumps in this city!" I yelled from the back of the motorcycle.

"Our Governor, Zayed Khan, installed them," Jack responded. Zayed Khan had been an enemy of the Taliban, an initial ally of Coalition Forces, and had brought order and relative prosperity to Iskandar. He rebuilt schools, planted trees, and paved roads. "To help stem the rising numbers of pedestrian casualties, now that people are driving faster!" We drove over a speed bump where, sadly, Zayed Khan's son had been shot and killed in his SUV a month before.

We rode up to a popular hillside park that sits below James and Billy's prayer mountain, complete with an old MIG and several Russian helicopters for decoration, a snack bar shaped as a blue metal chicken, and a large outdoor swimming pool (sans chlorine). Zayed Khan's flying saucer-shaped guesthouse hovered over the park on top of a nearby hill. We dismounted and watched about fifty men frolic in the deep pool, some of them barely able to swim.

"Looks like some of those guys are just swimming in their underwear!" I observed. Pretty strange for ultra-modest Afghanistan, and not a pretty sight.

"Not sure Zayed Khan will appreciate that too much." Jack leaned closer and whispered: "There is a darker side. ZK maintains his own army and police force and really runs the show here." He explained that ZK substantially invested in the infrastructure of the city—ingratiating himself to many in Iskandar—but also became an extremely wealthy and powerful man during his tenure as governor. Detractors complained about censorship and human rights abuses in the city, particularly for women. "Zayed Khan calls himself the emir of our part of the country. Trouble is brewing between him and (President) Karzai."

Half a dozen bearded men with whips entered the pool compound and drove the swimmers out. "Did ZK send those guys?!" We watched with a mixture of wonder and amusement as the men tucked their whips away and carried eight, giant, pink swan paddleboats into the pool. "Nope, it is just paddleboat time!" *What a country!*

The motorcycle was a great way to connect with my new ancient city. I had never been much of a motorcycle rider, but a few weeks of cabin fever and the onset of culture shock prompted me to borrow Dr. Jack's dirt bike for a few jaunts around town. I didn't have much Dari yet, but it was important to me to be out in society as much as possible. My second day of riding ended with a spill into a jewey, right in front of a group of young Afghan men playing volleyball in the central park. Thankfully, my worst nightmare was blunted by the fact that this particular jewey had dried up in the summer heat. But I had a motorcycle lying on top of me, my calf burning from contact with the exhaust pipe, and, worst of all, a significantly wounded ego. The volleyball players just stood there and laughed as I tried to negotiate out from underneath the fallen bike. *Thanks a lot for the help! Glad to provide you some entertainment!*

I decided it was time to buy my own ride. Christine was right; motorcycles in Afghanistan have risks, but I found this new means of transportation to be therapeutic. There was something to be said about the joy of flying down a dirt road, hair blowing in the wind, weaving around zaranges (auto rickshaws) or exchanging a thumbs up with a passing convoy of American Hummers. Freedom. I made my case to Christine. "Sweetheart, the merits of a sound mind over here outweigh the risk of having to spend some time in a hospital bed. I'm just in a better mood after I ride." Somehow, she eventually agreed, but Christine strictly forbid any daddy-daughter riding in Iskandar.

We purchased a seventeen-year-old Suzuki 250cc dirt bike in a steel-shipping container, fresh from Japan. Now that I had my ride, I needed to find an immersion environment in which I could practice speaking Dari. Christine and I had just begun full-time language learning, but there was a lot of English spoken at the office. On a motorcycle ride early on, I'd spotted a gym next to the stadium in the central park. *Perfect,* I thought to myself. *I can listen to Dari while rebuilding my body from some of the weight I've lost from Giardia and Pashtun's cooking!*

Remembering his childhood home of India from his country manor estate in green East Sussex, Rudyard Kipling penned the verse:

Oh, East is East, and West is West, and never the twain shall meet, till Earth and Sky stand presently at God's great Judgment Seat.

But sometimes East and West do meet, and that mixture can brew up shocking absurdity. Kipling would have loved the Afghan gymnasium.

One morning I summoned my courage and walked into the gym for the first time. When they saw me, the guys running the place turned off the Hindi music video they had been ogling on the fuzzy TV set that hung in one corner of the gym. They put on a bootlegged copy of *Commando* in my honor. From that day forward, every time I showed up at the gym the dancing Indian girls lost their screen time and a young Arnold Schwarzenegger came on. (When I explained to my new buddies that Arnold was now governor of the most populous state of my country, that made perfect sense to them.) Most of the weights were homemade, but everything was present for a complete workout. Ten minutes into my first workout, I noticed a young man to my left doing some very interesting aerobic exercises. I tried not to smirk. *Maybe that is good for you, sport, but it sure looks goofy!* A few minutes later, a skinny young man ripped off his shirt and walked over to the mirror. He started flexing without shame, accompanying his motions with spirited sound effects: "OoooAAH! POW!" I almost dropped the barbell on my chest. Then I thought about it... the transparent vanity on display was almost refreshing. *Which is more vain, to sneak looks at yourself in a mirror during a workout at the gym, or to openly flex in front of others like you might in private at home?*

I finally worked up the courage to go to the gym in the evening. The place was so full of men (including a judo class in one corner) that four of us worked in with each bench or weight set. Being that I spoke very little Dari, the guys exercising with me decided that I must know very little about weights. I was their apprentice. Thirty minutes into the workout, I heard some clapping in a corner. Assuming it was an awards ceremony for the judo students, I tried to keep exercising. But my new weight–master had other plans. He grabbed my hand and instructed: "*BiyA, Berem!*" ("Come, let's go!") Against my better instincts, I allowed him to lead me into the fray.

We got there in time to see a small fellow pull off his shirt and start flexing for the crowd. I swallowed a laugh, condensed it to a silly grin, and turned to the guy standing next to me. He wasn't laughing at all. "He is very strong!" he said with admiration. Another lightweight pulled off his shirt and started the routine. He added some impressive and well-coordinated grunts, which only led to louder applause. The procedure was repeated several times, until I found myself being pushed toward the middle. *Oh, no. This a BAD situation!* Help, I wanted out! *How did I get into this! Totally surrounded! Culture Shock, Afghanistan!* Then guys started pointing at me… "Take your shirt, off!!" they commanded. I was pushed to the middle of the crowd…

Top, the Collins family enjoying a break from hiking outside Iskandar City. Ellie with Hassina and Pashtun, bottom left. With her blonde hair and blue eyes, Ellie was an instant attraction in Afghanistan, with men and women constantly vying for her attention. Bottom right, Ellie and Matthew on his beloved motorcycle.

Everyone has been made for some particular work,
and the desire for that work has been put in every heart.
—Rumi

Love risks everything and asks for nothing.
—Rumi

Chapter 6

My Home is with You

I walked upstairs one evening and did a double take. "Matthew, look what Jack found in the bazaar today!" Ellie, almost a year and a half old, was sitting on a plastic training potty. Crouched next to her in the shower room were Uncle Jack and Aunt Audrie, gently holding her hand in a plastic bowl with warm water. Next to Ellie was another plastic bowl with cool water. "She is learning quickly," nurse Audrie smiled. Dr. Jack agreed. "We will have her trained for you in no time!" Ellie beamed at me, proud as a peacock.

Tiffany and Dr. Jack had never been able to have children of their own but quickly became Ellie's doting aunt and uncle. Ellie would walk into their bedroom in the morning, sit on the edge of the bed, and read books with Aunt Tiffany. She was starting to respond to Tiffany's Spanish. In the evenings, she would climb up on Papa Rodney's lap while he watched an episode of *MASH* and share his popcorn dinner. We had been in Iskandar for only three weeks, but as the only child in the staff house, Ellie had already gained an uncle, three aunts, and two grandparents.

Sometimes Christine and I would take her out on short shopping excursions with us, where *dukondars* (shopkeepers) would try to win her heart with a piece of candy, despite Christine's protests. I'd carry her on my shoulders or in her backpack carrier where she would wave like a rock star as Afghans vied for her attention. The cheek pinching at the bazaar was a little too much for her, though. Afghans love children but can be a little rough with their displays of affection. In crowded places, hands would protrude from burqas and pinch her cheeks. Sometimes, she would pinch the women back.

Our office staff adored Ellie and did their best to secure her friendship. Ghulam, our battle-hardened guard, had a soft spot for Ellie. His preferred method over the years to win her affection was to raise his walking stick above his head and to shake it at her. He would then break into laughter, usually at the same time she was running in the opposite direction in panic. Sometimes he would take off his prosthetic leg and shake that at her as well, laughing hard as he hopped on his remaining leg. He couldn't figure out why his attempts at wooing her weren't working.

Our main activity the first six months in country was Dari language study. Persian is a descriptive language, and the Dari ("Redneck Persian") spoken in Afghanistan is especially so. A rose is an "elephant flower," a turkey an "elephant chicken," and a rabbit "donkey ears." It also is an ancient language, a window into a beautiful culture, thousands of years in the making. When complimented for something special, an Afghan will reply, "Your eyes are beautiful!"

In the mornings, Christine and I would sit side by side in Aziz's small classroom learning grammar and basic vocabulary. Christine and Aziz were patient with me; while I was pretty quick with the grammatical structure of the language, it became clear early on that I was the turtle at Dari vocabulary. Having learned fluent French in her childhood, Christine was quicker, smarter, and more disciplined with her studies. When we were moving too quickly through a chapter for my brain to keep up, I'd stall by asking Aziz questions about Afghan culture. He knew exactly what I was doing, but this being an honor culture, he played along.

"So when we enter the guest room of someone's house, where should we sit?"

"The seat furthest from the door is the place of highest honor," he explained. "But is always best to sit halfway up, because village elders could walk into the room after you. The master of the house will honor you by asking you to come sit closer to the high position."

"Aziz, I was walking in the bazaar the other day, and a dukondar invited me to come to his house for dinner. Should I have said yes?"

"He was just being polite. An Afghan will always ask you three times if the invitation is real. He was just honoring you as a sort of greeting."

"What about tea? People are always saying 'Chai Bukhoren!'"

"If he has tea in front of him, and he motions to you, then you can sit and have tea with him. Tea allows even poor Afghans to practice hospitality."

"I have heard a lot about the famous Afghan hospitality. But will an Afghan really give his life to protect me if I am his guest? Why would he do that, especially if he doesn't even know me? He might not even like me!"

"He would. His family honor depends on his ability to protect his guest. If he couldn't protect you, the entire honor of his family and tribe would be damaged. His children would not be able to marry, and no one would do business with any of his relatives. Protecting guests is the highest priority."

"I've noticed that the men here go first. In my culture, holding a door for a woman is a sign of respect. Should I do that here?"

"Please do not, Mr. Matthew! Her relatives would think that you were interested in her, and it could be dangerous for you. She might be beaten at home for this! It is best to never make eye contact in public with an Afghan woman."

By now, Christine would give me a look that said, "Let's get back to work!" I'd slip one more question in:

"I've noticed that when people greet one another, they spend a lot of time dramatically inquiring about each other's well-being and health. They ask all the questions at the same time, so no one is really listening to the other person."

Aziz laughed at his own cultural practice. "This is just a way of showing respect. The greetings are long, but they show that the person is more important than the task. It is good that you always do this. It shows that you honor our culture, just like Miss Christine does by covering her head."

When greeting each other, Afghan women especially add intonations and gestures of great joy. They repeatedly kiss each other's cheeks as if it has been years since they have seen each other. I found it amusing to watch the ladies on our team participating in this ritual; sometimes they overdid it. But I tried not to tease them; they were just trying to adapt to the culture. I got used to the greetings, but they seemed more dramatic when done in English. I was at the clinic with Dr. Jack and Dr. Maleki one day when a fellow Pashtun doctor walked into the room. Impressing us all with his command of English, he swept across the floor and cried out: "Dr. Maleki, my dearest! My heart is so happy to see you!" With that, a bear hug and multiple cheek kissing commenced. The Pashtuns are the fiercest warriors on the planet, but they also can be the most flowery, with men wearing nail polish, picking flowers, and dancing for each other at weddings. Years later on a visit to Jalalabad, deep in Pashtun territory, I asked the office manager if he would go down to the bazaar and get me a phone card.

"Mr. Matthew, just ask me for my head, and I would gladly give it to you!"

"I really don't want your head. Just a phone card."

"All you have to do is ask, and I would give you my head!"

Christine, Ellie and I would eat lunch with our team and Afghan staff, trying to use as much Dari as possible during that meal, and then spend the afternoon in a combination of personal study and practicing with language helpers. Language learning was humbling. I had a master's degree but felt like a kindergartner in conversation.

"Peace be upon you. How are you? Are you good? How is your family? My name is Matthew. I am from Texas. I work for NGO. We do doctor and school and village helping. What is your name?"

In the afternoons I'd try to get out in the community to practice my new vocabulary. Often I would slaughter it. I walked into one trinket shop, where a guy was really proud of his rock collection. "Your rocks look very delicious!" For some reason, I always mixed up *makbul* (beautiful) with *masadar* (delicious). But at least I could blend in. With dark hair, hazel eyes, my beard grown out, and wearing a pair of dusty shalwar kamis (called *paran tombons* in Iskandar) and my long *desmal* scarf, I passed for a Tajik on the streets of our city. I learned the Afghan gait, puffed my chest out a couple inches more, and strutted like a true land pirate with a determined face but a slightly lost look in the eye. I knew when I truly blended into the crowd because the sideways glances disappeared and people started knocking into me. Getting lost in the crowd was, for me, freeing. It was great antidote to the first stages of culture shock. *Maybe I can't say a whole lot yet,* I thought to myself, *but I'm engaging with the culture...physically!*

I'd head toward Iskandar's eight-hundred-year old mosque, passing people selling cloth, wool, secondhand clothes, and hundreds of shoes on the street until I reached the gardens of the mosque compound. Many considered it to be one of the finest examples of

Persian architecture anywhere, with blue, handmade tiles covering the facades and towering minarets. After decades of war and neglect, restorative work slowly continued with tiles painstakingly being made by hand within the complex.

One day I'd ducked inside and was watching several men on prayer cloths going through their prayer rituals, prostrating themselves toward Mecca. They were reciting their prayers in Arabic, a language that most Afghans do not understand. A young university student approached me and politely started conversation, in good English. "Excuse me, but I feel that you are not on the right path. The true path is of submission to the one true God." We spoke for a while, and I learned that Afghans think that all Americans are Christians and that we believe in three gods (God, Jesus, and Mary), never pray, and are sexually immoral.

Near the mosque was Iskandar's blue glass shop. The aged owner, Sultan Ahmed, often sat in the doorway and would bid me welcome with an oversized handshake and an offer of tea. Glassmaking goes back in his family for centuries, and on certain days his small factory—several doors down to the right—would be in operation. His son enthusiastically explained the process of making blue glass, unchanged over the centuries here, as a hunchback skillfully worked with his hands, feet, and mouth in a blazing hot environment.

Sultan Ahmed had a great selection of blue glass in his shop, accompanied by all kinds of treasures made centuries ago, along with trinkets recently crafted in India to look old. Muskets and swords from dead British soldiers, ancient Greek coins from Alexander's day, four-hundred-year-old Persian cylinder seals, century-old Turkmen carpets, *buzkashi* whips, and stone oil lamps hand-carved over a thousand years ago were all on display. The gray-bearded shopkeeper next door had some of the same, plus a staggering collection of shotguns made in the frontier villages of Pakistan.

Saying *"khuda hafez"* ("God be with you") to Sultan Ahmed, I'd walk through the crowded material bazaar, through a sea of blue burqas punctuated by some black head-to-toe (but open-faced) *chawder namazes* worn by more progressive women. I passed several burqa-clad women weeding through a large pile of bras, holding them up for estimation—all officiated by the gray bearded bra-seller. At the end of the street lay Iskandar's impressive gold bazaar, selling an astonishing amount of gold for a country with one of the lowest gross national products (GNP) in the world. This economic anomaly was made possible by the cultural practice of the bride price. If a man wanted to marry a woman, he would need to first pay a hefty price to her family in animals, cash, and gold, signifying her value. (This became a problem for me in that Christine was asked at weddings, "Why are you wearing so little gold?") I'd continue walking past shops selling nuts, raisins, and numerous spices until I arrived at Iskandar's imposing mud fortress, first built by the Greek army of Alexander the Great more than two thousand years ago.

On my "language jaunts," I almost always ended up at the fortress, easily my favorite place in the city. The first time I walked through the gate, a friendly ANA (Afghan National Army) soldier showed me around. We climbed up the highest tower in the "newer" section of the fort— only several hundred years old—for the postcard-perfect view of the ancient mud citadel and its eighteen towers. Below us were centuries-old neighborhoods of mud homes surrounded by walls and maze-like streets, fronted by workshops where men carved up old tires to make sandals, buckets, and saddlebags. Climbing down narrow staircases, we explored a large, partially underground room below this tower, where truckloads of out-of-circulation afghani currency had been dumped. We tramped around in the sea of millions of old afghani notes, throwing them up in the air and generally having a good time. I found old British rifle cases and slings in all the rubbish. A few months later, after the ANA had moved out of the fort, I tried to take Christine into this room to show her the money. Two Afghan National Policemen (ANP) yelled at us:

"Stop! Don't go in there! It is dangerous!"

"Chi? Muskel nis! Chand ma pish, inji amadum. Khatarnak na bud!" ("What? No problem! A few months ago, I was here. It wasn't dangerous!") I was quite pleased with what I could communicate with my limited vocabulary and was trying to show off a little for Christine. She wasn't that impressed and let me know that I should listen to these men with AK-47s.

"You don't think it is dangerous, huh? Come with us."

They led us to a side room where they had amassed a small collection of land mines and unexploded ordnance.

"You don't think it is dangerous in there? We found this underneath the old money in that room you want to go play in!"

It took me a second to remember the right word. *"Uhh...Bebakhshen!"* ("Pardon me!") *Whoa. And why do I have such a hard time remembering that word?!*

After wandering along the walls of the newer section of the fort, I'd walk up the ramp and through the centuries-old wooden doors guarding the ancient citadel. Genghis Khan, Timur, and others laid siege to this very structure. In the early days, I found bullet and artillery casings and even a few bones lying on the ground inside. I'd climb a dark spiral stairway leading to the top of a tower, eighty feet above Iskandar's old city, with a bird's eye view of all the action on the streets below. Bullet pockmarks crowned the tops of shops built into the side of ancient mud buildings, while crowds of pedestrians, carts, and rickshaws bought and sold vegetables, goat heads, and other local culinary delights.

Many have written about the quality of the evening light in Afghanistan. One early evening I stood on a tower, basking in the glow, reflecting on battles that had been fought on this very spot. I stood where a young British lieutenant had stood, 170 years before, directing the defenses of the city against Persian attackers. A player in what is known by historians as *The Great Game*, this young British spy originally came to Iskandar with dyed skin and

Afghan dress, posing as a Muslim holy man. When the Persians (aided by Russian advisors) attacked the city, he gambled his head (several players of *The Great Game* lost theirs). He changed back into his military uniform, presented his services to the Iskandari court, and helped organize the city's defenses, inspiring the Afghans to fight to the end. Iskandaris remember this young Brit for valiantly saving the day when Persian artillery had breached the walls and foot soldiers were pouring in through one damaged section. While the city's defenders scattered, he charged forward into the breach, inspiring the Iskandaris to fight harder to save the city.

A jingle from my mobile phone rudely interrupted the battle being played out in my head.

"*Salamaleykum*... Hi, Sweetheart!"

"Where are you? Are you getting some good language practice, Matthew?"

"Yes! Profitable afternoon. Learning a lot."

"Don't forget our date tonight. Tiffany and Catherine are watching Ellie, so we should really leave in the next thirty minutes. Hurry home from the fort!"

"Uh, right! Will be there in twenty minutes!"

An hour later, Christine and I sat on a carpeted platform, looking out at the lights of Iskandar. This was our first date in Afghanistan, at a hillside restaurant shaped like a flying saucer (in similar fashion to ZK's guesthouse, which hovered on a hill above), but the lamb kebabs were good and the view fabulous. We could never let our hair down in public, so we could not touch. Christine had to keep her head covered. Still, she looked beautiful to me, the blue of her kabuli chawder matching her eyes. They sparkled in the evening light.

"This is a step up from Pashtun's cooking!" I said between chews.

"You shouldn't be so tough on her, Matthew. She does her best."

"Slimy okra basted in oil. Soggy squash in double the oil. How do you make rice so oily?"

"OK, you are right!" Christine laughed. "She might not be around much longer. Tiffany caught her wearing Sadie's dress this morning!"

"Jack was telling me that Afghans do strange things when they are about to quit their jobs. Maybe Hassina could start cooking lunch for everyone. Actually, I shouldn't complain. You are the one who has to cover your head whenever you go out! I sure do appreciate you."

"God has been good to us, Matthew. He has really taken care of us here."

"Did you see Audrie and Jack trying to potty train Ellie the other day?"

Christine laughed, then quickly glanced to the side to make sure no Afghan men had noticed. She lowered her voice a bit. "It will never work. She is way too young. I tried to tell them that."

"She loves the attention," I replied. "All the uncles and aunts, and she loves Hassina. Ellie knows it is her when she shows up for work, still in her burqa!"

"She is adjusting well to life here," Christine said. "Sometimes she tries to cover her head with a scarf when she sees me doing it!"

I took a sip of my ZamZam Cola, an Iranian imitation of Pepsi. "Never thought it would be this smooth. I feel like we are safer here than I expected. When people write and ask about danger, it really feels like the war is far away, in a different country."

I thought for a second as I chewed on a kebab.

"Hey, Christine, we are doing OK, aren't we?

"What do you mean?"

"You and me. It's a full house. Not a lot of privacy. Plus, a male-dominated culture outside. I want you to know that I love you and respect the way you choose to take the lower position in this country."

"I love you, Matthew. My home is with you."

Little did we know that the danger that pervades Afghanistan was about to turn its head toward us.

Top, a fortress built by the Greek army of Alexander the Great more than two thousand year ago. This was Matthew's favorite place to visit in the city. Matthew, left, standing at the gates of the old fortress.

'I feel sure I am right when I say that the less the Afghans see of us,
the less they will dislike us.'
—Frederick Roberts, 1880

If you can keep your head when all about you are losing theirs,
It's just possible you haven't grasped the situation.
—Jean Kerr

Chapter 7

The Rites were Still

Flying

Several days later, I was out in the bazaar practicing my Dari:

"What, this *very* expensive! This is a kharedji price! Very bad! Give me a good price! Please! *Bizamat!* (Without trouble!)" I wildly gestured for emphasis and stormed out of the shocked dukandar's little shop. We were arguing over the price of a cheap, plastic fan. He wanted 800 afghanis ($16) for a fan worth 750 afghanis ($15), something Zelme called the "skin tax" on us kharedjis. *Ridiculous!* I was really just trying to use the new words I had learned that week—often, to get them to stick—but it was hard not to get caught up in the horse-trading. I glanced back to look for a crack in the dukandar's resolve, but he looked mostly perplexed about what rock this stingy kharedji had just crawled out from underneath.

I was about to enter for the second round when my phone rang. It was Sadie, our team's grandmother/security officer. She took her job more seriously than I did, at least at the time.

"Matt, where are you! I just got a call from ANSO. There is an emergency! You need to get back to the office now!" ANSO stood for the Afghanistan NGO Safety Office, an organization that kept us apprised of security issues and sent out emails every time there was any incident in town, from a complex suicide attack down to someone throwing a rock through a window. Sadie spent a lot of time reading ANSO reports.

"Hi Sadie, how are you? I'm kind of in the middle of something important here."

"Aman Khan has just defeated Zayed Khan's troops south of Iskandar! They are moving north toward the city!"

"Yeah, hasn't that been the rumor over the last couple days?" I asked. Several of Zayed Khan's rival commanders had made gains in their turf battle with our governor, and rumors had flown around that the rival commanders were going to try to attack the city. We had been in a state of "lock down" for two days, bags packed for evacuation, and I was glad to be done with that.

"This is SERIOUS, Matthew!"

"You sure they are not crying 'wolf' again?"

"ANSO also sent us a follow-up email. They say there are up to a hundred Taliban fighters rumored to be with Aman Khan who will be looking for Americans!"

That last part sounded pretty bad, so I abandoned my battle for an Afghan price on a fan and sped back to the office in the LLC. Kaka opened the gate, and I noticed the BLC parked there, a small lake of radiator fluid leaking underneath. I checked in on my family—Ellie was taking a nap—and then walked into Rodney and Sadie's office, which functioned as our NGO's nerve center at the time. I overheard Zelme saying something about the bad guys being able to reach the outskirts of the city in one hour, and then Sadie's phone rang. Zelme walked out to get the latest word on the street from Ghulam.

"That was the PRT; they say they advise all American citizens to come immediately to their base, if we can make it there in the next thirty minutes. If not, we should hide in the basement. They are sending an email with more information." *Whoa. This sounds pretty serious.*

Rodney and I read through the email from the PRT, another of the acronyms I was learning that stood for "Provincial Reconstruction Team," basically a small US military base tucked into a neighborhood of Iskandar city. Zelme ducked back into the office. He maintained his trademark poise but was clearly worried: "People are saying that Aman Khan's soldiers will attack Iskandar, and they have Taliban with them. Maybe only thirty minutes away from the city."

Rodney looked at me. "What do you think?"

I dunno; I just got here and am not in charge yet. Don't want to be chicken, but this could be bad. One thing is for sure: Ghulam and Kaka sure won't be able to do much to protect us if Talibs come to our place.

"Let's go!" We sent our Afghan staff home, quickly grabbed our go bags, money, and vital documents, and jumped in the LLC. The BLC was out of commission, so Dr. Jack and I took off in this little vehicle with Christine, Ellie, three other ladies, and all their bags crammed into the back seat. Rodney and Sadie stayed behind to finish buttoning down the place; we might not be back for some time. Chaos reigned on the streets, with everyone either trying to get out of Dodge or find their way home in a hurry.

"You do know where the PRT is located, right?!" I asked Jack, as he weaved through human, vehicular, and donkey-cart traffic.

"Pretty sure. Been by there once before."

The American-run PRT base was located in an upscale neighborhood of Iskandar and blended in well. We drove around the same city blocks several times until some local teenagers—standing on a street corner, watching all the entertainment—flagged us down.

"Hey, that way!" They pointed us in the exact direction of the PRT.

"Well, that was embarrassing! They knew exactly where we were running off to!" Jack executed a fast three-point-turn, just missing a lonely wooden cart piled high with watermelons. It was an amusing scene, minus the fact that thirty minutes had already passed.

We arrived at the American PRT and I jumped out to help the women get inside.

"We have some American women here who need protection!" I said to a young Marine guarding the PRT gate, hoping that I came across cool and official. He and his team were busy trying to hold off a small crowd, which included a group of about ten well-armed men from other countries, each carrying an AK-47, many clips of ammunition, grenades, and a sidearm. They were paramilitary dress but were begging the marines to let them in. One of them grabbed my arm and yelled with an Aussie accent: "Tell them that I am your brother!"

We showed the Marines our passports, and the ladies stepped through the razor wire-shrouded gate. I shouted to Christine and Ellie that I loved them, then jumped back in the LLC to go back with Jack to the office for Rodney and Sadie. I felt relief to have Christine and Ellie in a safe place but was eager to get back to them as soon as possible. The LLC's clutch started slipping, but we had no choice but to keep driving. At least traffic had dissipated; everyone had taken refuge inside. Jack and I arrived at the office, decided we were still better off with the LLC than the BLC, and told Rodney and Sadie we had to leave now.

"Sadie, we have no time! Let's go!" Now I had become the hyper one. With Rodney and Sadie in the back seats, we limped the vehicle back to the PRT. This time the streets were empty; every time we rounded a corner it felt like we might encounter bad guys and a hail of bullets. *This feels like a bad Western movie!*

Walking into the PRT compound was kind of a reverse culture shock. Welcome back to America! These guys were living it up with air conditioning, hamburgers, a big screen TV, their assault rifles and machine guns scattered all over the place. I almost tripped over an M-60 trying to keep up with Ellie, who was toddling around making friends with soldiers in the middle of all this. One soldier brought her a large bag of candy. Next thing we knew guys were going back to their rooms, rifling through care packages, and bringing her handfuls of candy.

"Thank you, but she really doesn't need any more candy!" Christine objected.

I butted in, with Ellie's candy bag. "Yes, she does. Fill it up!"

Lieutenant Colonel Irving, commander of the PRT, stepped up and addressed us.

"Welcome to Club Med! We know it's plush; we'd appreciate it if you help keep that our secret here in Iskandar. The situation is spotty. We have Special Forces units in play and are trying to communicate with Aman Khan that if he crosses a certain line, he and his men will be subject to airstrikes. If worse comes to worse, we have a convoy lined up outside and big guns to blast out of here if need be."

I had been kind of hoping for a helicopter evacuation but asked if there was still time for US civilians in the city to make it to the PRT.

"I'd say if they can get here now, they should do so."

I stepped outside into the courtyard and called James.

"Matt, we are good here at Billy's place. Let me tell you what we are doing. We are praying together right now and really sense God's peace and protection."

"Look, James. I really think you guys should get over here! There is still time."

I called him a couple times, and we went back and forth; I was concerned for James' family, whom I've known for years, but also knew that I needed to respect his decision. I certainly respected his faith, and maybe they were safer there in a non-descript house than out on the street, trying to get to a well-fortified target. I agreed to keep him updated with what I was hearing. An American diplomat stood out in the courtyard talking on a satellite phone with the governor, president, and leaders of both sides, trying to broker a cease-fire. Rumors were flying around and people were predicting the city was going down.

I went back inside, ate a hamburger, watched on the big screen some of the Summer Olympic games going on in Athens, and waited things out with my family and team. Ellie fell asleep on my shoulder. At the end of the day, American Special Ops units managed to broker a cease fire about fifteen miles from the city.

Lt. Col. Irving gave us a wrap-up briefing, ending it by saying: "It is safe for you to go home now. I guess they are homes? Or to whatever you call the places where you live."

We arrived back at our office and staff house emotionally tired but happy to be home. I tucked Ellie in her bed, said a prayer over her, then suggested a movie to the team to help us unwind a bit. "How about *Blackhawk Down?*"

"Absolutely not!" Christine and Tiffany shouted in unison. Dr. Jack and I endured a chick flick with the ladies.

Nearly a month passed, and though we experienced several false alarms, things calmed down and life continued as normal for a summer in Iskandar. The bazaars were full of vendors selling everything from pomegranates to cell phone cards. Local Toyotas and NGO SUVs vied with bicycles, animals, push-carts and pedestrians for supremacy of the roads in an organic chaos. And the sky was full of kites. I ventured out on a few more "language jaunts," but (almost) never without first filing my flight plan with Sadie, who did her best to keep tabs on everyone's location at all times.

I put Ellie to sleep each night on my shoulder, pacing her room and singing songs to her. Especially a variation of Toby Keith's country-western song, "Huckleberry" in which Ellie became my Huckleberry and I asked God to protect her.

Then I'd tuck her into her pack and play with her stuffed Lambie. I'd pray: "May the Lord bless you and keep you. May the Lord make His face shine upon you, and give you peace. Amen."

Zayed Khan had been weakened by the advances of his enemies. Finally, at the opportune moment, President Karzai made his move: he sacked him from his position as Governor of Iskandar. The UN came out on the same day with a statement praising the move as good for the country, and American warplanes and helicopters flew over the city passing along the message: *"We are here!"* The idea being to let Zayed Khan's supporters know that there should be no funny business.

We sat down at the office to eat lunch. Hassina was cooking now, and lunch had improved. I worked on her chips, which I really liked. Ellie chewed on tomatoes, eggs, and nan. We talked about the fighter jets circling the city above.

"Did you know that when the American pilots climb out of their planes and take their helmets off, some of them are women?!" Hassina exclaimed, wide-eyed.

Some of our Afghan staff found this hard to swallow.

"When we took Rodney and Sadie to the airport this morning, Zelme and I saw a lot of ANA troops coming into the city," I commented. "Must have been at least eighty of them guarding the bridge and checking vehicles. They sure are taking this change seriously!"

Dr. Jack looked up from his plate: "Tomorrow could be an interesting day."

We got a call late that night from ANSO, warning of potentially violent anti-Western demonstrations the next day from Zayed Khan supporters. They were angry at Karzai, but even more so at his Western backers, particularly the United Nations and the

United States of America. Our concern was that they might turn their anger against NGOs like us. Dr. Jack and I had been planning to go with Zelme, Aziz, Ghulam, Dr. Maleki and Mirwais out to a village clinic the next day for training with a large group of community health workers. I volunteered to stay behind with the women, and we agreed that Mirwais would stay as well just in case things went south. I called James and let him know that tomorrow could be dangerous. He assured me that they would stay close to home.

Crack, crack! The next morning I awoke early to the sounds of distant gunshots. *Nope, not dreaming about 24, those are real.* I walked into Ellie's room, scooped her up, and carried her back into bed with us. The gunshots died down after a while.

I was studying Dari at my desk upstairs at 9:00 that morning when automatic gunfire resumed with a vengeance, this time closer to us, and from multiple directions. I started hearing sounds of yelling and screaming from an angry mob. Soon I could smell the smoke from a burning building. "OK, it has hit the fan," I told Christine and the ladies on my team. Let's get down to the basement!" On the way down I ducked into Rodney's office to get our cash and vital document out of the safe and into my backpack, just in case we needed to make a hasty exit. Inside was James, checking his email.

He looked up and asked: "Hear all that gunfire?!"

"Yeah, but what are you doing here?! You told me you were going to stay home today or at least close to home!"

"This is close! My house is just a few miles away!"

I shook my head. "Everything in Iskandar is just a few miles away... you live on the other side of town!"

Bam, bam, BAM! The gunfire was getting closer.

James looked at me: "I've got to get home now! Pray for me, bro!"

I was angry that he had blown off my warning the night before but even more worried for his safety now. I agreed that James needed to get home to his family; he was going to have to drive through this. I said a quick prayer for James and he took off in his van, out the gate into a city turned dangerous. I emptied the safe, grabbed the satellite phone, and looked through Sadie's desk files for other important documents. I smelled more smoke and heard the rotors of helicopters flying just a hundred feet above.

As I was finishing up, James called. "Matt, I wonder if some of this is celebratory gunfire? Crowds out, with lots of guys shooting guns up into the air!"

"Call me when you make it home!"

I walked down into the basement and asked the women to pray for James.

"I thought you said he was going to lay low today at home with his family," Tiffany responded. "What was he doing here?"

"I thought so, too! But some guys are stubborn, you know? You got to hit them over the head with a baseball bat to get them to listen to you!"

Catherine let me know that even if this was true, that was something I should tell him and not them. She was right; I shouldn't have talked about my brother behind his back and regret it to this day. We prayed for James, and he called back a few minutes later.

"Matt, you called?"

"No! Where are you?"

"Almost home, but your phone has called me several times. Must have been pocket calls. You were saying something about hitting a guy over the head with a baseball bat! Just saw the craziest thing: a helicopter hovering a few feet over the road, rotor blade angled forward, holding back a crowd!"

My stomach dropped; I felt like I had just been hit over the head with a baseball bat! *I need to be careful with what I say... my mouth is my biggest problem!* I later apologized to James, who hadn't even realized that I was talking about him. He forgave me, but it hurt him. I learned a life lesson in the heat of that moment, one that another James wrote about two thousand years earlier:

So also the tongue is a small member; yet it boasts of great things. How great a forest is set ablaze by such a small fire! With it we bless our Lord and Father, and with it we curse people who are made in the likeness of God. From the same mouth come blessings and cursing. My brothers, these things ought not to be so (James 3:5, 9–10, ESV).

Things seemed to quiet down outside around 11:00 a.m. I went up to the top floor of the office, looked out the windows, and noticed smoke coming from several different directions in the city; US helicopters were hovering over the smoke. The first reports came in from ANSO and the PRT. That morning a large mob had attacked one of the city's UN compounds. After ransacking and setting fire to part of the building, they moved on a rampage to attack other compounds belonging to foreign NGOs. The mob had grown in number as opportunists— lured into the fray by the hopes of looting offices—joined the crowd of angry Zayed Khan supporters. Many locals had wandered into the streets to see what all the fuss was about and had been quickly swept up into the mob. When they tried to leave they'd been beaten by organizers from within. The ANA (Afghan National Army) had rapidly been dispatched to contain the mob's destruction. Judging by the thousands of gunshots that we'd been hearing that morning, they had used restraint, mostly firing up into the air. But they had been too late to stop the mob from destroying a number of foreign NGO offices or from gaining control over the central square kilometer of town—right where we happened to be.

I walked into the courtyard to the guard shack to check in with Kaka. Mirwais was out on the street, trying to figure out where the mobs were headed next. He assured me that we were fine and should stay put. "I feel safe enough to take a nap!" he yelled, with bravado that was less than convincing. Ash from nearby fires blew into the courtyard.

The PRT sent out an email encouraging Americans to come over, then called several minutes later to withdraw the invitation. Fighting had broken out on several streets around the PRT so it wasn't safe to try to get there. We stayed hunkered in the basement. Tiffany, Catherine, and Audrey played with Ellie and helped Christine keep her distracted until she fell asleep.

Bam, bam, bam, bam, KBOOM! The ground shook as fighting resumed around 1:00 p.m. I ran outside to get a report from Kaka but found the guard shack empty. I swallowed, hard.

Now we have been abandoned. Just me to protect the ladies and Ellie. What will I do when the hoards break through the gate?! God, please help me!

Just then, our smaller gate opened and a somber Kaka slipped in. He greeted me and then reported that fighting was taking place near the hospital, with many fatalities, about two blocks away. He'd heard that foreigners had been killed. Mirwais had abandoned us for the safety of his home.

In 2003 Rodney had chosen to rent a compound for our NGO in the modern part of the city where most of the other international NGOs in town were located. Armed police patrolled our street every hour during the night. Conventional wisdom had always been that we were located in the safest part of town. But now we were right in the middle of the hot zone. Thousands of angry Afghans were heading in our direction.

I ran upstairs one more time to get a better look.

The sky was full of acrid smoke from burning compounds, while the noise of automatic gunfire—punctuated by grenade blasts—slightly obfuscated the shouts of the mob outside.

"Down with Karzai! Death to America!"

Staying low, I glanced out the window. American military helicopters buzzed nearby buildings at a hundred feet, flying around the plumes of smoke and competing with dozens of kites for airspace.

Don't cut down the kids' kites, I thought for a fleeting second.

I needed to get back down to the safer basement area to give the women an update but paused for a moment to collect my thoughts. *What am I doing here?*

That wasn't the real question that was tormenting me. I was asking myself why I had brought my family to Afghanistan.

God, I believe that You called us here. I feel a spirit of fear gripping my heart; Lord, help my unbelief, and give me courage! Help me know what to do now! Please protect Ellie, Christine, and the ladies!

I glanced out the window once again and assessed the current situation. We had only two guards at the office and one had already fled the scene. So it was up to Kaka and me to protect four American women and my precious one-year-old daughter. Trying to evacuate was not an option...not only would we be driving through angry mobs, but trigger-happy ANA soldiers had our part of town blockaded in. *Not a lot of options...please help us come up with something!*

Kaka rushed in with new word from the street. The mob had torched a NGO compound around the corner and was coming our way. Unlike many NGOs, we had chosen to try to fly under the radar; there was no big sign on our gate. I hoped the mob would pass by, but of course everyone on our block knew we were there. *Will they sell us out?* Kaka was yelling so quickly that I couldn't understand much he said, except for the word *khatarnak!* (dangerous!) Catherine, the most proficient Dari speaker on our team, helped me out. "I don't understand everything, but he says it isn't safe for us anymore here. He says we should hide in Zelme's house across the alley. Fatima is there, and expecting us." *A new option; risky but at this point probably better than staying here.*

"OK, time to go!" The women prepared to evacuate our office compound from a small side gate opposite from Zelme and Fatima's house. The trick was that we needed to cross the alley completely incognito. I was already wearing a pair of Afghan shalwar kamis, blending in nicely. Catherine donned a blue burqa—the traditional,

all-enveloping Afghan garment that covers a woman head to toe
with only a screen to look through. We didn't have enough burqas
to go around, so Christine wore her chawdar namaz—the garment
that the more "liberal" minority of local women wear—resembling
a large sheet, covering all of the body like the burqa except for the
face. When slightly hunched over in the necessary walking posture with the garment held right below the chin, from a distance
Christine looked like an Afghan woman. We tucked Ellie under
Catherine's burqa, pretending that this was a big game so as not to
alarm her.

I cracked open the gate and glanced outside. Holding our
breath, we slipped out into the alleyway two by two and crossed
over to Zelme's home. Fatima quickly opened the gate and brought
us into her thick, mud-walled house. I didn't think anyone out on
the main street noticed. We all understood that Fatima was risking
her own life to protect us.

The situation outside continued to deteriorate. The sounds of
angry people and automatic gunfire were now coming from the
main street, just on the other side of the wall of the house where
we were now hiding out. I got on the phone with Zach, Iskandar's
security warden. He was calming and professional. "You guys are
doing good, Matthew. I'm in contact right now with the American
military. Describe your position as best you can so they can spot it
from the air."

I gave him the position of Zelme's house, just to the east of our
NGO's compound, right on the corner of the main street and the
alley we had just darted across. "To confirm our position, there is a
maroon, twenty-foot steel shipping container full of rice for one of
our projects in the courtyard of the house. I'm standing next to it
right now."

"Roger, Matthew. Standby."

I looked up at the kites in the smoky sky and hoped that none
of the bullets being fired in the air would fall on my head. I leaned

against the shipping container and acknowledged to myself that I was now in culture shock. *I'm not sure I'll ever understand this place!*

Zach came back on the line. "Matthew, I just spoke with the American commander, and they have tagged the house from above and have over-watch by helicopter. Your position is too hot for a military extraction. Advise that the safest thing for you to do is to lay low for the time being."

I ducked back inside Zelme's house, where Ellie was dancing around. Audrie was on the phone with her dad, wiping away tears as she told him that she loved him. I had been trying to get through to Dr. Jack on his satellite phone with no success. He called me at 4:00 p.m. from the edge of town. The connection was fuzzy, so I had to almost yell into the phone to be heard. Tiffany kept shushing me, afraid that hostiles on the other side of the wall might be able to hear.

"Jack, the city downtown is under attack! We are in the middle of it but are safe for the moment."

"Zelme and I can see the helicopters and smoke from here."

"Jack, don't come home!"

"What? Come home?!"

"*Don't* come home!"

"Did you say you want us to come home?!"

"DON'T COME HOME!" I yelled into the phone. "It's not safe!"

"Sorry! I can't hear you!"

The line went dead. I tried to get him back for the next thirty minutes.

Tak! Tak! Tak! Loud knocking at the gate. We froze. *What to do now? No basement to hide in here! TAK! TAK! TAK! TAK!*

To our great relief, it was Zelme, our fearless office manager! He'd made it through the ANA blockades on foot and navigated his way through the mob back to his house. Casting aside the taboos of his culture, he embraced his wife right in front of us and kissed her on the cheek. He explained that Dr. Jack and the rest of our staff were fine ... they were at Zach's place, a guarded compound in a government-controlled part of the city.

By 5:00 p.m. Zach and I both decided that we needed to get out of there. It would be too dangerous to spend the night with the mob still controlling the street. As far as we could tell our office still had not been attacked, and the BLC was parked inside our office compound. Zach instructed me to put our NGO's magnetic sign on the top of our vehicle, and at 5:30 sharp an American helicopter would fly above to help escort us outside the combat zone.

Zelme and I peeked out the door of his gate. A group of young men was gathering at the street corner outside our office ... not a good sign. We darted across the alleyway and let ourselves into our office compound's side entrance. We quickly loaded the Big Land Cruiser with evacuation bags and locked up the office as tightly as we could. The women, still concealed in Afghan garb, crossed back to the office two by two.

At precisely 5:30 p.m. we sped out of the gate, a crazy Zelme at the BLC's wheel. Despite driving at amazing speeds, he managed to not hit anyone and got us down roads that were not barricaded by the ANA. Ten minutes later, Zach welcomed us into his protected compound. We watched the remainder of the day unfold on BBC television.

The true heroes in Iskandar that day were the American soldiers. They rappelled out of helicopters and drove armored vehicles through NGO compound walls to evacuate European aid workers—just as armed, violent mobs were breaking down the main gates. Despite the fact that bullets and grenades were fired in their direction, American forces strictly adhered to non-lethal methods of defense. American soldiers were injured doing their jobs that day, but incredibly not one foreign aid worker was hurt. A number of Afghans died. Christine and I bowed in prayer together and thanked God for His protection of our team, family, and especially little Ellie, who was quite enjoying her day and all the attention she was getting.

That evening Dr. Jack and I climbed to the roof of Zac's compound to watch the action from a distance. We were just a couple miles away from our office and all the rioting, but it was a different world in this part of the city. The bazaars were open, people were standing around pointing at the sky, and every rooftop was full of spectators. The sky was a brilliant orange from a dust-enhanced sunset. We could barely make out our office from the rooftop... the sky above it was still full of smoke and helicopters, but the kites were still flying.

Part III

Endure

Fall, 2004

To Our Dearly Loved Friends and Family,

Just a quick update: We have had excellent health and especially Ellie has been doing much better since our last email update. She is adjusting very well to this new culture. Since she has her cheeks pinched by the people here, she now thinks it is fun to pinch other's cheeks as well!

We do need your prayers that we could maintain love for the Afghan people and contentment living in such a different culture. Many times I have to fight back frustration and even anger at the way women are looked at as being non-entities. Just the other day, we had an Afghan electrician helping Matthew install a fan. He demanded that he should have hot tea. So, putting on my headscarf (because it would be extremely inappropriate to have my head uncovered in the presence of a man), I begrudgingly knelt down and put the cup of tea at his feet. This little headscarf I wear inside when men are around is actually nothing compared to what

I wear outside our walls. The full chawder covers all of my body expect for my face, and this gets very hot and hard to manage carrying a toddler on my hip and a bag of groceries underneath the veil. I have to remember not to laugh in public or draw attention to myself. Today a friend and I stopped and got an ice cream bar (yes, ice cream!) along the road, but we could not eat it with others watching so we had to stoop down and face a wall to eat it quickly before it melted. All this to say that the way women are viewed really does take a toll on me, and I thank you for praying that God would give me love for the people and a gracious attitude when inside I'm screaming: "It's not fair!" Someone who truly helps me (when all around the culture says the opposite) is my husband. I am thankful for Matthew as he serves and helps me with adjusting to life here.

Thankfully we didn't have to evacuate a few weeks ago due to the political situation ... but please do pray for peace in this country right now. Things are not stable as we await the elections, and we have to have bags packed to evacuate at any time. We count it a privilege to be here and want to stay!

Thank you for your prayers, friendships, and emails that daily encourage us. We love you all and do miss you.

With Love,
Christine

*Count it all joy, my brothers, when you meet trials of various kinds,
for you know that the testing of your faith produces steadfastness.*
James 1:2–3 (ESV)

Kharedji: a foreigner, an outsider.

Chapter 8

These Crazy Kharedjis

Things settled down in Iskandar, although I had trouble going out
without looking over my shoulder. Fall brought relief from the heat
and dusty winds. Our community health work was moving forward;
Dr. Jack secured funding to add another clinic with coverage in
forty more villages. Christine and I continued with full-time language study, although I gotten a little more involved in the project
work. I was ready to get to work and try to make a difference in my
new country.

One November evening, over Tiffany's awesome Navajo tacos,
she cleared her throat: "Hey everyone, Jack and I have an announcement. We are pregnant!" Tiffany and Dr. Jack had been married
for eleven years and had never been able to have children. They

were content and had used their mobility to serve the poor in some unique places, but inside their hearts was a desire for children.

"Congratulations!!" Hugs and backslaps followed. Our Afghan friends were sure it was the Afghan water. I had a different theory.

"You've been watching too much *24* and were too amped up. Now that we finished season two last month, you could settle down in the evenings and perform your husbandly obligations!" I slapped Jack on the shoulder.

Dr. Jack shrugged, but it was easy to get a reaction from Tiffany. "Matthew! That has never been a problem for us!"

I knew that God had blessed their obedience. This was a beautiful example of the promise made in Psalm 37:4: "Delight yourself also in the Lord, and he will give you the desire of your heart."

The next week some of Dr. Jack's former colleagues came to visit. Rick Donlon was a pediatrician working in inner city Memphis, Tennessee. In med school, he made a pact with three buddies that they would devote their lives to using their medical skills to serving the poor. Moving to racially divided Memphis, they started Christ Community Health Services (CCHS) in 1995. They set up their first clinic in Binghampton, Memphis' most medically underserved neighborhood, but commuted to work from nice houses in the affluent, white suburb of Germantown. After several years, they realized that if they were really going to make a difference in this community, they needed to take the lower position and go all in. They sold their houses and moved into the hood. People in their affluent, white mega churches thought they were nuts. God blessed their faith; within three years they grew to twelve doctors serving the poor in three inner-city clinics. They started house churches in their community, taught neighbors to grow vegetables in their backyards, and played a lot of basketball. Eventually they became convicted that they shouldn't get too comfortable in their hood but needed to also go to the nations. So they sent Dr. Jack and Tiffany to Afghanistan in the spring of 2004.

Dr. Rick brought a group of four other doctors from CCHS with him to Iskandar. I was impressed from the start with this group. They were humble, eager to serve, took their faith in Christ seriously; themselves, not too much. They already had taken risks and learned to overcome fear with faith. Dr. Rick's faith was contagious. (Under his leadership, Christ Community Health Services became the largest primary health care provider in Memphis, serving over 57,000 patients each year in eight health centers and four dental clinics in the poorest neighborhoods of Memphis. They also made a difference overseas in the hard places, from Afghanistan to Darfur. In August 2014, Dr. Rick left CCHS to take things to the next level in Memphis with Resurrection Health.)

We took Dr. Rick and team out to the villages to conduct mobile medical clinics. We started in the friendly village of De Khak, where Harbob had invited us to come see patients and then stay the night. I knew that the entire village was going to want to be seen so I had concerns about how we were going to handle crowd control.

"Let's just let Harbob and the village mullahs handle this," Dr. Jack had responded.

"I'm not sure that is a good idea. We needed a good system to make things work in the Philippines."

"Well, they know how to handle their own people better than we do!" Jack had been around three months longer than I had, so I backed off.

We set up shop in a crude mud home near the edge of the village and converted the large rooms into makeshift exam rooms. Christine helped sort out the medicines and turn another room into a pharmacy. Harbob and the village leaders policed the doors to the house, first admitting only those with the most serious illnesses.

After an hour or so of seeing patients, the system completely broke down. We were besieged by a mob of over a hundred villagers pushing to get to the front of the crowd of waiting people.

The village women were the most unruly and aggressive, crawling through the windows of the house and even through Rodney's out-stretched legs as he made a last-ditch effort to protect the hallway. Hardly culturally appropriate! Dozens of women filled the hallway and crammed into the ladies' examination room, shutting down our operation (and making me concerned for the structural integrity of the house). Harbob and the village elders finally pushed their way through the crowd of women and drove them back out of the house with sticks. But the women refused to move back from the doorway, standing their ground and just ducking as Harbob systematically bopped their heads with his stick from right to left, resembling something of a sprinkler system. One gray beard turned to me and said, "See, you have got to beat them to get them to obey!" *Well, isn't this wonderful? We have treated 30 villagers so far today and beaten 40 Afghan women with sticks! Not what I had in mind.*

I grabbed a notebook from my backpack and started tearing up pieces of paper to try to institute a voucher system. But with the mob of women packed around the doorway it was impossible to implement. Dr. Rick, who had been busy with a patient, ducked his head out of his exam room and realized what all the noise had been about. Wearing a red, long-sleeved Arkansas Razorbacks T-shirt emblazoned with the phrase "WOO PIG SOOIE" (hardly cultur-ally appropriate colors or subject matter for a conservative Islamic country), he charged the crowd of women, growling and flailing his arms like a bear. Standing six-foot-four with plenty of muscle, Dr. Rick was an imposing sight. The Afghan women screamed and ran from the doorway. Rick pursued for a few yards outside the house, continuing to growl and flail like a grizzly, capturing the attention of the entire village of De Khak and burning a memory into their collective folklore.

Time froze for a moment. There was Rick the kharedji (for-eigner), growling like a bear in front of a mass of shrouded Afghan women. There was the crowd of several hundred traditional village men, bearded mouths open in shock. There was me, totally exposed in front of the house, nowhere to run. And now, we were going to die. *I hope it is quick; a hail of bullets from an AK-47. This might put us on heaven's Darwin Awards list! Not what I had in mind!*

Dr. Rick ceased his antics as if the realization had suddenly struck his cerebral cortex: "This was not a good idea!" A few, long seconds of silence passed, the crowd too stunned to react. I resisted the urge to cover my privates. Then everyone broke out in laughter! Dr. Rick went back to his patient; we regrouped and reorganized so that we could resume caring for these villagers and their children. And I managed to convince Harbob and the mullahs to use their sticks only as barricades.

By evening, the team had treated hundreds of patients but run out of vital medications. Zelme and I drove back to Iskandar, racing the clock to make it to the drug bazaar before closing to resupply what the team would need for the next day in the next village. Christine and the women slept on toshaks in a mud house full of Afghan women, telling stories and being forced to take turns dancing for the group. The guys partied with Harbob late into the night as he choked on his water pipe loaded with very bad tobacco. I got to check in on little Ellie, who was already sleeping like a princess when I got home and still asleep at the crack of dawn when Zelme and I took off for De Khak in the BLC, loaded up with boxes of medicines.

A few days later we sat around the downstairs living room of our staff house with Dr. Rick and his team. John, a young doctor, had brought his guitar along, and we were having a good time singing worship songs together. Ellie soaked up the attention, spinning around in the center of the room with her arms outstretched, worshipping God in her own little toddler way. We debriefed the week and concluded that there were better ways to serve Afghans with short-term medical teams. Most of these villagers would get sick again soon, and the level of care we provided was not available to them on a long-term basis. Worse, we had competed with the Afghan health care delivery system, creating higher expectations in the villages we had visited. We needed to work smarter to empower long-term sustainable development. We decided it would be better to invest in training Afghan doctors. Over the next few years, Dr. Rick would bring back teams of doctors from CCHS to provide continuing medical education to Afghan physicians, helping them to raise the bar of medical services in their country and building some great Afghan-American friendships along the way. They encouraged us more than they know.

Winter quickly set in and the temperatures dropped. We learned that winter is a tough time throughout Afghanistan. Most Afghans pretty much button things up and just try to survive the winter, waiting eagerly for spring. Electricity was unreliable, especially during the winter months, and our current was too weak to support more than one small electric heater that we placed in Ellie's room. It was about as effective at heating her room as a match inside a freezer, so we set it up a few feet from her pack and play, close enough to take the bite off the chill, but far enough away (I hoped) to not be a fire hazard. We used a combination of kerosene and propane heaters, but they had their disadvantages (like burning eyes, the risk of carbon monoxide poisoning, and the fact that most propane tanks available in Iskandar were rejects from Pakistan or Iran). We were thankful for the long underwear and wool socks we had brought, lessons learned from our Mazar experience. Ellie looked like a little Eskimo in her fleece, full-bodied pajamas. We couldn't leave the propane heater on in our room while we slept, so we bundled up and snuggled under alpaca wool blankets that I had bought once upon a time in Peru. The temperature in the room was sometimes near freezing when we woke up, so Christine and I would both pretend to still be asleep, hoping the other person would get up to light the heater. Usually I lost.

We really couldn't feel sorry for ourselves, though. I went out to the villages where many people didn't own socks. I would sit on a toshak and rub my cold feet, covered in two pairs of wool socks. The guy sitting next to me, and his children, would be barefoot. *OK, my feet really are not freezing.* They would burn goat dung in a mud oven for heat. No one even thought of trying to heat a room, though. It was all about proximity to the heater. In some villages they would sit around a *sandali,* one of mankind's more socially brilliant inventions. This efficient heat system utilizes a small (and low) table, thick wool blankets, and a bowl of hot coals. Ten people can fit their feet under this table, close to the hot coals. The blankets, which are attached to the table, wonderfully retain the heat when pulled up over the body. The sandali provided warmth and fantastic opportunities for communal interaction. Stories were told, relationships deepened, and traditions passed down generations around the sandali. I heard fascinating tales of Afghan history and learned much about Afghan culture sitting around a sandali for hours at night in a mud house out in the villages.

We celebrated Christmas in a land that didn't know Christmas. Christine had brought along our Christmas stockings, but I felt we needed a tree.

"You know, Zayed Khan planted a lot of pines in our city parks; maybe we could borrow one of those."

Christine wasn't seeing it. "You are crazy, Matthew. Can you imagine the headlines? Kharedji arrested for cutting down one of Iskandar's rare trees!"

"I wouldn't cut it down; I'd dig it up. Middle of the night, dressed in black. I'll put it back after Christmas!"

I was half joking, but Jack, James, and I actually found an Afghan nursery just outside the city that had pine trees. We found one that could pass for a Christmas tree. We paid 150 afghanis ($3 USD) for it, dug it up, and proudly brought it back to the staff house. I looked high and low in the bazaar and finally found strings of gaudy plastic fruit lights. But when we pulled all the plastic fruit off, we had little white lights. The team added ornaments—some homemade, some that had been brought across the sea for the occasion. It wasn't the most sophisticated Christmas tree, but it was beautiful to us. One night I walked out to the guard shack and invited Ghulam in to check out the tree. We sat in front of the Christmas tree and drank tea together, two men from vastly different backgrounds—one from privilege and comfort, the other a survivor of countless battles who had spent much of his life struggling to put food on the dastarkhan (tablecloth) for his kids. *"Besiyar makbulas"* (very beautiful), he said several times over, as we enjoyed a quiet moment of peace together.

Kaka greeted us on Christmas morning. *"Eid e Christmas Mobarak!"* he roared. "Eid of Christmas, Congratulations!" This was the closest thing he knew to "Merry Christmas!" Kaka was the spitting image of an Afghan Santa Claus so we took photos of him proudly wearing a Santa hat while holding Ellie. Driving around Iskandar on Christmas Day, it was remarkable to be in a country where no one celebrated Christmas. People went about their business, buying and selling used clothing in the dusty bazaar, pushing carts loaded with potatoes or sacks of rice down the muddy street—just another day in Afghanistan. On one hand, it was kind of depressing; on the other, it was liberating from the distractions of Western materialism. We remembered the reason that we celebrate Christmas: the Creator of the universe, entering our world as a baby, to save us!

Christine and I realized that we were getting tired. The cold, the culture shock, the monotony of language learning, the stress of constantly having to think about security ... we needed a vacation. One weekend in January I met Trent, a British NGO worker who was part of a prestigious mountaineering club in England.

"So, have you found any places here where you can rock climb?" I asked. I had lovingly packed a rope and climbing gear, but everything I had found so far had been made of flaky sharp rock or shale. Nothing worse than having a handhold break off while climbing up a route.

"Everything I've been on is crumbly," Trent responded. "I did spot a mountain near the airport that looks interesting."

I knew the exact place he had in mind. It was a large pinnacle protruding somewhere between fifteen hundred and two thousand feet from the ground by my estimation. We determined that it was a waste of time to bring ropes or equipment. The rock was going to crumble.

This pinnacle had been calling me as well, ever since the first day I landed in Iskandar. About two hours after meeting, Trent and I were in the Big Land Cruiser heading out toward our new conquest. Leaving the main road, we drove off-road for twenty minutes, trying to get as close to the base as possible so that we could park the vehicle in a place where we could keep an eye on it the whole way up. Passing behind a small hill, we were surprised to find a garbage dump hidden from view of the main road. We couldn't really drive any closer to the base of our mountain than the dump, so we parked about fifty yards away. We traversed the edges of the dump to get up to a ridge that led to the base of our mountain. Because of the cold, the smell wasn't overpowering. I noticed thousands of flies enjoying the garbage, but within minutes we had left the dump behind and were beginning our ascent.

A third of the way up, things got dicey. Even the large pieces of rock that looked solid from a distance turned out to be little more than a combination of sharp, quickly fragmenting rocks and dirt. The handholds were not trustworthy...several times I started small avalanches (and once almost fell to my death) by thinking that a handhold was solid. After a little while Trent decided it would be best for both of us if he led, so I was the one getting peppered by the small rocks that became dislodged with each step up. We were climbing with friction as our sole ally, a tricky balancing act between pressure and motion.

The real problem was that this mountain was steeper up close than it looked from a distance. We were halfway to the top when we had to make a decision. We stared at a small chasm in the spine of rock that required a flying leap from a ledge to a lower boulder. It would have to be a perfectly straight jump; to both sides of us were vertical cliffs, dropping hundreds of feet. We thought we could make the jump, but once committed there was no turning back. "Geronimo!"

Once across the chasm, we continued climbing up the vertiginous spine of rock, only a few feet wide ... on both sides hundred foot fatal drops promised a spectacular, thousand foot tumble down to the valley floor. The view was getting better by the moment, but a sudden blast of wind could have blown us right off our narrow footing and sent us sailing down the mountain. Eventually, the spine gave way to a wider—but more steeply inclined—final slope up to the summit. We were free climbing at a sixty to seventy degree angle on a mountain composed of loose rock and now covered in most places with ice and snow. I slid for a few heart-stopping seconds but managed to arrest my fall on some compressed snow, hugging a boulder (that thankfully held) with my right arm. *Sure hope Trent knows what he is doing! No way we are going to be able to descend this route! And no choice, at this point, than to keep climbing to the top!*

It has been said that wisdom is thinking long term, but in certain moments of peril I have found it helpful to compartmentalize a bit, to think "baby steps." At this point, my goal was just to make it to the top of the mountain alive. Once on top, we would have to find another way off the mountain. *If only we had parachutes!*

The view from the top was spectacular. We were actually only about a mile above sea level, but from our perspective we might as well have been up in the Himalayas. To the west a range of jagged, snow-capped peaks continued as far as the eye could see. To the east a great plain extended for miles until another range of vertical hills broke the brown monotony. Toward the north was the ancient city of Iskandar, comprised of mud-created homes and courtyards, thin trails of smoke clouding the horizon a bit.

The daily Kam Air 727 flew five hundred feet below us, banking right as it made its final approach to Iskandar's airport.

I took a deep breath. "Sure is beautiful up here!"

"Brilliant!"

I decided to broach the topic on both of our minds: "So, how do you think we will get off this thing?"

"It appears that we will have to tackle the dodgy bit." He was referring to the western route that led to a range of mountains, punctuated by what looked like vertical cliffs.

"If we can't find a passage down the cliffs, we're in big trouble." I was stating the obvious.

"Indeed."

"You are more experienced, Trent. In your opinion, what do you think our chances are of both making it down today, alive?"

"Seventy percent, at best."

I took quick inventory. No ropes or gear that could help with descents. I had thought to throw a flashlight in my daypack but had nothing to start a fire with—plus, nothing to burn up here! No tarp, blanket, or emergency shelter. Neither of us was dressed warm enough to likely survive the sub-freezing nighttime temperatures on this pinnacle. Discovering a weak signal on my cell phone, I thought about calling the military base next to the airport to ask them to send a helicopter. That would be embarrassing and expensive.

Trent called his father in England to tell him that he loved him.

I decided I should give Christine a call: "Hey, Sweetheart! How are you?"

"Hi, honey! Are you having a good time? You sound fuzzy!"

"Well, yes! It's beautiful up here."

"Are you being safe?"

"Of course! Listen, the reception is not really good up here, but if I don't make it home by 6:30, please call the American PRT and ask them to send a helicopter to the sharp mountain just off the main road a few clicks south from the airport! They should look for two guys on top!"

"Honey, I thought you were going to be home by 6:00! Don't forget that we have guests coming over then!"

"Yep, I'm planning on that. Just in case!"

"And don't forget to pick up the nan on the way home. Love you! Please be careful!"

"I love you ... very much." Click. *Not sure she got my point! Maybe not a bad thing ... if we get off this, it would be good to be allowed to go rock climbing again!*

Time was running short so we started probing the west side down. It was much icier, and sure enough, scattered with formidable cliffs. We would push it as far west as we could descend, and then traverse to the north when faced with impossible vertical drops. We both knew that we were at a point of no return ... it was too late to go back to the summit and then try to climb down the way we had come up before dark. Trent and I had no choice but to take risks as we reverse climbed down cliffs. We jammed our hands into cracks in the rock and used deeper inside crags as handholds. Several times these handholds broke loose. Wonderful therapy for my prayer life!

We finally reached a place where we found some goat droppings on the side of the mountain. We celebrated. *If mountain goats can make it down from here, maybe we can! God, please forgive me for being reckless today. I should have put my family first. Please help me make it down to them!* The mountain became more forgiving, and thirty minutes later we were making great time by sliding down snowfields.

We made it to the bottom, elated to be alive. The only problem was that we were now on the valley floor to the northwest of our mountain, and we had parked to the southeast. We trekked toward the vehicle at significant speed, trying to beat the onset of dusk with our sore and scraped limbs. We made it to the north side of the garbage dump and followed a trail right through. Trent was interested in the garbage. He began taking pictures ... in fact, more than he did of our climb.

"This would be a brilliant project! We could recycle the glass, plastic, paper..."

"Fascinating. Let's keep moving."

"This could employ hundreds of locals ... become self-sufficient in a year! We could set up an assembly line for the glass, set up a small factory..."

I just wanted to make it to the vehicle. Not only was I exhausted, but also the smell was starting to get to me. But the flies were gone. *Strange! Where are all the flies?*

We soon found out. Arriving at the Big Land Cruiser, we were stunned to observe that a massive migration of flies had occurred while we were away accomplishing our manly feat. I had accidentally left my window cracked open an inch. The flies had moved to warmer pastures.

"This is the most incredible phenomenon of nature I've ever encountered!" Trent, the biologist, excitedly began. "Somehow they instinctively recognized that the inside of your Land Cruiser was warmer terrain! How could they have sensed it from so far away? Was there some form of communication involved?"

"This is absolutely gross!" My feelings of euphoria at surviving the mountain had now fully morphed into profound disgust. This was bizarre ... surreal even.

The entire ceiling, seats, dashboard, and floor were covered with thousands of flies. When I opened the door, the cloud of swarming flies became so thick I could barely see through to the other window. Doing our best to keep our mouths closed, and blowing air out of our nostrils, we swept the flies out of the BLC with long pieces of brush that we found on the ground. Flies swarmed everywhere, into our ears and clothing. *I would pay a hundred bucks for a broom right now! Unbelievable!*

We eventually realized that the only way we were going to get rid of them was to drive with the windows down and the back doors open. Squinting to minimize fly contact with my eyeballs, and doing my best to keep them out of my other orifices, I drove the BLC for about a mile down the dirt track toward the main road. Instead of vacating the BLC, the majority of the swarm went into a state of paralysis and clumped together on the ceiling, doors, dashboard, and on us. The ceiling of the Big Land Cruiser was almost completely solid black. Flies started falling from the ceiling by the hundreds into our hair and open collars. *One thing is for sure... going to be sick for the next few days!*

"Cold-blooded creatures. Their circulation is slowing down as they get blown by the freezing air..." the biology lesson from Trent resumed.

We stopped once again and started cleaning out the BLC with weeds. We swept out over one thousand paralyzed flies. Maybe two thousand.

Feeling a little happier, we made it to the main road and started for home at faster speeds. Freezing, we closed the windows and cranked up the heater. Within minutes, we had at least a thousand flies once again swarming the cabin.

"Great! They warmed up."

We made the rest of the trip home with the windows down, stopping several times to sweep out flies with the best tools we could find. Arriving at our office compound, Ghulam looked at me in disgust. I promptly went out to the bazaar and bought some bug spray, emptying the contents of two bottles into the air ducts and everywhere else in the vehicle where I suspected colonies to be hiding. Then I took a very long shower.

Zelme was even less happy with me the next morning. What had I done to his vehicle over the weekend? Not only was the BLC full of hundreds of dead flies, there were still dozens buzzing around inside. He drove the BLC on official business all the time; now he was going to have to live with flies for weeks. I repeated the procedure with the bug spray, this time with a group of Afghan staff watching their boss—now turned lord of the flies—sweeping dead flies by the hundreds into the bushes. I had a difficult time explaining to them how I had managed to import this colony of flies into our compound. Ghulam and Kaka just shook their heads while Zelme fumed. Aziz suppressed giggles. They were all pondering the same question that puzzles all Afghans who rub shoulders with foreigners in their country: "Who are these crazy kharedjis?"

It was time for a vacation ... for our sake, and for theirs.

Top, Mattew (on right) spending time with the locals in De Khak. Above left, Christine organizes medicine and supplies for a local village. Above right, Dr. Rick in his trademark red Arkansas Razorbacks T-shirt. Dr. Rick made a lasting impression on the patients he served and was a huge encouragement to the Collins family during their time in Afghanistan.

Now it is not good for the Christian's health to hustle the Aryan brown,
For the Christian riles, and the Aryan smiles
and he weareth the Christian down;
And the end of the fight is a tombstone white
with the name of the late deceased,
And the epitaph drear:
'A Fool lies here who tried to hustle the East.'
—Rudyard Kipling

Chapter 9

Planes, Trains, and Auto-Rickshaws

Saturday, February 12, 2005, 10:00 a.m.

Sadr Khan stroked his gray beard as he paced back and forth on the ice-covered runway. The air temperature had just risen above freezing, and I was trying to convince him to open Iskandar International Airport's runway for landing.

"The twin engine King Air is designed for sub-optimal landings, especially on snow." I had no idea what I was talking about.

"And the UN pilots are experts at ice landings, perfect safety record." They were from South Africa.

Sadr Khan looked up at the snowy mountains beyond, stroked his beard, and fiddled with his radio. He had been managing this airport for decades and had dealt with Russians, Mujahedeen, Taliban, US Army Special Forces, and now this pesky American.

"Tell you what. What if we drove our Land Cruiser up and down the airstrip to help melt the ice? As you can see, it is already getting soft!"

Sadr Khan grunted his approval, and for the next hour Zelme, Dr. Jack, and I sped up and down the runway in the BLC, crisscrossing the UN's fuel truck in a race against time to melt enough slush so that Sadr Khan would allow our plane to land upon arrival.

A few weeks before, Christine had expressed her doubts about taking a vacation from one chaotic, third-world country to another chaotic, third-world country.

"Are you sure that India is the right place?"

"Sure, sweetheart. India's got some beautiful hotels."

"I've heard it is pretty crowded."

"We will go up to the Himalayas. Plenty of fresh air and trees."

"Sounds cold. We could use a break from the cold weather."

"But the hotels up there have good heat. And the weather will be great in Delhi and Varanasi. The women there wear colorful clothes instead of sheets over their heads. We can travel all over without worrying about getting blown up...Delhi Fort, the Taj Mahal, the Ganges River in Varanasi, Wildflower Hall up in the Himalayan foothills!"

"Let's be careful to take it easy while we are on vacation. Traveling too many places with Ellie sounds more exhausting than relaxing."

"Absolutely. India is a great place to shop, and I think we could really encourage Tammy and Douglas."

Spending time with my sister and her family (who had been working in India for years) had cinched the deal, but Christine knew better about the relaxing part. She already had watched me mark up a *Lonely Planet* travel guide to India. I tried to explain to her how relaxing the first-class compartments were on Indian night trains and showed her photos online of some of the nicer hotels we planned to visit.

After a good bit of negotiation with Christine, I had pre-booked us on three overnight trains, four day trains, and four hotels in different parts of the country. We also would be staying one night with some friends in Delhi and several nights with my sister's family in Varanasi. Being that I'd paid for all of this in full upon booking, it was important that we make it to Delhi on time to start our odyssey.

I started watching the weather online about a week before our vacation, and things looked bad. The forecast called for snow in both Kabul and Iskandar for the next ten days, so I went out and bought tickets on Ariana Afghan Airways for us the very next day to Kabul. For five days in a row we packed up our bags, said goodbye to our colleagues and staff, and drove out to the airport. Each morning the Ariana operations rep told me on the phone that the plane was coming that day. Each day we would sit in the sub-freezing cave of an airport for several hours until we would hear the dreaded "*Cancelled Shud!*" Then we would drive back to our home at the office, say an awkward "hello" to our colleagues and staff, unpack, and try to be productive for the last few hours of our day.

This was our last shot to make it to Kabul in time to connect to Delhi, and I had tickets for all three scheduled flights that day. Kam Air had flown a plane into a mountain in a blizzard the week before so was out of the running. Ariana and PACTEC had just cancelled their flights that morning, so the normally conservative UN was our only hope. I wasn't sure if we were really melting snow with the Land Cruiser or just packing down slush into ice, but our effort evidently meant something to Sadr Khan. After an hour, he walked out of the terminal and told us that he had just given our plane permission to land.

All the way to Kabul was fog and snow. Christine was airsick and I really needed a bathroom, so the turbulence was helping neither of us. Our flight time ended up being much longer than normal because of thick cloud cover over Kabul. After circling above the clouds for over an hour, the captain turned around and told us that we were low on fuel and would make an emergency landing at Bagram. Suddenly, they found a hole in the clouds above Kabul and made a quick decision to go for it. As we descended through the mountains, the fog once again enveloped our plane, and we were truly flying blind. At one point, the clouds cleared just enough for me to see large rocks just off our left wing. Then everything went white again. Holding Ellie on my lap, I asked God to let us make it one more time. Thirty long seconds later, we dropped below the cloud cover and found ourselves flying low over Kabul city. After landing, the two pilots exchanged a look and shook hands.

Two days later, we made it to Delhi and were on vacation! The first adjective that comes to mind for India is *crowded*! As we made our way from New Delhi to the train station in Old Delhi, the streets became less orderly and more cacophonous. Trucks, cars, motorbikes, rickshaws, pedestrians, and animals all vied for position on the roads and sidewalks. We were used to seeing herds of goats and sheep parading through town in Iskandar, along with horse-drawn wagons and the odd camel, but not the bumper to fender gridlock of humanity or the numerous cows in modern Delhi that had right of way. One taxi driver explained to me that he would go to jail if he accidentally hit a cow.

A second description of India would be *sensual overload*! As we arrived at the train station, we found it to be a microcosm of India—thousands of people from every caste and economic position, packed into one dirty, large terminal. Grasping two bags and chasing after the two *coolies* who had our larger bags balanced on their heads, I pushed through the crowd, stepping gingerly over emaciated elderly bodies that lay sleeping on the cement. Or were they dead? Beggars pulled on my clothes while hawkers persistently tried to sell used clay mugs of chai. Christine followed a step behind, clutching Ellie and her diaper bag. We finally found our train, but it was departing late and the doors would remain locked for another hour. After arguing with the *coolies*, who wanted four times what our driver had said we should pay for carrying our bags, we sat down on our luggage and observed our surroundings. A group of laborers loaded sacks of flour and crates of live chickens onto a cargo car next door, while several smartly dressed men read their newspapers on a bench next to us. None offered Christine and Ellie a seat. Down next to the track an old man bathed using a water spigot and tin cup, and another fellow defecated on the track right in front of the watching world.

'Isn't this great?" I asked Christine and Ellie. I got a reproachful look from my wife, but Ellie seemed to be enjoying the colorful sights, sounds, and smells.

Douglas, who had been living in India for too long, had described first-class cabins on Indian trains as "luxurious." Climbing aboard, we found our cabin, complete with four sleeping berths and garbage strewn about.

'Matthew, I thought you said that we would have a private cabin. I'm not sure it will work sleeping with strangers in the room. Especially with Ellie!"

'Don't worry, sweetheart. Indian Rail's website promised a private first-class cabin. We just have more room to stretch out!"

I went on a search for the steward responsible for cleaning the cabins. Stepping into the next car—which happened to be third class—I realized how good we had it and headed back to our cabin. That is when I discovered that we did have cabin mates. After a sleepless night getting off at each stop to make sure we didn't miss our connection, we finally arrived in Kalka at 7:00 a.m., jumped off the train, and found our "toy train" to Shimla.

Completed in 1903, the stretch of narrow-gauge track from Kalka up to the former British hill station of Shimla is a marvel of engineering. Winding through the foothills of the Himalayas, it tunnels through 121 mountains and crosses no less than 345 aqueducts. The train itself was just a little bigger than one you might find at a zoo—fully enclosed, each car had about twelve rows of seats and squeezed three tightly seated passengers from window to window. Another set of seats faced ours but with quarters so close that we were politely rubbing knees with our new set of Indian friends. The train was pulled by an antique, coal-fed steam engine. Sure to be a quaint and unique experience, I thought. Despite a serious travel hangover, I was starting to feel pleased with myself. I shot Christine a little "it must be great to have me as your man" smile.

The first fifteen minutes of the five-hour trek were pleasant. Once we cleared the pollution and garbage of Kalka, we chugged up into a green, lush mountain valley. "This is going to be as pretty as the Alps," I whispered to Christine. Then the thick clouds rolled in, and it began to rain. We began to experience the southern reaches of the same system that had been dumping snow on Afghanistan for the past week. We quickly learned that this antique "toy train" had no form of onboard heat, and we bundled Ellie and ourselves up with every layer of warm clothing that we had not left behind in Kabul. The wind howled, and the little train rocked back and forth on the tracks. "I'm starting to feel queasy, and it is freezing in here!" Christine whispered. All of the Indians seemed to be having a great time.

An entire family in the front of our small train car decided that it would be a great time to light up. I was annoyed that we—especially my one-year-old daughter—were having to consume their second-hand smoke but decided to let the other Indians onboard take care of business. Being a deferential lot, several families sitting in front of us decided that we could all use some fresh air. Lowering their windows, frigid air and rain rushed in, pelting those of us sitting toward the back. "This is unbelievable!" I whispered to Christine. "If they don't close those windows in the next five minutes, I'm going to climb over everyone and close them myself. While I'm at it, I'll put out those cigarettes!" Incredibly, other passengers responded by lowering their windows. By now, our car was a wind tunnel, and it was all we could do to shield Ellie from the nearly freezing rain. I looked around and noticed that everyone was wrapped in wool blankets that they had brought from Delhi, with big smiles on their faces, enjoying the fresh air break from Delhi smog.

By the time we arrived in Shimla, Christine was thoroughly nauseated and we were both popsicles. The views had been of fog the entire way. "Let's never do that again," my dear wife implored.

"Excuse me sir, but are you Mr. Collins?" a finely dressed Indian enquired with an almost British accent.

"Yes."

"Right this way. Allow me," he said, grabbing my bag and covering us with his umbrella. We were already soaked. He led us to a beautiful, black Mercedes.

"How was your train journey, sir?"

"Fantastic scenery."

We ended up at The Cecil, a colonial luxury hotel dating back to the days of the British Raj. I had written a letter to the general manager explaining that we were aid workers in Afghanistan and were wondering if they offered discounted rates to folks like us. When we arrived, we discovered that they had upgraded us to their largest suite. With teakwood floors, hand-knotted rugs, antique handcrafted furniture, and a palatial marble bathroom, our three-roomed suite was handsome indeed. The rain let up, the clouds began to part, and sunlight streamed in through the mahogany-framed windows. The views of the mountain range to the south were spectacular. We quickly began to forget about the train journey—and Afghanistan, for that matter. White-gloved attendants and waiters offered their services, from attending to our laundry to heating up the beautiful, marble indoor pool—with a view—to our desired temperature. I soaked with my daughter in a hot tub, overlooking the snow-capped Himalayas, and a jealous monkey started howling at us and banging on the window a few feet away. We opted to dine in our own living room that night and returned from a long swim to find a candlelit table waiting for us laden with fresh flowers. Tuxedo-clad waiters served us a five-course meal. Christine flashed me the look...

The next day we decided to stroll along the scenic promenade into town. We visited Viceregal Lodge, the residence where the British viceroys ruled India during the summers, and later carved up a map of India, creating havoc in this part of the world for generations. We ducked into Christ Church, a mid nineteenth-century Anglican Church that looks as if it were plucked from a village in Yorkshire. Arriving at the main town square, aptly named "Scandal Point" due to a rendezvous between a viceroy's daughter and a local boy, we noticed several horses being held by Indian guides. Ellie loves horses... she got excited every time she saw a horse pulling a load of bricks down the street in Iskandar. So I thought that this would be a good time for her to get her first real horse ride.

"How many will ride, *sahib?*" the owner asked, wagging his head back and forth in friendly Indian manner.

"My daughter and her mother."

"And you, *sahib?*"

"I'll walk. I'd like to take some pictures of them."

"Are you sure you are able, *sahib?* Why don't you take a second horse?"

Come on, I thought. *When will the touts stop? All I want is a five-minute horse ride for my daughter. The last thing I want to do is parade around the square on a horse looking like a stupid tourist being led by a guide.*

Two hundred rupees seemed high for a short ride, but I was tired of negotiating and we were on vacation after all.

Christine and Ellie mounted the horse, the guide took the reins, and they were off! I pulled out my camera, told them to smile, looked up, but they were gone at a heavy trot. Running behind, I managed to catch up and to snap one shot. The horse and guide showed no signs of letting up, so I kept jogging behind at an altitude of 7,000 feet.

So this horse ride is going farther than the town square, I thought. *Surely we will turn around when we get to the edge of town.*

No such luck. The trotting continued out of town and up a trail ascending the highest point of the Shimla ridge. The views were great, but my energy was focused on trying to keep up with the horse. Occasionally the horse and guide would pause for a moment, wait for me to stumble up to their position, and then take off again as I stood there panting.

I'd hear a "Hi, Daddy!" from a grinning Ellie, and an "Are you all right, honey?" from Christine as they trotted away, further up into the fog-enveloped heights.

"I'm fine!" I'd manage to exhale, doubled over in my attempts to breathe.

"Your face is red and it sounds like you are wheezing..." Christine's voice trailed away as her steed whisked her up into fog.

After forty-five minutes of trotting up hill, neither horse nor guide showed any signs of fatigue. My lungs were burning and my head was swirling. I told myself that it must be the altitude but knew in my heart that I had gotten out of shape in Afghanistan.

"This is great exercise. Don't worry about me. Are you and Ellie warm enough?" I choked out.

After a thousand-foot climb and nearly an hour of jogging, we reached the destination that our horseman had in mind all along...Jakhu temple. Dedicated to the Hindu monkey god, Hanuman, this temple is perched at the very top of a mountain and is inhabited—appropriately enough—by packs of aggressive monkeys. The views looked to be beautiful ... however we weren't able to see much due to thick clouds that had moved in during our trot up. A local caretaker attempted to trade a banana with a particularly cheeky monkey for the return of an old woman's glasses.

By the time we got back to the hotel I was showing initial symptoms of pneumonia.

The next day we transferred to another hotel further north into the Himalayas. The setting to the Oberoi Wildflower Hall is spectacular. The cousin to the Cecil, this British, colonial-style hotel only ups the ante in style and architecture. Everything is built out of teak, mahogany, and crystal, and a doorman in turban and uniform completes the effect. The hotel is perched on the ledge of a cliff with amazing views for miles into the snowcapped mountains of the *Shrikhand Mahadev* range. Wildflower Hall's intricately tiled indoor pool is fit for a palace: this water-filled mosaic is appropriately lit by crystal chandeliers and looks out through giant, mahogany-framed windows to the mountains beyond.

Our favorite activity was to hike for several miles over deep snow through a forest with views of unspoiled mountains as far as the eye could see. The weather was pleasant—just a few degrees above freezing and sunny—with even the occasional light snow shower while the sun was still shining. We would then retreat to the hotel and either sip tea in front of a roaring fireplace or take a dip in the outdoor Jacuzzi, which was perched on the edge of the cliff with million dollar views. Despite all the luxurious splendor of the place, I spent a good amount of time in the steam room just trying to clear my lungs.

After two nights at Wildflower Hall and a huge English breakfast, we bid an almost tearful goodbye and began our journey back to third-world India. Christine said there was no way we were taking the "toy train" down, so I hired a sleek hotel car to drive us through the mountains down to Chandigarh, where we would pick up the train to ancient Varanasi via Delhi.

The first thing that should have tipped me off to what was coming was that the white-gloved driver had a pile of "comfort bags" in his glove compartment. *What kind of driver has a stack of barf bags in his car?*

The road from Wildflower Hall to Shimla, and then down to Kalka, is one of the windiest in the world. In addition to the mountainous geography, the British engineers had other reasons to give this road some extra curves. They had very cheap labor and were paid by the crown per mile.

So we were driving for about half an hour—listening to classical music—when the first waves of nausea hit my wife. Christine decided to sit in front, and I kindly requested that our driver take it easy on the curves. He nodded but nothing seemed to change.

After an hour of impressive resistance on the part of my wife, the floodgates broke loose. Our driver was kind enough to stop for a moment while she filled the first of his "comfort bags."

"Excuse me sir, but where should I place the bag?" I asked after being handed the bag by my white-faced wife.

"Set it on the road."

I immediately objected. As a lover of nature, one of my greatest pet peeves is the littering of any kind on God's green earth, and quite frankly, I can't think of a worse way to litter.

"*Sahib*, that bag is not staying in my car. Leave it out on the road!" the driver insisted. "There are no rubbish bins along this road."

Feeling guilty, I gingerly placed the folded white bag next to the road.

It was not to be the last. Making up lost time to compensate for the stops, our maniacal driver took 180-degree hairpin curves at breakneck speeds.

"Please slow down around the curves!" I begged.

"I am driving slow, *Sahib*."

"No, you are not! If you would just slow down we wouldn't be having to stop every ten minutes!"

Over the next several hours, my poor, dear wife used up every one of our driver's "comfort bags." Truly, the capacity of her stomach was a wonder to all. We left a trail of white barf bags dotted behind us through the foothills of the Himalayas.

Halfway through the journey, Ellie gave me the look and then proceeded to throw up all over my lap and the back seat. I used every wet wipe in the diaper bag attempting to clean up the aftermath.

"Listen, we are out of comfort bags and wet wipes. My wife and daughter are very sick. You have got to slow down. I'm paying for your services, so I'm the boss! No more than 20 km an hour on the curves!"

"You will miss your train, *Sahib*!" came the reply.

"I don't care if we miss the train! My daughter better not throw up again!" I was not a happy camper.

The entreaties died on the ears of Mad Max. He raced through the mountains at breakneck speeds, tearing around curves that left me white-knuckled not only for the well-being of my wife and daughter but out of fear for our very lives. By this point, I was feeling green.

Mad Max was ready to get to Chandigarh and be rid of his foul-smelling passengers.

Suddenly, Ellie gave me the look again. Deftly, I moved her face toward the floorboard, but I was too late. The seat, my pants, and her entire body were now once again covered with vomit.

The car came to a screeching halt. Christine opened the door and leaned over, dry heaving now. Ellie was crying, and I was really upset with Mad Max.

"Now look what you have done! I don't have any more changes of clothes for her and nothing to clean up with for that matter!"

"There is some newspaper in the trunk, *Sahib*."

I stormed over to the trunk, pulled out a folded newspaper, and did my best to clean up the mess. By now I had crossed over to the dark side and was shamelessly discarding used, vomitous newspaper by the side of the road. A mangy dog approached and started eating it. Just then, a troop of rather large monkeys noticed that the dog was on to something. Approaching and surrounding me, they eyed my daughter's pink shoes, which I was trying to wipe clean with newspaper. I decided then and there that they were going to get them over my dead body. They began with the old "distract and grab" trick. To counteract, I spun around in circles, holding the monkeys at bay with violent, swooping kicks with my right foot. Mad Max leaned passively against the driver's door, watching the action with a smirk.

I was about to explode into a desperate fit of rage, but then suddenly time slowed and I could see the picture from above. There was Christine, sitting in the passenger seat, dry heaving. There was Mad Max, unhelpful as ever, watching the action. Ellie was lying in the backseat crying. And there I was, on the side of the road in the middle of the Himalayan foothills of northern India, spinning around like a fool, being ambushed by primates, ready to sacrifice my life for a pair of pink, vomit-covered shoes. I started laughing. It was all quite hysterical. The monkeys were either tripped out, or decided they really weren't going to get the shoes from me, and moved away to greener pastures. I walked to the car, got in, and told Mad Max to get going.

We made it to our train in Chandigarh with a minute to spare. The other passengers clearly noticed that we didn't smell too fresh, but at least we were out of the mountains. Five hours later we were in Delhi, where we were able to get cleaned up and change clothes. Another eighteen-hour train ride later we arrived in Varanasi in northeast India.

When Mark Twain visited Varanasi, he described it as "older than history, older than tradition, older even than legend, and (it) looks twice as old as all of them put together." Certainly this city— which can be traced back at least 3,000 years—gives Iskandar a run for its money for ranking within the top ten, oldest presently inhabited cities of the world. While most of the buildings are less than a few hundred years old—thanks in part to the Afghans who destroyed the city in 1300 AD—the traditions of Varanasi and its inhabitants are ancient. Varanasi is potent enough to send all but the most stoic of souls into the depths of culture shock but remains a place of keen interest to anthropologists, hippies in want of enlightenment, and travelers who wander off the beaten path.

My brother-in-law is of the first variety, and the highlight for us was getting to spend time with him, my sister and their children. Douglas helped to make some sense out of the chaos as he was able to provide insight into the practice of Hinduism that permeates the city. Tens of thousands of temples to Hindu gods fill the city, but the distinctive feature of Varanasi is the Ganges River, which flows right through the center of town. Hindu pilgrims journey here from far and wide to bathe in the river, a ritual that they believe washes away all sins. Devout Hindus come to Varanasi to die, believing that to expire in this city offers final relief from the process of reincarnation—basically the Hindu version of heaven. To help the deceased along the way, relatives burn their bodies along the *ghats* that line the river and dump the ashes (and more sometimes, being that firewood tends to be scant) into the river, which they believe to be both divine and the most pure form of water on earth.

We took a boat ride early one morning down the Ganges. As Douglas lectured on the history and practices of Hinduism, we watched thousands of people bathing in the water, washing their clothes in it, brushing their teeth with it, and drinking it. Along the same stretch no less than thirty sewers continuously discharge into the river. Studies of water samples from the Ganges in Varanasi show a fecal count three thousand times that of water deemed potable. I tried to wrap my mind around the intersection of faith and reason within Hinduism as I watched swimmers navigate their way through floaties, and as ponytailed hippies eagerly nodded in reverent awe at the wisdom of mostly naked gurus seated along the *ghats*.

The *ghats* themselves had an otherworldly, Indiana-Jones kind of feel, but the place felt oppressive to me. Walking along the Ganges and looking into the eyes of beggars, worshippers, and gurus, I sensed a great deal of fear and despair, not peace. I asked God to guard our souls with the peace of Jesus Christ and prayed that these souls would come to know Him.

Delhi felt crowded, but Varanasi was claustrophobic. I explored the city on Tammy's moped, having a little fun swerving around the cars, motorcycles, auto-rickshaws, and cows. Hindu's believe that cows are the highest form of life and worship them. Traffic stops to allow cows to lazily wander down the street, eating food put out by families who struggle to feed their own children. On my final day in Varanasi, I nearly impaled myself on the pointed longhorn of a bull that must have missed a turn somewhere in Texas and ended up in downtown Varanasi. Swerving left, I felt the point of his horn brush the side of my shirt just under my right armpit.

Saying goodbye to Varanasi, we took another fifteen-hour train ride to Agra. This particular train had no first-class compartment so we rode in second class, attempting to sleep on folded down beds along with dozens of other travelers. Christine was worried that someone might abduct Ellie if we both slept, so I took the first shift. Reyansh, a fellow traveler and local political science professor, attempted to help me stay awake with a lecture on international politics that spanned late into the night. "India will be the dominant world superpower within the next ten years!" Etc., etc. When I finally did sleep, I dreamt about opening a travel agency across the street from a beach somewhere. I'll fly people up to Wildflower Hall and tell them to stay away from Indian Rail.

We arrived in Agra, home of the Taj Mahal. Agra is a city full of touts and pollution, with little more to see than the Taj Mahal and

Agra Fort. But the Taj Mahal is everything one could imagine and more, worth the entire trip to India.

The Taj was built in 1641 by a heartbroken Mughal emperor named Shah Jahan ("King of the World") as a tomb for his second wife, Mumtaz Mahal ("Jewel of the Palace"), after she died in childbirth. The Indian tourist board likes to describe it as "The Ultimate Monument of Love," but I couldn't help but wonder if lovely Mumtaz had the choice between a big mausoleum built for her posthumously or her "King of the World" husband emptying out his harem during her lifetime, which she would have chosen. Regardless, the Taj Mahal is an incredible monument. Impressive at first glance for size, beauty, and symmetry, it gets only more beautiful under scrutiny. The inlay work is exquisite in design and mind-numbing in scope, with thousands of stones—including jasper, agate, malachite, lapis lazuli, and turquoise—laid out in beautiful patterns perfectly hand cut to fit within the chiseled marble. The same is true for the *pietra dura* scrollwork—all quotations from the Quran—that embellishes the huge vaulted arches. The entire complex took more than 20,000 laborers twenty-two years to complete, and legend has it that Shah Jahan rewarded his chief architect and skilled laborers by amputating their hands to make sure that they never built anything like it again. (What a guy!)

While strolling inside the Taj complex, I couldn't help but be impressed by Shah Jahan's devotion to symmetry. He was so obsessed that everything within the complex be symmetrical that he built a faux mosque facing east to mirror the impressive red sandstone mosque that faces Mecca. When Shah Jahan died, his son buried him with little fanfare just to the right of the large shrine dedicated to his wife in the middle of the mausoleum. In a twist of Indian irony, Shah Jahan's body throws off the entire symmetry of the place.

Frankly, that didn't bother me too much. What did bother me was walking out of the mausoleum to discover that my shoes had been stolen. I had brought only one pair of shoes on this trip; now

I was walking around the Taj Mahal complex in my socks. Not that this drew much undue attention to myself... Ellie had already done that. One rather nice part of Indian culture is their love for children. Ellie—with her blonde hair, blue eyes, and flirtatious smile—attracted movie-star fanfare as she rode around in her back-pack carrier. Our entire experience at the Taj Mahal was one of being mobbed by the masses, all wanting to have their photo taken with my one-year-old.

Finally escaping the mobs of Ellie's groupies, we found the Taj Mahal's lost and found. No, the thief hadn't experienced a change of heart and turned in my shoes.

"It was foolish for you to leave your shoes outside the steps, *Sahib*."

I had left my shoes along with hundreds of other shoes. Cultural etiquette demands that you take off your shoes before going into the mausoleum.

"Oh, really? Where should I have left my shoes?" I was feeling just a little perturbed.

"You should have left them with the shoe-minder, *Sahib*," came the response, with a tone that let me know it was my fault that my shoes were stolen.

"Can you help me out here? I can't exactly walk the streets of Agra in my socks. Do you have any extras?"

"Come with me. I'll show you the way."

The lost-and-found man led us out of the complex and across the street from the main entrance (all in my socks). There stood one refreshment stand and five different vendors selling shoes. After examining each of these shops to see if my shoes were on display, I settled into bartering mode.

"A good day to you, *Sahib*. So you need a pair of shoes?" Mr. Indian Used Shoe Salesman stated the obvious.

"How much are these sandals?" I pointed to a cheap pair made from fake leather.

"A hundred bucks."

"A hundred rupees?"

"One hundred dollars, *Sahib*."

"You gotta be kidding me."

"They are handmade from camel leather, *Sahib*."

He had me, and we both knew it. Turns out that a white guy standing in the dirt in India in his socks has poor leverage, and I needed something to get me back to Afghanistan in the dead of winter.

A few days later, friends in Iskandar asked about our vacation. "Did you love India? Was it a refreshing trip for your family?"

Christine responded with her normal smile. "Matthew always plans the best vacations."

She then leaned over to me and whispered, "The next time we are staying in just one place. How about a beach somewhere?"

We needed a vacation from vacation.

Top Left, Christine, in traditional dress, and Ellie pose for a picture during the family vacation in Varanasi, India. Bottom, Christine and Ellie take a horseback ride in Shimla, North India, shortly before trotting up into the heights. Top Right, a family portrait in front of the Taj Mahal (right before Matthew's shoes were stolen).

He who wants a rose must respect the thorn.
—Persian Proverb

To be happy for an hour, get drunk; to be happy for a year, fall in love;
To be happy for a life, take up gardening.
—Chinese Proverb

Chapter 10

The Museum

One of our goals when we came to Afghanistan was to move into an actual Afghan community as deeply as possible. If we were going to make a long-term difference in this country we needed to understand it, something that few kharedjis ever achieve. Most foreigners come on six-month to one-year contracts, live in comfortable compounds behind armed guards and razor wire, and never begin to learn the language. We enjoyed living in the comfort of our office/staff house for the first eight months in Afghanistan but realized quickly that it was not helping us develop relationships with Afghans beyond those with whom we worked. In order to better learn language and to get to know Afghanistan, we needed to live deeper in Afghanistan.

By February 2005 I was on the hunt for a house in Iskandar. I looked at more than twenty houses with a property dealer and finally found a workable house in a good part of town that had everything we were seeking. I explained to the owner that I understood the reservations that many Afghans have with allowing foreigners to live in their communities. We planned to live in a way that showed respect to their religion and culture. The night before we signed the contract and began moving in, my would-be landlord came by the office. He apologized and explained that the deal was off. Some of his neighbors had come over and explained that a foreigner could not be allowed to live in their neighborhood.

"But as I promised before, we will live according to your culture. My wife always covers her head when she goes outside, and we never eat pig or drink alcohol!"

"No, no. This is not the problem. We like you, Mr. Matthew. I would have made a lot of money from your rent. The problem is that you are American. My neighbors say that if something happens to you in our neighborhood, the American military will bomb us and take me to Guantanamo."

"Mushkil Nis! (Not a problem!) I don't work for the US government, and they don't care what happens to me!"

"I'm sorry, Mr. Matthew. The neighbors have decided "

"Loken, I Mushkil Nis! Rasti!! (But this is not a problem! Really!) I can sign a release form that promises the neighborhood will not be held responsible if anything bad happens to me or my family."

"Mr. Matthew. Please come anytime to my house and have tea. But this discussion is finished!"

And that was that. My first real taste of Afghan xenophobia left me discouraged. *I'm not sure they really want us here. How do we go deeper in culture when they won't let us in?*

Christine and I prayed a lot while on vacation in India that God would provide a house for us in Iskandar where the neighbors would accept us. It seemed that the Afghans were glad to have us foreigners around for the money and services we provided but tried to keep us bottled up in compounds, separated from their society. Most foreigners were glad to comply, but I wanted to break through the wall of separation. After we returned to Iskandar, I stopped by the property dealer, just a hole in the wall office several doors down from our office.

"*Salaam Aleykum*, Mr. Matthew! *Khushamaden*! (Welcome back!) *Safar Shuma Bakhair ti Shud?* (Did your journey pass safely?)"

After all the greetings, he got down to it. "I have found a big house for you with a large garden, but I do not think you will like it. It is very old and spoiled. The price is good."

"Please talk to me about the garden."

"It has many mulberry, pomegranate, and almond trees. They are very old. And grape vines!"

"Will the neighbors allow a kharedji to live in their neighborhood?"

"They are open-minded, Mr. Matthew. The *saeeb khune* (owner) is a doctor who lives in Germany."

The next day we walked through an ancient-looking gate into a large compound to find an eighty-year-old, mud-brick mansion. The builder was a famous Iskandari who had once owned a significant portion of the land on the north side of Iskandar city. He built this large house for his two wives; one lived on each end of the long cobblestone hallway. The home was built with mud and straw; its walls were three-feet thick, covered with baked mud bricks on the outside. *These walls look like they could absorb a tank shell!* The rooms had soaring curved ceilings, topped by a mud roof. It was still the rainy season of early spring, and I looked for leaks. *How about that... only one small leak in all these rooms! Fifteen leaks at our modern, concrete office and growing!* The doors were constructed from local timber before the days of doorknobs; they were closed and fastened by metal chains. *If Christine gets mad at me, she could easily lock me in my room!* The house had a large front porch, with an exposed log and timber ceiling, and a great command of the front courtyard. I fell in love with the place right away: *I shall call you "The Museum."*

Waheed, the owner's nephew, showed us around. "My grandfather built this house eighty years ago."

"Besiar Jaleb! (Very interesting!)" *He must have built it while he was still a young buck! Eighty years ago!?*

We stood under a mulberry tree, one of four that looked at least eighty years old, looking up at the imposing brick columns that fronted the porch. The mud walls of the courtyard were lined with mature pomegranate bushes. A grape arbor stood against the front wall of the compound, while younger almond and apple trees demarcated a large, square-shaped yard of mud infested with weeds. I noticed an ancient well that was drying up but still had enough water to keep the trees alive during the heat of summer. I could imagine this courtyard transformed into a beautiful garden, Ellie swinging under a tree...

"No one has lived here for years. My relatives keep telling my uncle that he should knock it down and build three new houses on the property."

Don't do that! This is to be our home! I tried to play it cool. "I think this amount of land is worth a lot of money here in the middle of the city."

"Yes, it is! But my uncle has many good memories growing up in this house. He says they can knock it down only after he dies."

We walked out the gate, hands tucked behind our backs in pensive Afghan fashion. We strolled past neighboring gates. *Perfect position for security. At the end of the alley, not visible from the main street. Any bad guy would have to pass thirty neighboring compounds, all honor-bound to protect us, IF they invite us to move into their neighborhood as their guests.*

Waheed continued. "Almost half of the neighbors are our relatives. My family is an important family in Iskandar; many of our relatives live in Germany and Holland."

I decided now was the time to ask the big question. "How would your relatives feel about a kharedji family living in the neighborhood?"

"We are educated people and would welcome you. Your family would be under our protection." *Wow. That's it!* Afghan protection, based on their culture of honor, is stronger than cement, razor wire, and armed guards.

"What would your family ask for rent?" *Now they are going to shoot the moon. A thousand dollars a month? Two thousand? Here comes the kharedji price!*

Waheed leveled his eyes with mine, projecting the serious look of one not willing to negotiate. "We would require $350 a month in rent. And you would need to do all the repairs yourself."

I couldn't believe it. This was a godsend. Perfect place in the city, local protection, amazing potential. I wanted to do the renovation myself, and Waheed said the family was willing to sign a three-year contract. But it would be a hard sell with Christine... The Museum was in a sorry-looking state. Both electricity and city water came into the compound, but neither worked inside the house. Few of the old wooden windows had glass remaining, and none of the eighty-year-old doors closed properly. The Museum didn't have an inside bathroom or kitchen. Everything needed a fresh coat of paint, but first hundreds of cracks in the walls and ceilings would need to be plastered. The floors in the rooms were made from a flaky plaster, so I'd have to re-plaster or cement them before I could put any kind of carpets down. The back yard was filled with knee-deep garbage. The last guy who lived there had cows, and by the smell of things, they had spent some time inside during the winter. The Museum was a definite fixer-upper.

I brought Christine over for a look. She noticed the bad condition and smell.

"Matthew, you have got to be kidding. This place would take months to repair! You don't have that kind of time. You are still studying Dari and getting involved with project work already." It was evident from her tone that she thought I should be putting more time into language study.

"Sweetheart, I managed a large building project in Mozambique. A lot can be accomplished in a little time with cheap labor. This can be done in a couple weeks!"

We walked through the house together. She looked out a broken back window.

"Look at all the trash in the back..."

"Look at the grape arbor back there," I responded. "And the two mulberry trees. You know how rare trees are in Afghanistan. We can turn this courtyard into an oasis. Think about how much Ellie will enjoy the freedom and space to roam."

"I don't know, Matthew. The house is much bigger than what we planned. And it has no indoor plumbing. Or kitchen."

"Sweetheart, this place is special. Don't worry, the next time you see The Museum I'll have it all fixed up. You will be impressed. Three weeks!"

I signed a three-year contract on The Museum and immediately set about hiring a crew to fix it up. The largest task was going to be all the plastering and painting...I hired a paint crew on day one and also put the foreman in charge of repairing the doors and windows. Then I hired electrical and plumbing crews, and a mason and tile worker to put in a kitchen and bathroom. I hired some local carpenters to build shelves and a cupboard for the kitchen, complete with a large granite countertop mined from the mountains of Afghanistan. A group of laborers worked outside pulling weeds, cleaning out garbage, and hauling gravel for the back courtyard. I planted grass seed from Holland and seventy rose bushes, purchased from a local *gulkhune* (flower house) for a dollar a piece.

It didn't take long to learn that renovation is done a little differently in Afghanistan. In a storeroom that I was turning into a bathroom, I explained to the plumbing crew that they should gently chisel out just enough space for the pipes in the mud walls. I returned to the room a few minutes later to watch a gray-bearded man take the first chop out of the wall with his pickaxe. It was better for me not to watch. I came back a couple of hours later to find an entire section of wall missing with pipes running across the open expanse. The workmen dismissed it with a wave of the hand—don't worry yourself, Mr. Kharedji, it is nothing to rebuild a wall. When the plumbers put a drain in the wrong place, they simply rubbed a flammable compound on the PVC pipe, lit it on fire, and bent and extended it to where I said it should be. I wanted to install a ceiling fan in our living room, but the electrician was sure that it would sooner or later fall right out of the mud ceiling. One day while I was walking through a bazaar around the corner from the house, I noticed a large beam of wood leaning up against a carpenter's workshop. Within an hour, that wooden beam was installed across the ceiling of our living room and we were hanging the fan from it.

The neighbors were interested in the renovation. I would stop by the house to check on progress and find my next-door neighbor supervising the workmen. Afghan men dress in earth tones but prefer to paint the interiors of their homes in vibrant colors like pink, green, or purple. I was going with the light browns and beiges, which didn't meet with the neighbors' approval.

One day Waheed asked, pointedly, "Who chose the colors for the paint?"

"They were my choice. It will look good when everything is finished." He just shook his head, but several weeks later when everything was finished and we had Afghan rugs laid and pictures up on the wall, he decided that the overall effect was beautiful. Most of my self-appointed Afghan consultants thought that I should cement over the cobblestone grand hallway and cover it with *farsh* (thin, industrial-style carpet that most Afghans use to carpet their homes). I chose to re-grout the stone tiles and to varnish them, completing the effect of a cobblestone street running through the middle of The Museum.

Fazl Ahmad came into our life during this project. We would need a *chaokidar* (unarmed guard) for our house in the near future, and Ghulam was campaigning for his son. I needed a couple of extra laborers for the courtyard renovation and decided to see what kind of work ethic this young man had. I told him to show up at 7:00 a.m. sharp and to bring a friend. Fazl Ahmad was the friend. The first job was to pull thousands of weeds that had grown up between the clay tiles in the courtyard over years of neglect. I'd look out the window and see Ghulam's son sitting on his duff, but Fazl Ahmad would be still going at it. A few days later it was hauling wheelbarrows of gravel all day.

By now Ghulam's son was showing up for work looking stoned, but Fazl Ahmad was ready to rock and roll with work each morning. During the last week of the project, a fight broke out among some of the workers. At first I ignored the commotion outside, but after a few minutes I decided I'd better intervene before the entire neighborhood showed up. I walked into the courtyard to see our manic/depressive painter and Ghulam's son—both armed with bricks and with fire in their eyes—ready to smash each other's craniums. Fazl Ahmad was holding back his friend. Later that day Fazl Ahmad mentioned to me that he was not only an expert in pulling weeds and hauling gravel but also proficient at gardening and masonry. I hired him as my family's first chaokidar.

Three weeks and just over three thousand dollars later, the renovations were complete and we were ready to move into The Museum.

The Museum was rustic and beautiful at the same time, apropos for life in the ancient city of Iskandar. I brought Christine over to see her new home, and she was impressed. My Afghan neighbors also liked our "antique" house; my teammates thought it looked like Zoro's place on the inside. Both helped us to move in.

The day we finally settled into The Museum, Fazl Ahmad reported that he had seen a *djinn* (something similar to a demon) in one of the side rooms of the courtyard. With a wild look in his eyes, he described her big eyes, teeth, and long gray hair. He wanted to go to a mullah, pay him to pray a certain prayer over a jar of dirt, and then to sprinkle the dirt around the courtyard to keep the djinn away.

"I have another idea, Fazl Ahmad. Some of my friends from work are coming over this evening. They are followers of *Issa Massih* (Jesus Christ). We believe that He created the world and has power over everything, including djinn. We will pray to Issa and ask Him to get rid of this djinn."

Fazl Ahmad was good with that, and the entire team came over that evening. James and Billy also came with their families. I gave everyone the grand tour of The Museum, room by room. Our bedroom at the end of the great hall, with a dresser and wardrobes I had shipped over and assembled. A local carpenter had made the bed and chairs. Ellie's room, opposite ours, with her books and toys. A combination schoolroom and workout room, with elliptical machine and Olympic weight set, also shipped across the sea. Our living room, complete with an oak futon, toshaks, and bookcases for all the books that had served as "stuffers" in our shipping crate. The brand new kitchen, attached to a small dining room with wooden table for family dinners. A guest room, which Catherine would be moving into for the foreseeable future. The large cobblestone hallway, covered with maroon Afghan rugs and lined with toshaks, suitable for entertaining large groups. My carpenter friend had framed several puzzles that Tiffany, Christine and I had worked, along with a large world map, which hung in the middle of the hallway.

We stepped out onto the expansive front porch and prayed for God's protection and blessing on all who would enter. I remembered to pray about the djinn. When we were finished, Billy had a special request. "Matthew, would you mind if I anointed your doorpost with oil and prayed one more time for your household?"

"Sure, Billy." We had quite a big doorpost to anoint, but I hadn't thought of this before. I ran to the kitchen and grabbed a plastic jar that I assumed to be vegetable oil.

As he prayed, Billy anointed my doorpost. But it smelled like vinegar! We were all squinting by now; Billy eloquently concluded his prayer.

"Uh, Billy, I think you just anointed my doorpost with vinegar! Sorry about that! Hope you didn't just curse my place!"

We all shared a laugh. "I'm sure God understands, Matthew!"

Fazl Ahmad never saw the djinn again.

We enjoyed the advent of spring out in our beautiful courtyard. The almond trees blossomed white, the grass grew nicely, and the pansies and roses that I planted the month before bloomed in all their April glory. Fazl Ahmad enthusiastically jumped right into the gardening scene, bringing bags full of mystery seeds that he assured me would produce much better results than my flowers. Within a month I had sunflowers and corn stalks growing in all of my flowerbeds, choking out most of everything else botanical. My neighbors loved the courtyard; they would come over, run their hands over the grass while raving about the near-paradise beauty of it all, and Fazl Ahmad would bask in all the glory. He had a tender heart for small animals, making little houses for crippled birds out of cardboard and wire. Ellie's first pet was a turtle that he found in our yard. After showing it to me, he gave it freedom in the streets of Iskandar—thinking that Christine and Ellie would be scared of such a beast. Upon realizing his error several hours later, he searched high and low for the turtle and brought it home that evening. We built a swing for Ellie and hung it together from the mulberry tree in the front yard.

We celebrated Ellie's second birthday in April, and she became the delighted owner of two bunny rabbits. Fazl Ahmad put his masonry skills to good use and built a mud house for them in the corner of the front yard. Christine subjected them to thorough examinations and determined they were both female. She was wrong. Much to Ellie's delight, soon we had a growing rabbit colony.

We emailed a video of Ellie to our families in April, with a special announcement.

"Baby!" she exclaimed.

"Where is the baby?" I asked.

"Baby!" she pointed at Christine's tummy.

Turns out we had brought back a little souvenir from India!

One day in early May we sat out in our front courtyard on blankets in the cool of the evening, enjoying Christine's amazing chicken salad. The grass was coming in nicely. Ellie tugged on my sleeve until I got up for the fifth time and spun her around and around, first by her arms, then by her legs. We spun around until I couldn't stand, but she was hardly dizzy.

"Will you look at that," I gasped, trying to keep down the chicken salad. "She can run in a straight line! We have an astronaut in the making!"

A neighbor's flock of forty or so pigeons dive-bombed our courtyard. They had little bells tied to their feet, making a tinkling sound as they changed course, flying over our heads and barely clearing the courtyard walls. It took me a few weeks to realize this was a man-made addition and not the discovery of a rare species of Central Asian bird. They looped around, putting on quite the show.

I leaned back on the blanket, next to my wife, and said, "I am so thankful, Christine. I never imagined that we would live in such tranquility. In the middle of Afghanistan!" *I know there will be some rough days ahead; best to enjoy the moments of peace. It is a good thing that God knows the future, and I do not.*

"God has blessed us so much, Matthew. I'm so thankful for you, finding this house, all your hard work." She gave me a light kiss.

"This house is an answer to prayer, for sure! I'm thankful for our neighbors. I don't know how many times Waheed has come over and helped me replace fuses out in the electrical box."

Over time, we became even more thankful for our neighbors. The Husseini family invited us into their community, providing a deeper entrance into the culture of Afghanistan. They invited us to their family weddings and funerals, treated us to traditional Afghan meals, and did everything possible to make our lives in Afghanistan as comfortable as possible. During the days that our house was without power, our next-door neighbor connected The Museum to his electrical system so that we would not go without. He refused to allow me to pay him back. When the neighborhood got together to cement our muddy alleyway, the Husseini family refused to allow them to charge us a higher portion than any of the other Afghan families.

I was most grateful for the protection that our neighbors provided for my family. We were their adopted foreigners, and they were intent on keeping us safe. When things got a little more dangerous on the streets, they let me know. Some of the information they provided was more timely and reliable than the daily security updates I received from ANSO. When I traveled outside Iskandar, my neighbors kept an eye on my family. We felt safe in The Museum, under the protective covering of our neighbors, but ultimately under the sovereign protection of God. The Museum became our oasis, a place of refuge and tranquility throughout the remainder of our time in Iskandar.

The Museum, a place of refuge and tranquility that housed the Collins family during their years in Afghanistan.

Our school is the place of freedom,
We give our heads for this freedom.
Our lesson teaches us the ways of freedom,
Our course is the desire of freedom.
—Akram Osman

Chapter 11

Iskandar University

Much of the "War On Terror" in Afghanistan has been a reincarnation of a centuries-old battle for land and power between various Afghan tribal groups. The war between the Taliban and Northern Alliance was essentially a fight between the ethnic groups of the Pashtun in the south and the Tajiks and Uzbeks who had seasonally banded together in the north. As descendants of Genghis Khan and his rude Mongol invaders, the centrally located Hazara people have long been picked on by both sides. The Pashtun Taliban massacred them, piling Hazara corpses in Kabul city parks. Cobbling a country together from these tribal "nations" is no easy task, but there is one place in Afghanistan where this is happening every day: the university.

Afghanistan's universities are the battlefields for the minds of the next generation of Afghan leaders. Students from various tribal backgrounds learn to think differently, to overcome tribal grievances and build camaraderie with fellow students, and to discover the power of unity in diversity. I had the privilege to teach cultural anthropology at Iskandar University part time for several years.

It all began quite suddenly and unexpectedly. I had been in Iskandar less than six months when I met an American named Tony. He was working with the leadership of Iskandar University, helping to improve their academics and to make them more compatible with universities around the world. He heard that I had a master's degree in intercultural studies and asked if I'd be interested in getting involved with the university.

The next day I climbed a set of rickety wooden stairs to the second-story office of the university's literature department. A group of five men sat in swivel chairs in a long, narrow mud and plastered room, with a gassy *bukharie* at one end taking the bite off the chilly air. The wall was lined with six computer workstations—gifts from USAID—that had been connected to the Internet for the three months that USAID paid for the expensive Internet service provider. This room was the literature department's faculty office and student research center.

The men all stood. I began my string of Dari greetings, but Tony quickly cut me off in English: "Matthew, this is Mr. Ramin, the dean of the literature faculty."

I persevered in Dari. "*As didane shuma khighly khushal shudum!*" ("To see you I have become very happy," the Persian equivalent of "Nice to meet you!")

"It is nice to meet you!" Ramin replied in English, shaking my hand warmly. He was young, sported a mustache and a nice pair of shalwar kamis, but seemed progressive.

"This is Professor Ibraham," Tony introduced. "He has been teaching English literature here for many years, longer than anyone."

"Hello," Professor Ibrahim curtly shook my hand. He wore a traditional gray beard and brown Western suit, vintage '70s, with vest, tie, and jacket. He sat back and eyed me with suspicion.

Tony introduced me to the other two professors and explained that they were paid very little (the going rate at the time for an Afghan professor was $100 a month), but that they were dedicated to providing their students with the best education possible.

"Our students are the future of Afghanistan!" Mr. Ramin responded.

"Ramin, how many hours of class does each of your professors teach a week?" Tony asked.

"It depends, but most of us teach eighteen- to twenty-five hours a week."

"Wow! All of your preparation and grading is on top of that?" I asked.

"That is correct," Professor Ibrahim answered.

"Mr. Collins here is an expert from America in world culture and sociology," Tony began. "He would like to come teach a course— in English—on sociology in your department. I think it would be valuable to your students to learn from a native English teacher, and the subject of sociology could really help your students develop respect for other people groups that are a part of Afghan society." *Whoa, whoa, whoa, Tony. Not so fast, Mr. Used Professor Salesman...*

"Actually, I just have a master's degree in intercultural studies. I could possibly develop a course in cultural anthropology in the future, but I'm not qualified to teach sociology."

I noticed the blank look on Ramin and Ibrahim's faces. *They haven't heard this term before.*

"Cultural anthropology is simply the study of cultures around the world," I explained. "For instance, most kharedjis who come to Afghanistan learn very little about your culture, but I think it important for all of us to try to understand Afghan culture and to respect your values while living in your country."

They liked this. *Brownie points!* "I think it is also important for your students to better understand the people groups of their own country. Obviously I couldn't teach about each tribe of Afghanistan but I could provide tools for research. Your students could teach each other—and me—about the various Afghan people groups in a positive way. Also, a course in cultural anthropology could help prepare your students to interact with people from other cultures. There are a lot of kharedjis here these days, and some of your students might study abroad one day!"

Mr. Ramin was very interested in this last part. "Perhaps you could teach a class on sociology and cultural anthropology?"

I explained that I was busy with work and Dari study. Perhaps we could continue dialogue about this and I could start thinking about curriculum and lesson plans for a class in cultural anthropology six months to a year in the future? *I'll have more time when I finish Dari study!*

But I was interested. I wondered what it would be like to stand in a classroom with some of the most isolated and ethnocentric people on earth, discussing ideas like culture shock, contextualization, and shades of cultural relativism? *Could this crack open the window to the outside world for some of these students?* More importantly, I wondered if this could help me wrap my mind around Afghan culture. As an NGO, we could do much better projects to aid the people of Afghanistan if we better understood them. *I could teach my students principles of cultural anthropology, and they could teach me about Afghan culture!* I had given talks about culture to groups but never actually taught a university course in it or developed a syllabus for it. *Well, plenty of time to worry about the details later!*

The next day I got a call from Mr. Ramin. "Matthew, we have discussed having you join our faculty part time and are in favor." This would be the first time they had ever had a foreigner teach in their department, quite the risk for all of them.

"Thanks very much for your confidence. You are very kind."

"We would like for you to teach a course in cultural anthropology to juniors and seniors, separate male and female classes, this next academic cycle."

My mind began racing. *This might give me only several months to prepare! I'll need to consult with some of my former professors to find appropriate curriculum.*

"That is very gracious of you. When does the next cycle begin?"

"Next week. Your first class will start in six days. Professor Ibrahim will sit in your class with you to observe. Unfortunately, we do not have budget for salary, but we appreciate your willing to volunteer your time."

I showed up at the university in a pair of khakis and an old tweed jacket that belonged to my grandfather once upon a time. Dr. Jack thought that I looked like Indiana Jones, but I felt more like Woody Allen. The get-up worked perfectly at Iskandar University.

I walked into my classroom—a long, narrow room constructed out of mud and covered in plaster—with butterflies in my stomach. Sunlight streamed in from an open window, illuminating dust while providing just enough light to see my students' faces. Sixty pairs of earnest brown eyes peered up at me from under veiled heads. Never before had I been granted permission to encounter the world of the opposite gender in this completely segregated society. I felt like I was walking on sacred ground.

"My name is Matthew Collins, and it will be my privilege to explore culture with you this semester. God has blessed me with a wonderful wife, Christine, and a little girl named Ellie." I spent a long time talking about Christine and Ellie. I shared how Christine covered her head in Afghan fashion, and Ellie liked to copy her mommy, covering her head in a scarf as best she could. They laughed. *OK, I think I'm connecting here. Very glad Professor Ibrahim is in here with me!* I asked them to please introduce themselves. They each stood in turn. "My name is Najibe, the daughter of Namatullah! I am very happy to take this course, to further my English skills, and to better understand all the culture of the world!"

Each young woman in my class introduced herself in similar manner, stating her father's name after hers, with great reverence. This demonstrated the core value of Afghan culture: honor. In the West, we value truth higher than anything else. That is why the President of the United States can be impeached for telling a lie under oath and why we feel guilty when we lie. Truth forms the basis for a society based on the rule of law. We stop at stop signs in the middle of the night—when no one is around—because we feel guilty when we don't. (Afghans would never do this!) Afghans value honor above all else and are motivated to do the right thing by the fear of shame (the loss of honor) at breaking a cultural norm. Family honor is paramount; the actions of the individual affect the reputation of the entire family, and this is considered most sacred. This principle keeps society morally pure (at least outwardly), teaches responsibility at a young age, and puts the needs of family honor above the rights of the individual.

"Culture is the body of knowledge shared by members of a group." I wrote the definition on the board. "This is why Christine covers her head in your country. She always dressed modestly in America, but over there a woman covering her hair is not an issue related to modesty. But Christine has learned this Afghan rule— this piece of knowledge that you share—and so she knows to cover her head in the presence of a man, because she is a virtuous woman! She has learned a piece of your culture." Sixty scarf-covered heads nodded in agreement.

These women proved to be my top students. I had some outstanding students among the male class, but the women understood what a privilege it was to be in their country's highest halls of learning. For years, they had been forbidden to have any kind of formal education and had bravely continued learning in the cover of their homes. They turned in their homework with pride and on time. I was continually inspired by their brave ideas about life and their aspirations for their futures. It was as if the university gave them the momentary opportunity to come out of their oppressive society and to become fully human for a while. They would debate concepts of truth and reality with one another and with me, demonstrating passionate values and beliefs. Then—at the end of their school day—I'd sadly watch them put on their chawder namaz and burqas and head out into the open streets with the slightly hunched, submissive walk of anonymous Afghan women in a male-dominated world.

"Contextualization is to effectively communicate an idea into the context of another person." I wrote the definition on the board. "It simply means to make ideas relevant to a given situation." *And there is nothing simple about it!* I appreciated the irony of my situation: here I was, an American man, in the middle of culture shock, teaching a class of Afghan women how to cross cultures. In order to successfully do that, I needed to contextualize my teaching to their understanding. But could I begin to understand their frame of reference? My cultural background and life experience was so different! I read from my notes, slowly. "Contextualization is necessary for successful cross-cultural communication. When we contextualize, we encode our message into a different form so that the person listening can accurately decipher the original intent of the message. To do this, we must first understand the culture and mindset of our listener." *Can't believe I'm teaching this to Afghan women... I don't come close to understanding their culture; I am from a different planet!* It seemed to make sense to the class, though. Mr. Ibraham nodded intelligently.

I found it easier to explain the concept to the guys. "It is the responsibility of the person crossing cultures to contextualize their communication, both verbal and non-verbal. Only 7 percent of communication is actually verbal, the words themselves. Fifty-five percent is non-verbal and 38 percent how you say it. But even communicating with gestures requires cultural understanding. In

America, giving someone a thumbs up is a compliment or means that everything is OK." I flashed them a thumbs up.

There was a collective gasp and double-take, then some muffled laughs.

Naser—one of the more vocal junior students in the boys' class—spoke up. "My Teacher, you must never do this in public. Someone might kill you! Do you know what this means in Afghanistan?"

"Yeah, I know. The Afghan birdie."

"What?"

"A crude insult. But in my country it is a nice gesture. So when an American convoy, with all their big guns, drives through a remote Afghan village and the children and farmers give the American soldiers the thumbs up, you mean that they shouldn't think 'they are saying that we are number one?'"

"No!" The guys thought this was really funny. We all laughed together, and no one laughed harder than Professor Ibrahim.

"Ethnocentrism is a critical attitude toward other cultures in which a person judges other cultures using his or her own culture as the standard. It comes from two Latin words: *ethnos*, which means culture, and *centric*, which means centered." I circled the Latin words with chalk, like an old-school professor from a movie I had seen somewhere.

Naser raised his hand. "My teacher, the culture in Afghanistan is the best in the world. And Afghan food is the best in the world."

"Thanks for your opinion, Naser, but that statement was ethnocentric."

"Yes."

"It is not a good thing to be ethnocentric. We are all naturally ethnocentric. This is an attitude to resist! We should each declare war on ethnocentrism!"

"But the Afghan culture is the Islamic culture, so it is the highest culture!"

There were challenges to teaching cultural anthropology to students who had been trained at an early age to believe that their culture was superior to all others. According to the Hanafi school of Sunni Islam—still taught and practiced in this part of the world—not only is every letter of the Quran the literal word of God, but its followers are supposed to exactly emulate its prophet as much as humanly possible. The *Hadith* voluminously helps apply the Quran and tells much about the lifestyle and habits of Muhammad. So if you want to be a good Muslim in Afghanistan, you should wash yourself the way Muhammad washed, eat the same kinds of food that Muhammad ate, lay down with the same posture in which Muhammad slept, etc. In conservative Islam, there is no separation between the mosque and state, no dichotomy between the spiritual and physical, so Islam is the center of all things. The Afghans view their culture as being almost entirely inspired by their religion. They are quite dogmatic about their religion, so every aspect of their culture is "the way it should be done."

"Naser, I am not saying that there are no universal absolutes in terms of truth, reality, and natural law." *Better tread carefully here.* "God has given us His laws, such as the sanctity of human life, and God's law applies to all cultures." *Think I said that right. Whew, Mr. Ibrahim is nodding.* "But many things in culture are just preference, such as food, music, marriage practices, and social structure. In fact, you will find diversity with these things even in Muslim countries. For instance, Indonesian food looks and tastes different from Afghan food. The same is true with marriage practices." Naser relaxed. I wasn't teaching blasphemy or heresy. "A foundational part of the study of cultural anthropology is that each culture deserves to be examined with optimism and should never be judged by using one's own culture as the standard. That is true with foreign cultures. That is true with different tribal sub-cultures right here in Afghanistan!"

After studying the basic principles of cultural anthropology, we looked at the different sub-cultures in Afghanistan—by far the most interesting part of the class for me. We studied twelve different ethnic groups, and I had the students do the research. Most of these ethnic groups were represented in the demographic makeup of my students. I sent them out into the villages to interview Tajik, Pashtun, Hazara, Baluch, Aimaq, Uzbek, and Turkmen leaders, and then they presented oral reports to the class of what they had learned. Studying and presenting different ethnic groups in a multi-ethnic classroom in Afghanistan could have turned disastrous, but to my delight it had the opposite effect. My students became fascinated by the sub-cultures that were different from their own and learned to better appreciate the wonderful diversity hidden just beneath the surface of their homogenous-appearing country.

During our final section of the class, I brought in various guest speakers from the international community to share about the cultures of their home countries. The students loved the speaker from Japan, thought that the presenter from Germany was much too strict, and were fascinated by the Finn's descriptions of life in Scandinavia.

One day I asked Peter, a friend from Uganda, to come talk with the class about African culture. Peter had been adopted and raised in Africa by a British humanitarian aid worker and knew more about designing projects than anyone I had ever met. Exceptionally bright, he had spent the past two years in Iskandar writing proposals for a Norwegian NGO, bringing in millions of dollars of funding for humanitarian projects into Afghanistan. He also had suffered raw Afghan ethnocentrism as a black man in the Afghan world. I thought Peter might have some valuable insight for the class from his own experience with culture shock when he first arrived in Afghanistan.

Peter began with a few nice comments about the positive things he had noticed in Afghanistan and then unloaded more than two years of cultural frustration on my male students. "The thing that shocks me the very most about Afghanistan is the way you abuse women!" he candidly started.

A young student named Jafar tried to counter that actually Afghans value their women. Covering them up from head to toe was showing respect for them by providing protection and shelter from the dangers of male society.

But it was too late. The tsunami was already headed to shore. Peter spent the next twenty minutes detailing the rampant practices of polygamy, forced marriages of underage girls, wife-beating, lack of equal rights for women to work or drive in most places, and the harassment of females on the streets of Iskandar. Peter spewed statistics accurately and unmercifully, and was entirely thorough in his prosecution. Somehow we ended up on a discussion of the merits of the burqa.

"Have you ever tried one on?" he challenged the class.

"Of course not!"

"Do you understand how much a woman can see looking through the screen of her burqa? About 30 percent, with no peripheral vision. Would you like to know how many women are run over by donkey carts and trucks each year because they can't see when they cross the street?" Silence.

Peter continued. "Many more of them injure themselves falling into the jeweys. You know they call the burqa their prison. Can you imagine having to wear that over your head, face, and clothes when it is 45 degrees[3] outside?"

"Actually, the burqa was not invented in Afghanistan. It was first invented in India," Naser countered, trying to defend his nation's honor.

Peter looked around at the deflated faces and finally realized that he had thoroughly shamed his audience.

"Well, you know, we also have some problems in Uganda," he tried to salvage a little of the room's dignity about a half hour too late.

"In fact, some things in my country even shock me! There are some people that still practice female circumcision!"

---

3 Peter was measuring temperature in Centigrade. 45 degrees C = 113 degrees Fahrenheit.

Up until this comment, all eyes had been on the floor. They now looked up in confusion.

"They don't know what circumcision means?" Peter asked me incredulously.

"Teacher, what is circumcision?" Naser asked quite forcefully, relieved to have a change in subject.

For a second, I felt like a deer in the headlights. *Great, here I am with a bunch of young men who—besides their mother and sisters—have rarely been in the room with an unveiled woman. How did our conversation degenerate to this?*

I reluctantly stood up.

"Well, in many cultures," I began, quite unsure of where I was going with this, "when a baby boy is born they do a little surgery on his, uh, private part."

"Yes, we know about this. But he said *female* circumcision!" Naser responded, with a look of confusion quickly morphing into horror.

Peter just stood next to the chalkboard, not helping me out one bit.

"Well, in a few tribal parts of Africa, they do a little cutting on young women. It's not normal or healthy and is in fact considered to be a violation of human rights!"

Every eye was glued on me. We all wanted a change in topic, and quick! But my mind had gone blank. I gave Peter a pleading look.

"One thing I really like about Afghanistan is the hospitality of the people!" Peter finally intervened, with a big African smile.

Ten minutes later, on the way to the girls' class, I whispered: "Don't say a word about circumcision in there!"

Peter started out a little softer with the young women. It didn't take long before one of them asked him what surprised him about Afghanistan.

Trying not to stir up the hornet's nest again, he took a different tact.

"My NGO is involved in health projects out in the villages. One of the things that shocked me about Afghanistan is how some of the fundamentalist beliefs really hurt the health and well-being of the people."

"Can you give us an example, please?" The challenge came from Najibe, one of my brightest, and definitely most outspoken, students.

"Women's health in the villages. Did you know that the uneducated mullahs out in some of the Pashtun villages won't allow a woman to bathe for fourteen days after she gives birth to a baby? It causes all kinds of infections!"

I covered my face with my hands. *Good thing Mr. Ibrahim is not with us today!*

"They don't even understand their own religion!" Peter continued. "The Quran says something about a woman being 'unclean' for forty days after childbirth, so they think it means that a woman shouldn't bathe for fourteen days! They think that this will protect them from djinn somehow! This is a real problem in the field of women's health! Ladies die from this in the villages, and we are always having to treat women for major infections out there. We ask them, 'Why don't you take a bath?' They respond, 'If I wash myself, I will shame my family and my husband will beat me! The mullahs demand it!' Quite frankly, this shocks me about Afghanistan!"

I peeked through my fingers and looked around the room. The entire class was shamed. Most of them were red-faced, looking down at their desks. *I have no idea what he is talking about.*

"What you are saying is not true! Our women would never do this!" Najibe decided to fight back for the honor of her culture.

"That's right!" chimed in much of the class.

"Really?!" Peter chuckled for a while, utilizing that beautiful African laugh. "You are all educated Afghan women. You know better, but you also know that this is a problem out in the villages!"

I realized, with some panic, that right now I was caught in an epochal clash between two cultures. In Afghanistan you never call attention to facts that shame people, and in Africa you never question the accuracy of an authority. Peter was not going to let this issue die.

"Don't tell me that this isn't true in the villages! My NGO works in hundreds of them, and this is a problem in many Pashtun villages where we work!"

"No!"

"We were out in a village last week. There was a young woman—perhaps fifteen years old—who had just given birth to her first child. She was very sick! Our nurse told her that she needed to wash herself every day if she wanted to get better. I felt so sorry for this girl...she was weeping! She told us that she wanted to bathe but if she did her family would disown her!"

"What you are saying is not true! Being clean is very important in Islam!"

Peter just laughed at the denials. He was not going to yield any ground, especially because he believed that everyone in the room knew he was right. "OK, how many of you deny what I am saying is true? Raise your hand!" He moved to the chalkboard to start writing down numbers. "This is a documented public health problem in Afghanistan! Go down to the WHO (World Health Organization) or UNICEF office, and look at the research!"

Fatima, a young mother of two who was finishing up her bachelor's degree in literature, couldn't take it anymore. "You are going to leave Afghanistan and tell the world that Afghan women are unclean!" She broke down in tears.

I looked around and saw damp eyes around the room. Peter began to realize what he had accomplished and finally decided to change the subject.

"Another thing that shocks me about Iskandar is the wall of separation between men and women in this society. Why can't girls and boys go to school together? Is this really the teaching of Islam or is this your culture?"

"In Islam, it is taught that it is not good for men and women to be together in the same room unless they are family," another student named Rehana responded. *I always thought Rehana was shy ... she never talks. She must be even more devout!*

"Really? Well, at Kabul University the boys and girls attend classes together!"

Rehana dug her feet in. "They are not real Muslims, then!"

"Really! In *Arabistan* (Saudi Arabia), they go to class together!"

"They are not real Muslims, either!"

"You say they are not real Muslims in Arabistan?" Peter asked incredulously. "Your religion started in Arabistan! Your prophet was from Arabistan! Every year thousands of Afghans make the hajj to Arabistan, because it is the center of Islam!"

It was time to intervene. I was still fairly new to this country but I knew that it was dangerous for foreigners to lecture Afghans about their own religion. Peter was leaving Iskandar for good the next day, but I planned to live here for a while.

"You haven't said much about the culture of Uganda," I finally cut in. "I'm sure the students would love to ask you some questions about African culture."

"Yes, professor. I have a question!" came a voice from the back of the classroom. It was Najibe. "Last night I watched a documentary on BBC about an African tribal group. They wore hardly any clothes at all. Please, could you tell us, sir, why you don't wear clothes in Africa?"

Touché. Chalk one up for the ladies.

I went back to my office a little nervous that day. I wasn't sure that I still had a job teaching at Iskandar University. In fact, I watched my back a little more than usual that entire weekend.

The next week I tried to test the waters a bit to see how much apologizing was needed. "Perhaps our African friend was a bit blunt. I probably should have asked him to talk about something other than culture shock."

"He was quite a shock to us!" Najibe replied. Then they all broke out in laughter. I was forgiven.

One day I walked into my classroom, and the women—with great enthusiasm and congratulations—informed me that it was teacher appreciation day. They escorted me to another room where they had a banquet set up for my fellow professors and me. Forty women stood in the room and watched the five of us eat. Then they presented us with presents... they gave me boxes of chocolates, two dress shirts, and several pairs of dress socks. *I knew my socks were a little scruffy!* We went outside for a big group photo. It felt almost scandalous to be surrounded by Afghan women standing only inches away, but I was really humbled by their appreciation. *These women are overcomers, worthy of the world's respect.*

Not everyone in Iskandar was a fan of the university. About halfway through my first semester, uproar broke out in the city with the university in the cross hairs. Two cheeky students in an Islamic studies course asked their professor for an apologetic on Islam. Reportedly the students were fed up with being told *what* to believe, and wanted to know *why* they should believe it. They wanted evidence for why this system of belief that they had grown up with was true and to understand why it should be imposed on the entire world. The professor was taken aback by the boldness of their question and wasn't sure how to answer. So he fell back to the normal recourse employed in this part of the world when faced with a question on religion for which there is no stock answer—he accused his students of blasphemy. A riot quickly broke out at the university, and the two students were beaten and thrown in jail.

Word quickly spread on the streets in town that these two young men had converted to Christianity (the rumor was untrue). The big mullahs in Iskandar organized large protests against the university. Thousands of turbaned men marched against the university, calling for the two young blasphemers to be publicly hung Taliban-style from the trees in the central park, right in front of the university. They wanted the university—a place where young students are taught the dangerous art of independent thinking and secular studies—shut down.

The literature faculty came under scrutiny, but Mr Ramin, Professor Ibrahim, and all one hundred of my students kept it quiet that an American was teaching in their department. Classes were cancelled for the week, and Ramin advised that I shouldn't come near the university until further notice. "So many Afghans are stupid and uneducated!" he exclaimed over the phone. "I'm sorry, Mr. Matthew. This will pass."

"Don't worry about me, Ramin. I really admire Professor Ibrahim and you for your courage. Please be careful!"

Finally President Karzai stepped into the fray. He made it clear that the fate of these accused young men would be decided by the courts and not by a mob organized by angry mullahs. After careful examination, the court found the two young men innocent of the charges of blasphemy. They were released and promptly fled to Pakistan out of fear for their lives.

Things settled down to normal, and I was soon back to teaching at the university but always conscious to keep a low profile. In between classes one morning an Italian journalist, accompanied by his cameraman, walked into my classroom uninvited. He introduced himself and explained that he was a writer for a large Italian newspaper.

"How long have you been working in Iskandar?" he asked, pulling out a notepad.

"Almost a year."

"Are you, um, a little nervous being here? I mean, do you ever feel that it is dangerous for you?"

"Why? This is a great place. Folks here are plenty friendly. I tell you what ... why don't you let some of my students ask you some questions about Italy? They have been studying some about

European culture. Class, we have an Italian guest with us today. He'd be happy to take a few questions."

With that, class began. Our Italian friend looked nervous. He had been in Afghanistan only a few days and wasn't used to taking questions. His cameraman stood at the back door and snapped photos while I sat on the front row, obscured by my students.

"Please tell us how Italian culture differs from the culture of the countries that neighbor it," Naser requested, in excellent English.

He started slowly but ended up talking about the Italian love for beauty, smart clothing, architecture, romance, good food and wine ... basically the "good life."

This didn't seem to impress my students.

"Can you tell us a little about marriage practices in Italy?" was the next question.

He explained that Italian society was free, so that young people could marry whomever they pleased. In some traditional families, the young man might ask the woman's father for his blessing, but it was really just a formality. He tried to explain the concept of dating and left out premarital cohabitation entirely.

Did I notice correctly that his hand was trembling?

"Could you tell us about your religion and to what extent religion influences culture in Italy?" asked another student named Mohammed Jami.

I was downright proud of my students. *Intelligent question, Mo!*

By now our reporter was clearly sweating. First of all, he explained, he wasn't really religious himself. Italy traditionally was a Catholic country. But the country had freedom of religion, and there also were plenty of Muslims living very happily and worshipping very freely in Italy—including the former king of Afghanistan. He was very sorry, but he had a pressing appointment so he really had to run. But it was great being able to talk with all of us. With that, he scurried out of the classroom. *Chicken!*

Two months later, I was in the middle of proctoring the final exam of my cultural anthropology class to about a hundred students scattered about an increasingly hot courtyard. Professor Ibrahim and Mr. Ramin circled the courtyard, helping to supervise. Alana, a woman old enough to have grown children, handed me her completed exam.

"My teacher, may I ask you a question?"

"Of course!"

"Several months ago we talked about reverse culture shock. If I remember correctly, you went home after living overseas for several years in Africa. I have been wondering. Do you ever completely get over reverse culture shock? How long does it take to get used to your own country again?"

There was a look of distant sadness in her eyes.

Alana went on to tell me her story—one I had been wondering about for months. She had lived in Germany with her husband and daughter for more than ten years. They were part of a large Afghan community of many extended relatives. She enjoyed her life in Germany, particularly the equality and freedoms that women have in that society. But she was never able to provide her husband with a son. Eventually her husband's relatives decided that it was time for him to take a second wife. For a while he resisted—he was a good man, she kept insisting—but finally yielded to his parents' demands. Being that German law forbids polygamy, he was forced to divorce her and sent her and their daughter "home" to Iskandar to live with her mother. Alana had been here a year and was still trying to adjust to the role of women in this society. She also really missed her husband. His new wife was a shrew, and even he was miserable with this new, younger model. Alana's saving grace was Iskandar University, the one place where she could be fully human.

It seemed a little awkward for me to be having this conversation with an Afghan woman, ten years my senior, in the middle of a hot, dusty courtyard with more than a few eyes watching. It was another heartbreaking story in a land full of them. But I sensed that it was somehow therapeutic for Alana to be able to share her story with a man who valued her identity as a woman. Our conversation would have been simply scandalous outside the walls of Iskandar University.

Over the next few years I taught several classes in cultural anthropology at Iskandar University. Eventually, the boys' and girls' classes combined, although they always sat on opposite sides of the room. Sometimes I played them against each other to remind the guys of the women's formidable intellects and to motivate them to work harder. My NGO helped the literature faculty develop a stronger Internet research facility, and I started a cultural anthropology discussion group. Eventually I brought on an American literature professor to teach on a more regular basis. Several of my former students received Fulbright scholarships to study in the United States.

One year Professor Ibraham brought several jugs of milk from his cows to my house on Christmas. The next day he showed up at my office with a cake he had made for my family, wishing us a "Happy Christmas." As we were sitting in my office sipping tea, he quietly stated, "We like you, Mr. Matt." Not quite sure that he had said it clearly enough, he repeated himself. "What I mean to say is, I *really* like you." He reached over, patted my knee, and said in English, "Actually, I *love* you!" I wasn't quite sure how to respond to Mr. Ibrahim's kind expression of appreciation for the friendship we had developed over the past years, so I changed the subject. "So tell me more about the class you plan to teach in American literature..."

And Jesus said to him, 'If you can! All things are possible for one who believes.' Immediately the father of the child cried out and said, 'I believe; help my unbelief!'
Mark 9: 23–24 (ESV)

I will say of the Lord: 'He is my refuge and my fortress, my God, in Him I will trust.' He shall cover you with His feathers, and under His wings you shall take refuge.
Psalm 91: 2,4 (NKJV)

Chapter 12

Angels Shall Bear

You Up

We enjoyed a peaceful spring of 2005 in Iskandar. More than six months had passed since the riots, and that day almost seemed like a bad dream. Dr. Jack and Tiffany flew back to America at the end of April for the birth of their son. They were to be gone for four months, so I was plenty busy managing our expanding health projects, teaching on the side at the university, and still taking Dari classes from Aziz. I stressed more about managing Afghan health workers and navigating the politics of inter-organizational NGO cooperation than I did security.

One May morning I saw in the news that *Newsweek* magazine had erroneously reported the desecration of a Quran by an American soldier at Guantanamo. *Newsweek* retracted the article, but the damage had already been done; violent protesting erupted around the Muslim world. On May 12 I read ANSO reports about violent protests in Kandahar and Jalalabad. NGO offices had been targeted by mobs; sadly, Afghans had died in the rioting. That afternoon we received an ANSO warning that several mullahs in Iskandar were planning protests in our city the next day following Friday afternoon prayers at the large mosques in town. They were likely to turn violent. Our neighbors warned us to stay inside, and the team planned to go into lockdown by noon.

I had difficulty sleeping that night. At 1:00 a.m. I got out of bed, walked across The Museum's hallway to Ellie's room to look in on her. She was sleeping peacefully, surrounded by stuffed animals. I asked God once again to please protect my Little Nut Brown Hare and just stood and watched her for a little while as she slept, outlined in the faint glow of her night light. Her breaths were peaceful. I whispered a memorized verse in the quiet of the night, written down two thousand years ago by a man well acquainted with dependence on a sovereign and loving God:

And we know that all things work together for good to those who love God, to those who are the called according to His purpose. (Romans 8:28, NKJV)

But didn't he get his head cut off eventually? I thought about all the horrible things that have happened to people, including Christians, since Adam sinned and brought evil into the human experience. *All things work together for good!* I knew the answer came from a view of life that extends beyond this physical, temporal existence. Jesus Christ himself told a guy struggling with faith:

For God so loved the world that He gave His only begotten Son, that whoever believes in Him should not perish but have everlasting life. (John 3:16, NKJV)

I believe in you, Jesus. I know that if I die, I have eternal life. Which I long for! But this was not my greatest fear. It was something happening to Ellie. *Could my faith survive that?* I thought about it for a while and gave her to Jesus once again. *She is yours. Please protect her, Jesus. And protect me from fear. I believe. Help my unbelief!*

The next morning my faith was to become sight.

At 9:00 a.m. we gathered with some expat friends to pray for the peace of our city. We met at the house Tiffany and Dr. Jack had rented, which they shared with Audrie. We sat down in Audrie's spacious living room on the second floor. The room had high ceilings (I never measured but estimate at least twelve feet) and large, glass windows that looked out into a walled, cemented courtyard below. The entire compound was about fifty yards back from the street in a secure location. One of the expat women took Ellie and two other small children up the stairwell to a third-floor room to play.

We began to pray for God's protection on us all. Suddenly, a piercing scream from the lady upstairs watching the children!

My brain raced at light speed. *No explosion, no shattered glass! Would have heard gunfire! Intruder?!*

I bolted—along with several other men—for the stairwell. I got there first and ripped open the door.

Ellie was lying on the landing, unconscious. *Oh, God!*

"Don't touch her!" screamed the woman upstairs. "She just fell from up here! She landed on the back of her head! I almost caught her foot!" She broke down and wept.

Ellie had tripped, stumbling right through the third floor railing, and fallen a very high story (at least twelve feet) before landing on the back of her head.

In nanoseconds, memories flooded my mind: Holding newborn Ellie at the hospital. Ellie devouring her cupcake on her first birthday (the same day we packed up our house in America to move here). Ellie swinging in the breeze in our courtyard, a big smile across her face. Now she looked lifeless on a cold landing in Afghanistan.

Oh Jesus, save her! I can't remember if I cried out verbally or just in my heart.

She opened her eyes.

I gasped, then got down on all fours. Christine and a small crowd were right behind me.

"Don't touch her! Her spinal cord could be damaged!" Audrie cried out.

What now? Dr. Jack just left! No trauma care in Iskandar! Help us, God!

Ellie started to cry and to wiggle around a little.

"She shouldn't be able to move like that if she's paralyzed! Right?" I turned to Audrie.

"I think that's right!"

There was no blood. Ellie started moving around more on the landing and crying a little louder. She rolled on her side to get up.

"Catherine, is that right?! She's not paralyzed?" My tone was pretty intense... I wanted confirmation from both nurses in the room.

"That's right. I don't think she could move like that if she had a spinal cord injury."

Catherine, Audrie, Christine, and I crowded around little Ellie. Others in the room started praying for her in the background. The two nurses checked her out as best they could. No apparent fractures; not even external bruising as best they could tell. No signs of a concussion.

"Can I pick her up?" I looked at Catherine.

"I'm not a doctor, but I think so."

Well, no EMS service here. "Audrie?"

"I think so, Matthew."

I gingerly picked up little Ellie, and she reached for my neck. She snuggled her head on my shoulder. Christine joined the hug, and then, along with Catherine, continued searching for any signs of trauma. Not a scratch. "Her pupils look totally normal," Catherine concluded. "It's a miracle!"

It was a miracle! *Thank you, God. Thank you.* Ellie had stopped crying by now, and I held her tight. For a very long time. With tears in my eyes. Eventually, she wanted to run along and play. We were glad to see her walk in a straight line, but she wasn't going anywhere out of my sight.

My dad is a head and neck surgeon. I gave him a call in the middle of the night, his time. "Dad! Sorry to wake you. Don't worry, we are all right. But Ellie had a fall. It is a miracle, but she seems OK. I need to decide whether we need to call for a medevac (medical evacuation) flight from Dubai."

He walked me through all possible symptoms of brain trauma, and we went through the checklist looking for anything that would point to internal bleeding or brain swelling. She checked out completely fine.

"And she isn't complaining of any pain? No headache?"

"None. No dizziness either. She is completely lucid. Still no pupil dilation."

"Check on that every hour for the next twenty-four hours. Through the night."

"Will do. Dad, this was a miracle. Angels must have caught her!"

"It was a miracle, Matthew. But really... our response shouldn't be amazement but gratitude. And praise!"

That night Ellie slept between Christine and me in our bed (something that soon became a bad habit). As I tucked her in to sleep, I read these verses from Psalm 91:

He who dwells in the secret place of the Most High shall abide under the shadow of the Almighty. He shall cover you with His feathers, and under His wings you shall take refuge. Because you have made the Lord, who is my refuge, even the Most High, your dwelling place, no evil shall befall you, nor shall any plague come near your dwelling; for He shall give His angels charge over you, to keep you in all your ways. In their hands they shall bear you up...(Psalm 91:1, 4, 9–12, NKJV)

Christine and I woke Ellie up every hour of the night to be sure there were no signs of concussion. There were none. In the middle of the night, as I laid next to Ellie, listening to her sweet little breaths, God's Spirit whispered to my soul: "I am sovereign and can protect your family as easily here in Afghanistan as in America. I have called you here to serve. Trust Me and obey." It was time to put it in gear.

I whispered back a prayer to heaven. "Thank you, Lord. I believe! Help my unbelief."

Story time with Matthew and Ellie.

In my experience, men who respond to good fortune with modesty and kindness are harder to find than those who face adversity with courage. For in the very nature of things, success tends to create pride and blindness in the hearts of men, while suffering teaches them to be patient and strong.
—Xenophon, in Cyrus the Great: The Arts of Leadership and War

Texas can make it without the United States, but the United States cannot make it without Texas!
—Gen. Sam Houston

Chapter 13

Remember the Alamo!

Rodney had long dreamt of expanding our humanitarian work into the mountains of Afghanistan's remote interior, to a place called Bahesht.[4] The tribal clans who lived in these parts were the poorest of the land and due to inaccessibility had been mostly passed over in the aid and development work in Afghanistan. In addition to a shortage of food, little medical care was available in this region,

---

4   Name of town changed due to security.

and people struggled to survive the negative 30-degree winters in their black tents and mud-walled houses, sometimes buried under six feet of snow. The area was infamous for its cultivation of opium in summer, and regional commanders were quick to wage feudal-type battles with one another. Due to mud, swollen rivers, and deep snow, the region was accessible from Iskandar only about half of the year. The only other way in or out was by a small plane, and that was spotty during the winter due to the region's Russian-built airstrips being covered in ice. During the spring they melted into mud pits. Very few foreigners ever visited this region. With only a few months left in Afghanistan, sixty-eight year old Rodney was chomping at the bit to get up there and check things out.

Early morning June 2, 2005, I woke up in my bed in The Museum, put on my shalwar kamis and travel vest, ate a bowl of cereal, then picked up my backpack. This was the first time I was to leave my family for more than an overnight village trip. I was a little uneasy. Our neighbors had assured me that they would take good care of Christine and Ellie while I was off traipsing around "The Wild West" of Afghanistan. I kissed my pregnant wife goodbye, then picked up Ellie. I sang to her John Denver's "Leaving on a Jet Plane" song, ending it with a kiss on the forehead and my improvised line: "Don't worry cause I'll be back again …"

I drove to the office, where I met my traveling companions. Robbie, our NGO's country director, had flown in from Dubai especially for this trip. He was no stranger to this part of the world; he had grown up in Kabul, Kandahar, and Tehran. At the age of twenty, he hid out in a Tehran hotel room during the Iranian revolution. Robbie spoke a variety of languages and had been all over Afghanistan, but this was to be his first trip up to Bahesht. Robbie's Dari was a little rusty, and we were not going to entrust the fate of our expedition to my limited Dari capacity, so Aziz came along with us to help translate.

James stopped by the office, and saw me in my Afghan village get-up. "Hey bro! Where are you going today?"

"Heading up to Bahesht. Up in the mountains!"

"Brother, be careful up there. I mean it!"

"Of course! Careful is my middle name."

James said a prayer for us, then Rodney looked at me. "You ready to go, Matthew?"

"Let's do this!"

A PACTEC Beechcraft 200 King Air dropped us off at Bahesht's dusty airport several hours later, and we took a quick look around the small provincial capital. Virtually all of the buildings were constructed from mud, straw, and rocks and were built on two sides of a swiftly flowing river that brought life to the province. The main bazaar was located at the center of town, with various goods essential to village life spilling out of small mud rooms and crude wooden stalls. No vegetables or fruit were available in Bahesht during the wintertime; the extremely ripe and expensive apples, oranges, and grapes we found had been shipped up from Iskandar on a treacherous dirt track over high mountain passes. Aziz and I walked past a butcher shop adorned by a freshly decapitated bull lying on its back, legs pawing at the sky. *Rigor mortis is setting in!*

This was Rodney's op. He had made arrangements for us to stay the night with a local, Afghan-run NGO, but the office manager seemed not to have gotten the radio message from Iskandar that we were coming. Being unprepared for guests, he took us down to the local "hotel" for us to get a bite of lunch. We climbed a rickety set of wooden stairs up to the dark second floor of the mud structure. About twenty turbaned travelers from villages all over the province sat on toshaks lining the floor, eating lunch with their hands and watching a small satellite TV set powered by a car battery.

"*Salaam Aleykum*" we said, placing our hands over our hearts, trying to fit right in.

"*Waleykum a Salaam*" several politely replied between chews. We were the first foreigners most of these men had seen.

The guy with the remote thumbed through the channels, ranging from *Al Jazeera* to *WWF* professional wrestling. He settled for a show on *Animal Planet* about a French beauty salon and spa for poodles. Afghans naturally detest dogs for being unclean animals; now we were watching French women in miniskirts bringing their pimped-up poodles to a salon where a shampoo and massage cost more than the average monthly income of the room. The entire room's gaze vacillated between the TV and us, staring hard and shaking their heads in wonderment.

"No, uh-uh, that is ridiculous!" Robbie protested.

"Only in France. Crazy French! Can you believe that?!" I objected, loudly, between chews of nan.

The men in the room weren't buying it. There were Afghans, and there were kharedjis. We were of the latter species, and kharedjis do things that make no sense. The mullahs were right to warn their flocks about materialists like us.

"Aziz, explain to them that we think it insane, like they do, to spend so much money on a dog's hairdo," I pleaded. "They should help feed villages and build schools." Aziz wasn't sure what to think or say, so he just ate, most likely wishing that he was back in Iskandar and not here with his present travel companions. I did my best in Dari to express disapproval of the TV show as I finished my lunch: *"Tuk, tuk, tuk. Khub nis! Divaneh!"*

We spent the afternoon visiting with government officials and the few NGOs that worked in the province learning more about the needs and opportunities in the region. Rodney arranged for a local vehicle and driver to take us to a distant village the next day to meet with Dr. Alana, a Scandinavian pediatrician who had established a small hospital. She also trained village women to become community health workers.

That evening we drew silty water from a shallow well in a bucket made from old tires to wash the dust off our faces, then settled in for the night on the floor of our host NGO's office. I pulled out my pocket New Testament and read from John's gospel by flashlight.

Robbie worked on a chapter from the latest biography of his hero, Bob Dylan. Aziz performed his evening prayers in the corner in Arabic, a language that he did not speak but had memorized.

Early the next morning I walked outside, rubbed the sleep out of my eyes, and did a double-take at the tires of the beat up Toyota Surf that Rodney had hired. They were the baldest I'd ever seen. *Slim pickings in Bahesht!* Impressively, the Surf faithfully bounded over the dirt track marked as a highway on Afghan maps, taking us past some magnificent scenery. I couldn't help but focus on the wild river, spying out some great kayaking spots. "That one looks like a class four rapid, maybe I'll get an inflatable kayak up here one day." My boss Robbie, the motocross daredevil, was looking the other way up at the boulder-strewn hills and mesas. "Just look at those places, Matt, perfect motorcycle riding! Can you imagine? The two of us on dirt bikes! We should plan a trip one day, across this part of the country, all the way to Kabul. It would be epic!"

Things got more difficult. Mechanical issues and a muddy road stretched our drive into a nine-hour trip. We had to get out and push through several mud bogs. At one dodgy bridge that crossed the river we opted to get out and walk across, then watched our Afghan driver slowly inch his Surf over the sagging wooden boards. But our chief obstacle proved to be another river just a few kilometers outside Dr. Alana's village. As we approached this scenic, cold river, it became clear that the Surf was not going to make it across. But the high water level didn't faze our Afghan driver. He clenched the steering wheel, focused his eyes, and put the pedal to the metal. His sheer determination took us farther than I imagined possible, but halfway across the laws of physics overcame magnificent willpower and the engine flooded and died. Cold river water started filling the floorboards. *Time to abandon ship!* Robbie, Aziz, and I salvaged our gear and carried it across the river, but Rodney climbed on the roof and coolly munched on peanuts while the drama unfolded around him. No sweat, a Kamaz truck lumbered along, and with a little monetary incentive pulled our vehicle right out of the river (with Rodney still on top). But the Surf's engine was dead. We paid the truck owner enough money to tow us to the center of the bazaar in town, providing plenty of entertainment for the good folks of Dr. Alana's village. "Hey, *Ali*, look at what the cat drug in! A couple of wet kharedjis!"

Dr. Alana was an impressive woman. Not only did she keep a fully operational hospital—complete with surgery—working off solar power in one of the most remote places on earth, she did it with a majority female staff. It was exciting to witness the professionalism and empowerment of the nurses and health workers, and just a little delicious to watch these dedicated Afghan women ordering the men around. "Sit down, wait over there until your turn!" And the men complied, for the most part. Dr. Alana had become something like the mayor of the town, riding around on a bicycle (normally only done by men) and advising the town council on difficult matters. The small PACTEC plane from Kabul flew overhead as we were walking to her house from the hospital and dipped his wings in salute. "Hel.oooo!" Dr. Alana took off her headscarf and waved it in the wind to the pilot. "He always dips his wings whenever he sees me!"

Over dinner in her mud fortress home, Dr. Alana told us about the isolated tribal people who live between Bahesht and her village, and one of her more notable patients, a feudal chief (some might say warlord) whose title, when translated into English, meant something like "Boss Lord." He ruled somewhere between 40 and 120 villages (depending on who we asked) and lived in a mud castle not too far off the dirt track that we would take back to Bahesht. Boss Lord was a part of the first *Loya Jirga* following Afghanistan's liberation from the Taliban, as well as a former rival to several larger warlords—the most notable being our ex-governor, Zayed Khan. Dr. Alana decided that it would be a good idea for us to meet him since we hoped to start community health initiatives in the poorest villages in his region. She sent a letter of introduction to his village by courier.

After saying farewell to Dr. Alana, we hired a different vehicle and headed back toward Bahesht. We found a better way across the river and drove through some beautiful, desolate places until we came upon two young men sitting on a boulder next to the dirt track in the middle of nowhere. They had AK-47s and palms raised in the air, signaling that we should stop. *Uh, oh.*

"*Salaam Aleykum*! We are not robbing you! Boss Lord sent us! Follow us!" With that, they pulled out a little motorcycle from behind their rock and set off. We followed them down an even more primitive dirt trail until finally in the distance a village came into view. A man approached us on a motorcycle with a group of people following him on foot, some armed. I squinted to see him better. The tall guy on the motorcycle had a long, salt-and-pepper beard, wore a white turban, and sported a pair of aviator sunglasses. *That's not Bin Laden, is it?! Maybe not a good situation!*

Thankfully my concerns turned out to be for naught. This was Boss Lord, and he welcomed us to his village. We walked through the thick wooden gates of Boss Lord's mud castle and entered a large room. Tribal leaders from many villages sat on the floor on toshaks that lined the walls, waiting to get their opportunity to request aid for their village or arbitration in a land dispute from their feudal chief. Boss Lord offered us the honored toshaks in the room and sat down on the floor across from us. He began by welcoming us to his humble home and then expressed his very high opinion of Dr. Alana. He said that friends of hers were guests in his slice of the country, something we were glad to hear, as it communicated to us—and to everyone in the room—that we were to enjoy his protection that night.

After several cups of tea, Rodney introduced our party, explaining our NGO's background and aspirations for work in Bahesht and the surrounding province. He was good at setting expectations at a lower level, but I thought we might need more value added from the start. Aziz did a fine job translating everything. Boss Lord seemed mildly interested in our health care initiatives but told us that if we really wanted to help their communities, we should come build proper schools and hire real teachers.

"We'd like to come help your villages improve their health!" I jumped into the conversation with too much enthusiasm. "Too many women die in childbirth, and treatable diseases are a major killer in these parts! We think we could make a difference by training community health workers in your villages!" I looked around the room while Aziz was finishing up translating the last part. I meant my spiel to sound inspirational, but these men were already bored. They were looking at the ground, picking their feet. "Boring kharedjis, thinking they can save the world with their projects. Seen one, Akhmed, you've seen 'em all." Boss Lord quickly arranged a marriage on the side, then shifted his attention back to me.

I changed tactics. "I've been teaching a class on sociology at Iskandar's University. We have been studying the different people groups of Afghanistan, and several of my students have written fascinating papers on the tribal people in your region. Could you tell us more about your tribe?" *This might be dangerous...*

Boss Lord, and the room, came alive. He explained how dozens of smaller tribal groups in the region had banded together over the centuries primarily for protection from larger adversaries. They were some of the most resilient people on earth, having a nomadic past but now mostly settled in remote mountain villages throughout several provinces. The government in Kabul meant little to them; they relied on tribal leaders for decision-making and governance. "We allow women to voice their opinion in counsels and even to have a say in their parents' choice for them of a husband," Boss Lord claimed. *Not bad for Afghanistan.*

Boss Lord told us stories of tribal kings from long ago who vanquished enemies, leaving behind impressive body counts. One poet-king of yesteryear created a mound in Ghazni out of a mixture of dirt and the blood of thousands of his enemies. His original plan had been to completely eliminate all human life in the region. But after he created his mound, he changed his mind and decided to spare some of the women and children. As he rode his horse across the dusty plain away from his monument, he composed a poem declaring how even his enemies were made of the same flesh as he and were, therefore, like brothers. And what a noble humanitarian he was for mercifully staying his genocidal hand! At least that is the gist that I got from Boss Lord as he quoted the poem at great length and with gusto. Aziz looked scared to death as he translated for us.

Boss Lord and his men regaled us with stories of their own great feats. He told the story of how Zayed Khan once sent a letter to him, suggesting that they ally together to fight a bigger enemy, Aman Khan.

"He wrote that we were like brothers and that I should bring my horses down from the mountains to Iskandar to help him fight."

"What did you answer him?" I asked, sitting on the edge of my toshak.

"I wrote back that it had been too long since we had a good fight. I told him that if he wanted my horses, he could come on up here to our mountains and try to get them himself if he dared!"

"What happened?" I noticed heads in the room slumping, but Aziz looked terrified. He was from Iskandar, and Zayed Khan had been his leader once upon a time. Did I really have to keep this conversation going?

"Well, he came up here and eventually he got our horses. But we killed more of his men than he did of ours!"

Nods and grunts of approval went around the room. I decided that it was time to try a grand entrance of my own into the conversation.

"You gentlemen remind me of the kind of people that live in the place where I grew up." Rodney flashed me an incredulous look:

"What are you doing?!" Robbie sported an ever so slight grin. He was enjoying all of this.

Beards, turbans, and eyes turned in my direction, intrigued to learn how such a boast from an uncooked foreigner like me could possibly measure up. I told them stories of Texas, with plenty of drawn-out Texan braggadocio and perhaps a slight blurring of the time periods. Robbie did his utmost to choke back laughter while Boss Lord's men sat in wide-eyed, reverent silence. I culminated with the story of the Alamo, which was received in the room with universal acclaim. Something deep within the Afghan tribal soul resonated with 257 vastly outnumbered Texans sacrificing their lives to protect their turf and to see how many Mexican soldiers they could kill before they met their fate. I noticed a distinct change in the expressions in the room toward me. I was becoming more than just a normal kharedji to whom Boss Lord had granted guest status... I was becoming a worthy, understandable human being—a bit more like them. As the story reached its grand, tragic conclusion, the men looked at me as though I had been standing there next to Davy Crockett and Colonel Travis.

"That is the greatest story we have ever heard!" one man with a thick beard declared.

"Do you know how to shoot a gun?" someone else asked. I might be an unbeliever, but I was on my way to becoming an honorary member of the tribe.

"Do you pray?" a turbaned man asked. Boss Lord broke in and declared that I was certainly a great guy but to expect that I prayed every day was to expect a little too much from a kharedji.

"I do pray!"

"No, you don't." Boss Lord answered for me, with a smile. Kafirs do not pray.

"But I do pray!" I explained that I believed in the power of prayer and made a practice of praying to God first thing every morning and every night before I went to sleep. I didn't face Mecca and my prayers were not in Arabic, but they were composed in my heart to God. I often prayed and sung to God in my heart throughout my day. *Especially when I'm in trouble, like maybe now.*

"We will see." Boss Lord let me know, with a smile, that this topic was concluded for now. Aziz gave me a look that said: "Please shut up ... I want to live!"

We had a great time in Boss Lord's mud castle in the middle of Afghanistan that evening. By the end of the night, we had been enthusiastically declared permanent guests of their tribe, and, much to his pleasure, I had bestowed upon Boss Lord the title of honorary Texan. "By the powers invested in me, by the Republic of TEXAS, I declare you an honorary Texan, with all rights and privileges ..." I was shooting from the hip now and have no idea how Robbie and Rodney managed to keep straight faces. For his part, Boss Lord decreed that all his people in all of his villages must treat us with the utmost respect and hospitality, and told us that we would have no problem running our health care projects in his villages. He would see to it that people in each village volunteered to be trained and to serve as community health workers.

Early the next morning, I awoke in the darkness. *Where am I?* There was Robbie, sleeping on a toshak. And Aziz on the one next to him. I checked my vitals. *Pulse, check. Appendages all attached, check.* I waited a few minutes then dug out my pocket New Testament and walked outside. I walked a hundred yards or so and sat down on a rock under a scrubby bush. I read from John 7, meditating on these words of Christ: "If anyone thirsts, let him come to me and drink. Whoever believes in me, as the Scripture has said, 'Out of his heart will flow rivers of living water'" (vs. 37–38). I started to pray, then looked up. Boss Lord and a small group of his men stood in front of his gate watching me. They were trying to figure out what I was doing. Is this kharedji praying?

Boss Lord asked me about it over breakfast.

"Every morning I try to read from the *Injil* and spend time in prayer. Jesus taught that we should pray in a quiet place, which can be anywhere. The idea is to pray sincerely to God and not show off for other people. I feel closest to God when I'm out in nature. For me, prayer is just talking to God, to my Heavenly Father. It is a personal relationship with the God who made the stars. I am a sinner, but Jesus made my heart clean so that I can know God."

"We Muslims greatly respect Jesus. He was a great prophet." Boss Lord seemed impressed that I took my faith seriously. "Christians are like our brothers, and we Muslims respect the *Taurat* (Torah) and *Injil* (Gospel). They speak much about our prophets."

They started asking me more questions about both books, and I did my best to explain the big picture story of creation to Christ. I also learned more about Islam. *Well, isn't this something? Back in America we avoid talking about faith and religion in public. Out here it is normal mealtime conversation!*

After elaborate farewells from Boss Lord and our new friends, we bounded over the dirt track back to Bahesht, getting seriously stuck in the mud only once this time. That afternoon we secured a vehicle to drive us to Iskandar the next day, then met with the newly appointed governor of the province. We walked into his office in our dusty travel attire; the governor wore a modern dark suit with maroon power tie. He received us warmly, listened to our ideas for health care initiatives, and strongly requested that we start a school to train the young men and women of Bahesht in English and computer skills so that they could be qualified for some of the higher level jobs that international NGOs and the military (NATO) were about to bring to town.

The next day before 5:00 a.m. Rodney, Aziz, and I said farewell to Robbie (who caught a PACTEC flight to Kabul later that morning) and commenced our trip back to Iskandar in a tank of a Land Cruiser that had been altered for durability while throwing all comfort out the window. We passed over the most treacherous, beat-up roads that I had seen in Afghanistan, matched by some incredible scenery. We stopped in one valley that reminded me of Yosemite.

Aziz and I stretched out our backs on wildflower-studded grass under an orchard, the sound of spring-fed streams gushing nearby. Views of purple mountain crags peeked through the treetops.

I chewed on a tall weed that I had plucked. "Your country has some beautiful places tucked away that most kharedjis never get to see!"

"I've never seen such beauty in my life!" Aziz responded.

Alas, our twenty-minute chai break had to end, and the rest of our bone-crushing trip had to commence. We passed through settlements of tribal yurts and the black tents of Pashtun *kutchis* (nomads). We missed a rocket attack in one village we drove through by a day. After fifteen hours of hard driving, we arrived in Iskandar dehydrated, covered in dust, really glad to be alive, and in serious need of a chiropractor. I limped through the metal gate into my courtyard, knocked on The Museum's front door, and embraced Christine and Ellie. It was sure good to be home, but like Rodney, I now had my sights set on a place called Bahesht.

Top, the beautiful, rugged terrain of Afghanistan. Middle, a mud-fort home of the region. Bottom, a dodgy river crossing. Afghan determination eventually gave way to the laws of physics, and the occupants had to abandon ship.

Success is the ability to go from one failure to
another with no loss of enthusiasm.
—Winston Churchill

Failures are finger posts on the road to achievement.
—CS Lewis

Chapter 14

Some of Our Ideas are

Just Ideas

Afghanistan revealed much to me about my own personal weaknesses, the importance of not taking myself too seriously, the necessity of holding tight to my faith, and the joy of giving to others. In other words: trust God, give it all I got, and laugh at myself—a lot.

I started leading the team in the summer of 2005. Rodney and Sadie had done a fine job laying the foundation for our team's work in Iskandar and were preparing to return to the USA to ride off into a West Coast sunset in an RV. It could have been awkward moving from a position of friend/colleague to that of regional director of our NGO, but everyone on the team made it easy, giving me a lot of encouragement and support. "Mr. Matthew will take our projects farther and higher than they have been before," Dr. Jack graciously promised Dr. Hakim, the Afghan Ministry of Public Health doctor who had oversight of our region.

In August Audrie and I flew to Kabul to attend a health review meeting sponsored by the Ministry of Public Health. A hundred and fifty Afghan doctors from across the country were in attendance. I was invited to speak about our community health strategy. I got up in front and made a case for the villages. The villagers were capable of solving many of their health care issues if we properly trained them. It takes a village! (I didn't really say that). I explained that we just needed to be willing to do the work to train community health workers and then monitor their progress with spot-checks in their villages by teams that we set up in government health centers. Village *shuras* (councils) could be empowered to help provide the right level of accountability to community health workers. "We can change the maternal and infant mortality rates and wipe out diseases like TB from Afghanistan if we start at the grass roots, village level, and empower villagers to help themselves!" I meant my spiel to sound motivational, but a hundred and fifty pairs of brown eyes just stared at me. Then courtesy applause. *This is not rocket science,* I thought to myself. *Why such an uphill battle?*

I sat down at my table and listened to the next speaker. *Wonder where Audrie went?* A few minutes passed, then Dr. Hakim burst into the room through a side door, white-faced in panic. He had everyone's attention. "Dr. *Saheb* Matthew, Miss Audrie's medical condition has rapidly deteriorated!" he shouted at the top of his lungs. *He knows I'm not a doctor! What! Where?*

I jumped up with three other Afghan docs and ran through the main hallway and out the front door to find Audrie lying unconscious on a dirty sidewalk. Her lip was busted and the side of her forehead bruised.

"Dr. Matthew, what should we do?!" Hakim looked at me, wide-eyed.

The irony was not lost on me that here I stood with four medical doctors, all hovering around unconscious Audrie, asking me, the one non-medical person present, what to do. The reality was that this was an awkward cultural situation ... They were Afghan men, asking permission to touch an American woman.

"You guys are the doctors! Check her vitals: airway, breathing, circulation!" *Good thing I watched* ER *a few times...*

"Yes!" Dr. Hakim exclaimed, and they got right to it. A few moments later, Audrie opened her eyes, and we helped her up. She looked like a busted-up boxer, but she would be OK. Audrie had started feeling bad, stepped outside for some fresh air, and then just blacked out. I made a mental note to keep a closer eye on her MS.

Clay and Susan, our good friends from America who had taken the chilly trip to Mazar-i-Sharif with us in November 2002, joined our team in August 2005 along with their children: Lucy, age eleven, and Jake, age nine. They brought with them a fresh wind of optimism. Susan, a math whiz, took over supervising all our NGO's accounting work. Clay, a gifted administrator, managed the Iskandar office and its growing number of Afghan staff. As we expanded our operations and project work, we gave them both plenty of work to do. All four jumped right into Dari language study.

In September three young guys also came out to work with our team as one-year volunteers. David was a second-year cadet at West Point. He noticed that the Mormon cadets were given two years, between their second and third years of study, to perform their two years of overseas service. Somehow he managed to convince the administration that though he was not a Mormon, he should be allowed to go serve overseas for two years as well! Thomas came to

Iskandar as part of the practicum for a master's degree program that he was working on in economic development. He was interested in its convergence with public health and later went on to become a medical doctor. Rustin had just finished his degree in plastics engineering and was trying to figure out what to do with his life. He had the melancholy personality of an undiscovered rock star and just wanted to make a difference. From the start, he wanted to roll up his sleeves and get his hands dirty. I quickly gave him the chance.

Our friend Harbob, the village leader of De Khak, brought a delegation by the office one afternoon to request help renovating their village's school. Like so many projects in Afghanistan, an NGO had built a mud schoolhouse for them previously, but the village had no skin in the game. The NGO did everything for the villagers but hadn't quite finished the project. Because some of the windows hadn't been installed, vandals broke into the school and stole some of the wooden planks that support the roof. As a result, part of the roof had caved in, and the dirt floor of the schoolhouse turned into mud during the rains of early winter. In previous visits to De Khak, I had noticed school children carrying empty rice sacks to school to sit on.

I wanted the village to *own* their schoolhouse, so I agreed that we would provide the needed wood, cement, and carpet, but that the village would have to provide the labor without expecting payment. This seemed like a new concept to them, but Harbob agreed. Rustin had been in Iskandar for only a week, but he had made the mistake of saying: "Coach, put me in the game!" I thought this would be a great cultural immersion experience so I drove him up to De Khak to supervise the pouring of the cement floors and the structural repairs to the roof.

"I can't believe you are just going to leave him up there in the village!" Aziz objected.

"It's only a few days, and it will be good for him!" I responded, tying down a load of wooden beams on the roof of the Big Land Cruiser. "I trust Harbob and his men to protect him, and we're sending him up there with a translator. He'll figure things out!"

Aziz just stood there, shaking his head, as Rustin, his translator, and I drove off on our little mission.

I inspected the work done so far on the school at De Khak while the villagers unloaded the wood. *Good... cement bags are all here and accounted for.* I walked through the dirt floor classrooms. *Rustin is going to have his work cut out for him.* "Now remember," I told him. "Your objective is to motivate the village men to do the work. Don't be a perfectionist, and don't do everything for them. Work alongside them and help them see the power of being a volunteer!" I left him with my satellite phone.

Harbob asked if I would take a young man named Mo from the village with me back to Iskandar, and I was glad for the company.

"*Inja Dest e Rast Begarden!*" Mo commanded, at a barely discernible fork in the dirt track.

"You sure that we turn right here?" I had driven back from De Khak enough times to be fairly certain of the way back to the city.

"*Bale!*" (Yes!)

It didn't seem right to me, but this guy was a local. *Maybe he knows a shortcut!*

An hour later, after about twenty dubious turns, each confidently determined by a fifteen-year-old Afghan, I had completely lost my bearings. *Maybe it wasn't too bright to plan on driving back to Iskandar on my own. This IS Afghanistan!*

Mo finally admitted that he, too, was lost. We drove on blindly, hoping to stumble upon some village that could point us in the right direction, until we got stuck in the middle of a huge sandpit.

I got out of the BLC and took stock of our situation. We were at least a three-hour drive from Iskandar, in the middle of nowhere. Our tires were completely buried in sand, no shovel. No cell phone service, and Rustin had my sat phone. *No coms!* Left my passport/NGO identification at the office. Gave Rustin all my money for miscellaneous construction supplies, $1.20 worth of afghanis left in my pocket. One rope; nothing to tie it to! No food, and worst of all, completely out of water. The early afternoon sun beat down. I kicked myself for not planning contingencies for the trip home...all I had been thinking about was getting Rustin going in De Khak! *Not too bright!*

Mo and I dug in the sand with our hands. It was infested with stickers, and our hands bled. We took turns pushing and gunning the engine, tires spinning deeper in the sand. We succeeded in only burying the BLC deeper down to its chassis. We were quickly losing hydration and strength. *Not a good situation, at all!*

Mo spotted a herd of camels in the far distance and took off running over the sand dunes...I watched him get smaller and smaller over the horizon. It looked as if he was talking with the camel herders for quite some time until I realized that the dot coming back in my direction was singular. *Aw man, his head is drooping.* Baking in the hot sun, I looked around the arid landscape to see if there were any other signs of life. Nothing. *Not sure how we are getting out of this one!* The thought occurred to me that now would be a good time to ask God for help. *Should have been doing that an hour ago!*

Before I finished my prayer, I heard the noise of an engine. *Can't see anything.* Evidently Mo heard it, too. He started running again over the sand dunes, waving his arms wildly. The sound got louder until a tractor popped up over a nearby hill. It was missing its front right wheel; two men hung off the left side as a sort of counterbalance. The driver sported a turban and a patch over one eye. *Sure hope that's not Mullah Omar...thought he lived in Quetta!*

Mo started sprinting, shouting something unintelligible, and the tractor drove right up to the BLC and stopped. *Time to find out if they are here to help or have other plans!*

I greeted the one-eyed driver and his two companions, my right hand over my heart. They pulled the BLC out of the sand and put us on the right track home. Mo finally arrived at the scene, panting like a dog, but profusive with thanks to our saviors. I was too embarrassed to offer our rescuers my pocket change; Mo gave them my rope.

I made it home that evening dehydrated, sunburnt, and plenty dirty. I smelled something fierce. Christine, now in her third trimester, was sitting in a wicker chair on The Museum's front porch watching Ellie run circles in the grass. I sat down next to her and downed a liter of water. I told her about the school, the sandpit, and being rescued by a three-wheeled, tractor-piloted, one-eyed Afghan.

"The Lord protects us, Matthew. You waited a little while to ask for His help."

"Yeah, I know. It's just too easy to slide back into self-reliance. You'd think I would have learned by now."

"We need Him every day!"

"Yes, we do!" I thought for a minute. "One of the benefits of living here is that I am much more aware of my dependence on God every day than I was back in America! Can you imagine? Some people there go to work every day in a cubicle!" *Poor souls.*

"Ellie and I are going to miss you next week, honey! It's hard to believe that in a week we will be in Dubai! And that in two months we will have a new baby, Lord willing!"

Rustin called me the next morning on the sat phone. We had a scratchy connection, but I understood him to say that there was no way these men were going to finish the job for nothing. "OK," I finally capitulated, "we will pay them with bags of rice and oil. We will make it a food for work project, but no money! They are still technically volunteers!"

The next morning Rustin called again. We had underestimated the amount of wood boards needed for the project. I dropped everything and went to a lumber mill to purchase another fifty long boards. Zelme and I tied them to the roof rack of the BLC, and I immediately set off on the three-hour drive north to De Khak. You would think by now that I would have learned—no more solo driving in Afghanistan!

Between two mountain passes lay a high plateau with strong winds, this day exceptionally so. I was driving along, feeling pretty good about myself, when a gust of wind snapped the cord holding down my boards and scattered them ten feet high in the air. A large Kamaz truck pummeled through my airborne boards, snapping them into a hundred pieces like twigs.

I pulled over and fought against the wind, attempting to salvage as many boards along the road as possible. Several other trucks passed by, further demolishing boards that were still lying in the road. Dr. Maleki and Mirwais just happened to be driving by on their way back to the city from a district clinic and saw their kharedji boss struggling against the dust storm to clean up his mess.

"*Chi Kar Mekuni?!*" Dr. Maleki yelled, unable to conceal a grin. "What are you doing?!" They couldn't mask their amusement. Here was this foreigner, thinking he is helping to save Afghanistan, making a total mess of things. What in the world did I think I was doing out here? I was asking myself the same questions: *What AM I doing here in this country?!* Mirwais and Dr. Maleki helped me salvage and load up a good amount of the wood, enough for the villagers to finish the roof of their schoolhouse.

I made it to De Khak and ducked into Harbob's house. Rustin, wearing a turban on his head, sat in a room surrounded by fifteen Afghan villagers. He just looked up at me and said, "You know, some of our ideas are just ideas." I gave my greetings to the room, then excused myself for a moment, and stepped outside. I laughed out loud for a good, long time.

Many foreigners who have worked in Afghanistan for a while consider the country a graveyard of effort. Whenever anything went wrong (which was often), Afghans like Dr. Maleki, Zelme, and Ghulam would throw up their arms, then shake their head and exclaim, "Afghanistan!" Perseverance is certainly an underrated quality. We got the schoolhouse finished in De Khak and had the satisfaction of seeing schoolchildren and teachers enjoying their new school with carpeted cement floors and strong ceilings. But I learned that if I didn't laugh at myself along the way, I'd eventually snap like that cord on the road to De Khak.

Top, an Afghan village. Bottom, schoolgirls sitting on carpet in their classroom instead of squatting in the mud.

Expect great things from God. Attempt great things for God.
—William Carey

Chapter 15

A Short Month Apart

Monday, September 26, 2005

I waved goodbye as my seven-month pregnant wife and two-year-old daughter boarded their flight for Kabul. They were accompanied by Catherine, who helped them navigate all the security checkpoints and pat-downs of two Afghan airports not designed with passenger comfort in mind. Christine and Catherine planned to attend a conference together in Kabul until Sept 29, when two other women would fly out with Christine and Ellie to Dubai. There they would stay at our NGO's staff house until the birth of our son, who was due Nov. 18. I planned to join them in Dubai at the end of October.

I felt like I left my heart behind at the Iskandar airport. *I'll sure feel a lot better when they make it to Dubai. Please protect them, dear God.* Once in Dubai, they would be in a safe, comfortable place with excellent medical care, but I wondered how I would survive without my family for a month. I reminded myself that this was the perfect opportunity to get up to Bahesht to open our satellite office and establish our education and health projects there. *Providential timing here—no way I could leave Christine and Ellie alone in Iskandar for a few weeks.* I drove home from the airport telling myself that this was good ... *I'll bury myself in work and the time will fly by!*

I managed a stiff upper lip until I pulled into our gate and saw Ellie's swing hanging from the tree—still and lonely. The tears streamed down, and I quickly walked past Fazl Ahmad's guard shack. *Can't let him see the tears.* He did, but I thought I noticed a compassionate look out of the corner of my eye. Or he may have just been concerned that I would starve to death and then he would be out of a job. It is hard for an Afghan to imagine a man cooking for himself or surviving on his own domestically for a few days. I walked into the tomb of a Museum and wandered around the empty rooms for a little while. I stared at Ellie's toys, imagining the little hands and wonderment in her eyes. "All right Matt...time to be a man!" (Yes, I was talking to myself.) The first order of business was to prove to myself that the Afghan notion was indeed wrong. "A man like me can cook his own food! Gonna boil some eggs, coming right up!" I turned on the gas stove, boiled up some water, and dropped two eggs right in. *"Muskil Nis!* (No Problemo!)" They exploded.

I got a call from Tony—the same guy who landed me the teaching gig at Iskandar University. In his spare time, he had started a leadership development institute training a dozen or so leaders in the business, government, and NGO sectors.

"Hi, Matthew. Got a favor to ask. Would you be willing to teach for me the next two nights? Hate to bother you last minute, but I've got to take a quick trip to Ireland."

"Uh...Tony. I'm about to fly up to Bahesht on Thursday. I won't be back to Iskandar for a couple months—lots to get done to tie things up here and get ready for the big trip."

"Just Tuesday and Wednesday nights. The topic is Attitude in Leadership. I've got materials, but you could base things on your own leadership experience."

I hesitated. "OK, Tony. I'll cover for you." *Can't believe I just agreed to this... at least I won't be moping around The Museum the next couple of nights!*

On Tuesday night I shared with Tony's leadership students about my half-baked plans to run up to Bahesht on Thursday and open a new office for our NGO, totally winging it. I talked about optimism, having a vision, and attempting great things—all the while trusting in God's sovereignty. I quoted one of my childhood heroes, Teddy Roosevelt:

"The credit belongs to the man who is actually in the arena, whose face is marred by dust and sweat and blood; who strives valiantly; who errs, who comes short again and again, because there is no effort without error and shortcoming; but who does actually strive to do the deeds; who knows great enthusiasms, the great devotions; who spends himself in a worthy cause; who at the best knows in the end the triumph of high achievement, and who at the worst, if he fails, at least fails while daring greatly, so that his place shall never be with those cold and timid souls who neither know victory nor defeat."[5]

I was talking more to myself than to the students. Somehow one of them decided that I wasn't a nut; he thought my talk was inspiring! He had a significant position with the United Nations and told me that when I got to Bahesht, his deputy there would be waiting for me to assist however I needed him. I thanked him but didn't think too much of it at the time.

---

5 Theodore Roosevelt, "Citizenship in a Republic" (Speech delivered at the Sorbonne in Paris, France, on April 23, 1910).

Thursday, September 29, 2005

Two days later, Rustin and I stepped off the plane onto Bahesht's dusty airstrip with our laptops, a satellite phone, several changes of clothes, a large wad of cash, and some big plans.

Sure enough, the Afghan leadership student/UN program manager who liked my talk came through. His deputy—a young man named Zeodin—promptly found us. "Welcome to f-ing Bahesht!" he greeted us in fluent English, wearing a pair of cargo pants and a broad smile. "I hate f-ing Bahesht! And it is f-ing Ramazan (Ramadan)! I hate f-ing Ramazan even more! Let's go have some tea!"

Clearly Zeodin had spent some time with American soldiers and practiced a more agnostic version of Islam than your average Afghan. I tried to explain to our new friend that we wanted to show respect to his culture and would refrain from eating or drinking in public during the daytime. Zeodin would have none of it.

"You see all these people?" He motioned with his hand toward the crowded bazaar. "All of the people in f-ing Bahesht are a bunch of hypocrites! They walk around looking hungry and thirsty during f-ing Ramazan, but they all eat in secret!"

I wasn't so sure, but we eventually succumbed to tea with Zeodin and his driver. For the next few days they took us all over Bahesht, introducing us to government officials and helping us find a suitable property to rent for our office. Every time I tried to thank Zeodin for his tremendous help, he dismissed it with a wave of his hand and said: "Don't thank me. I don't have a choice! It's my job!"

A lot of things came together at the last minute to make the start of our dreams in Bahesht a reality. Our first need was a safe place to stay while we looked for the right building to transform into an office. Being that we had some expensive equipment and thousands of dollars in our backpacks, neither the floor of the local hotel or the Afghan NGO where we had previously stayed seemed like good options. Just days before our flight, the director of the one large international NGOs doing projects at the time in the province had invited us to stay at his guesthouse for our first few nights in Bahesht. Word quickly spread of our plans to open a new office, and we woke up the first morning to find a group of people standing outside the gate seeking employment. Each morning the line grew, and Rustin and I began interviewing people for positions ranging from office guards to an office manager.

The local UNOPS base, which was temporarily set up in Bahesht to run the elections in this region of Afghanistan, also provided significant assistance to us. On the day that Rustin and I flew up, just before we crawled onto our plane, an Australian fellow approached me and asked if I would be willing to hand-deliver a large manila envelope to his colleague who would meet me at the airstrip in Bahesht. The envelope contained hundreds of hundred dollar bills, the full month's salary for all of the national and international staff at UNOPS in Bahesht. His colleague met me at the airstrip, expressed thanks for the unmolested envelope, and invited us to come by the UNOPS base to use their V-Sat Internet connection any time.

It was a good thing that he did, because our satellite phone was giving us all kinds of trouble. After a couple days in Bahesht, I finally managed to get a call through to Clay at our office in Iskandar. Through the static, he told me that I should sit down.

"Matthew, Christine and Ellie made it to Dubai and are OK."

"Thank God!"

"But listen! The doctor says the baby is coming early. She said you have two weeks to get there if you want to be on time for the baby, which I recommend."

"Two weeks! Christine isn't due until November 18! That's a month and a half still! Is the baby OK?"

"The baby is fine. We have booked a PACTEC flight for you. They are going to pick you up on Thursday, Oct. 6. In five days."

Five days! How am I going to get everything done in five days?!

"Clay, we have found a compound that will work for an office. The building is still under construction but mostly finished. Perfect position for security but sits on a big rock and has no well. We will need to pump water up from a nearby stream. No indoor plumbing so will need you to purchase all plumbing supplies in Iskandar and send up on a truck with David and the BLC, along with the V-Sat and solar equipment. I'll email you a detailed list when I can get to the UNOPS compound."

"Will do, Matt. We are going to send the satellite Internet and solar equipment to you from Kabul by air on PACTEC. Also sending you six computer stations for the training project that the governor requested. Aziz and I had fun purchasing those yesterday down at the computer bazaar. We will pack them in the BLC."

"Good deal. Let's hope they survive the trip up! Hey, we also need some heaters up here if the guys are going to survive the winter. Kerosene and propane are available up here but expensive and bad quality. One big kerosene heater, three propane. Already getting cold at night."

"Roger. Will keep you updated on Christine and baby by email. Check when you can. David, trucks, and supplies should arrive up there by Friday, October 7."

"The day after I leave. Rustin's gonna have a lot on his plate! He's going to have to become a diplomat up here as well. We've already met with the governor, UN folks, and the new ISAF commander. European guy. Likes to tell people his goal is to bring his family here on vacation next year."

Rustin and I signed a rental agreement for our office and filled our days hiring staff and overseeing the final construction work on our office. At the recommendation of the UNOPS chief, we hired a young man to serve as our NGO's Bahesht office manager. He was barely twenty years old, spoke English fluently, had excellent computer skills, and basically had just finished running the logistics for the elections in the entire province. He looked sixteen.

There wasn't a lot of food in Bahesht ... Rustin and I ate rice and oily beans twice a day with our new Afghan office staff. One day the PRT commander invited us for lunch at his tent base. Walking into their mess tent felt like cresting a ridge on the Appalachian Trail to find a town with restaurants and a luxury hotel. Prime rib was on the menu that day, with a full salad bar, apple or pumpkin pie, and a freezer loaded with Ben and Jerry's ice cream. We thanked the American taxpayers for those C-130s flying into Bahesht and loaded up on protein and sugar.

Thursday Morning, October 6, 2005

Clay got through to me on the sat phone.

"Bad news, Matthew. Your PACTEC flight today has been cancelled."

"What?! Weather is fine up here. You sure?"

"Yes, Matt. I'm sorry. Mechanical issues. We have you booked on the next flight, but that will not be until a week from today, October 13."

"That's past the two-week deadline, Clay! PACTEC can't come sooner?!"

"I'm afraid not. Any other options from your end?"

"Well, I've gotten to know the PRT Commander a bit. I could ask him if I can get out on a C-130. May need to go with Plan B. Hire a vehicle and drive to Kabul."

"That is at least a three-day drive, Matt. Maybe more. Quite a risk. Let me talk to some people before you consider that option."

"OK, Clay, but I can't just wait around indefinitely. What if PACTEC cancels their flight on the 13th? I can't just leave Christine in Dubai to have our baby by herself!"

"Understand, Matthew. The folks there are taking good care of her. We will figure something out. David got off first thing this morning ... he is driving the BLC, loaded to the gills. We are sending a second vehicle up with plumbing supplies and heaters; I sent Ghulam along for protection. They should arrive tomorrow."

The next day David pulled into our new compound at the wheel of an excessively dusty Big Land Cruiser. His lean frame was completely caked in dirt from head to toe.

"Welcome to Bahesht, your new home!" I swept my arm across our large dirt and gravel courtyard, still rough but with a great view of the town and river below. "How was the trip?"

David smiled, resembling a turn-of-the-century London chimney sweep. Black face, white eyeballs and teeth. "Oh, not bad. We did it in nineteen hours, not including a stopover in a village for some sleep on a dirt floor. The rivers weren't too bad, but the road was pretty sharp in some places." The road from Bahesht to Iskandar is nothing more than a single lane dirt track that snakes its way through some of the most rugged terrain on earth. I still have vivid memories of looking thousands of feet straight down from hairpin ledges, with only inches between our tires and the cliff's edge.

Five minutes after David pulled into our office compound the back left tire of the BLC went completely flat. We unloaded all of the supplies that he had brought up from Iskandar and then searched for the key to unlock the spare tire.

"Hey Dave, where is the key to the spare tire?" I yelled over my shoulder.

"What key?" David asked. "No one gave me a tire key."

"Good thing your tire didn't go flat between Iskandar and here! You wouldn't have been able to change it! What would you have done on the edge of one of those cliffs?!"

"Yeah, you are right. God's providence."

I thought about it for a minute. An Unseen Hand had guided this whole endeavor. There were too many variables coming together at the last minute to be pure coincidence: Boss Lord inviting us to work on his turf under his protection, the UN money envelope providing us with Internet access and logistics support, my last minute teaching at the leadership institute resulting in Zeodin's help, unexpected cooperation from the governor and PRT, David's safe drive up with no access to his spare tire. We removed the BLC's flat tire and took it to the bazaar in the back of a pickup truck. The tire guy at the bazaar found four nails in the BLC's tire.

That evening Rustin, David, and I gathered together in our new, rustic office. We were dirty and tired, and it still had no operating toilet, shower, or beds. We thanked God for His help in protecting and helping us start this new work in Bahesht. "Guys, there is still a lot of work to be done and the road ahead will be difficult. But you get to be a part of making a difference for the people of this remote province. We are in the palm of God's hand... that is easier to see over here. I was a little worried about this venture, but here we are and now I'm thankful. You guys are the answer to a lot of prayer. Rodney has been praying for this place for years."

Rustin and David nodded in agreement. They had asked their friends to pray as well. We knew our team in Iskandar was praying for us. I knew we had Christine's prayers.

"The truth is that I'm not sure how I'm going to get to Christine in Dubai. I fear missing the birth of our son. But I know God will make a way. Philippians 4 says that instead of being anxious, we should bring our requests before God—with thanksgiving. So thank you, God, for Your help so far, and please help me make it to my wife in time!"

The next several days we continued setting up the office, but my priority was finding a way out of Bahesht so that I could make it to Dubai before my son made his grand entrance into this world. The commander of the PRT got clearance from Kabul for me to fly out on the next US Air Force C-130 that came through town. Unfortunately, that flight was cancelled at the last minute due to mechanical trouble. It was going to be at least a few more days before the next C-130 arrived, not before Oct. 13, when I was scheduled to fly out on PACTEC. And even that would put me in Dubai possibly too late!

Sunday, October 9, 2015

Clay got through to my sat phone. "Bad news again, Matthew. PACTEC had to cancel their Oct. 13 flight. Some kind of fuel shortage."

"Clay, I can't just wait up here forever. I've found an Afghan with a Land Cruiser who will drive me to Kabul. Should be able to make it in three days, maybe quicker."

"I've checked into that, Matt. Not a good option. Talked with a guy who knows that remote area. Dangerous wolves up there!"

"What?! Wolves are the least of my worries."

"He says they roam the passes. They are hungry and aggressive. You have a flat tire or a breakdown, they attack."

Monday, October 10, 2005, 9:00 a.m.

I sat next to the governor in a room full of NGO workers and local politicians for three hours, learning more about the humanitarian landscape of the province. I introduced our NGO and explained the work in the province that we hoped to do. We planned to start advanced-level English and computer classes in a couple of weeks for about forty students initially (two hundred showed up the first day; Rustin and David had to quickly retool for more students). Then we would develop the community health project, working out of Bahesht's hospital and expanding eastwards out of a district clinic. Eventually we hoped to expand to nine districts if we could find the necessary funding and cooperation. Our NGO emphasized development but we might be able to assist with some emergency winterization aid projects down the road, such as road snow clearance and feeding displaced communities. Oh, did anyone have an airplane available? *If I can't find a real option for a flight out by the end of today, I'm hitting the road through the mountains tomorrow! Wolves or not!*

The UNOPS guy approached me afterward and said he could help. They had a plane coming the next morning to pick up sealed boxes of elections ballots. He thought he could get me on that flight to Kabul. I went back to the office much relieved. *Thank you, God! One afternoon left in Bahesht ... better make it count!*

We were still working on the water system at the office, so in the late afternoon David and I drove the BLC to a spring a few miles outside of town to fill our containers with fresh water. Two of our new Afghan staff came along as well. While they were washing the Land Cruiser in the river, David and I climbed up a small hill for a great view of the river and mountains in the distance.

We took in the view for a moment, then I spoke. "Man, I'm relieved to have a ride out. Looks like I'm going to make it to Christine in time. But part of me feels bad leaving you guys here. I'll be praying for you and Rustin every day!"

"Don't worry about us, we'll be fine. We have got ..."

Bam! David and I looked at each other. *Bam, bam!* We hit the deck.

"Someone shooting at us?!" David asked.

"Can't tell where the fire is coming from!" I responded. I craned my neck, looking around the landscape, still horizontal. *Bam!* "We better get off this hill!"

We climbed down the steep backside of the hill that jutted out into the river, unsure where the fire was coming from or if someone was even shooting at us. Climbing on river rocks, we inched back around the hill to get a view of our vehicle. Everything seemed fine. An ANA (Afghan National Army) Ford Ranger had arrived. Three Afghan soldiers were getting water from the spring.

"Good guys," I said to David. "Maybe one of 'em was just shooting his gun in the air or at rocks!" Relieved, we jumped across the rocks to get closer to the riverbank and back to the BLC when one of the ANA soldiers started glaring at me. He walked to his truck, grabbed his AK-47, and approached us slowly swinging his weapon back and forth. *He better be careful with that thing; he's pointing it right at us!*

We were still jumping across rocks toward the BLC when he made it to the riverbank. I stopped. David jumped onto my rock. *He doesn't look right! His eyes look strange ...*

Standing about forty feet away from us, he shouldered his rifle, pointed it in our direction, and... *BAM, BAM, BA BA BAM!* He fired several bursts into the river right next to the rock we were standing on. Bullets ripped into the water, just a few feet from my right foot. David and I exchanged a look of shock. Then he squared up his rifle, pointing it right at my chest. *This is it!* I thought, totally shocked. *He is going to shoot me. Totally exposed! Nowhere to run.*

I looked at him, slowly lifted my hands halfway in as non-threatening a posture as I could manage. *Don't show fear. No aggression, either.* I tried for a look that personalized. *We are friends. Just human beings. And I have a family.*

BAM! BA BA BAM! He fired another burst, just to the other side of our rock. My ears rung from the muzzle blasts.

He pointed the barrel right at my chest again, and my life literally flashed before my eyes. I saw Christine and Ellie. I wanted to hold them more than anything. *Please God, not now. Let me make it to my family!*

BAM, BA BA BAM! BA BA BA BA BAM! Two more bursts into the water, just feet away. I could smell the gun smoke from the rounds.

He lowered the AK-47 and just glared at us for a few long seconds. *No sudden moves... nothing to excite him. Those eyes look deranged!*

He walked away from us, back toward his truck, then turned, glared, and shook his gun over his head. The other two ANA soldiers acted like nothing had happened. He walked to the road and sat down on the dirt, cradling his gun.

"Whoah!" David and I looked at each other. "Let's get back to the BLC!"

We jumped across the remaining rocks to shore and walked quickly to the BLC. Our Afghan staff was angry... last thing I wanted was for them to start yelling at these ANA troops.

"I'll drive!" I barked at our newly hired Afghan driver. We were going to have to drive right past this deranged ANA soldier and his gun, and I wasn't sure if this guy planned to shoot us as we drove by. Either way, I wanted the reins.

We made it up to the road without further incident. A mile or so later I spotted an approaching convoy of European soldiers from the PRT in their Toyota Surfs. I jumped out of the BLC, hailed their convoy, and told them what had happened. One of them spoke passable English: "You need to go report this to our commander at the PRT."

"I'm reporting it to you now!" I was amped up. "The guy is just two clicks up the road, on the left. This just happened five minutes ago! You could arrest him now!"

"Sorry! There is nothing we can do about the situation. Please go make a report."

I stood there shaking my head as they drove off, then got in the BLC and drove to the PRT. As we approached the main gate, two armored Hummers drove up, and an American soldier jumped out.

I walked up to the Hummer. "Hey, how's it going?" He seemed surprised to hear an American accent in Bahesht, outside the wire.

"Good. We're just on our way to dinner."

"Yeah. Listen, we just had an incident about twenty minutes ago, about five clicks east of town." I told him about the trigger-happy nut in the ANA uniform. He ducked back into the Hummer and talked with his fellow soldiers.

"Sir, you could file a report with the Europeans, but I wouldn't waste my time here, if I were you. We've got our own place up a hill nearby. Would you mind following us?"

It turned out these soldiers were responsible for training the ANA in this part of the country, and they decided it was worth eating military rations another night to get to the bottom of this incident. It would be dangerous to have some Taliban in ANA uniforms running around in Bahesht. At their safe house, the American detachment commander, an Army Captain, spread out five sheets of paper on a table, each with forty black-and-white mug shots of Afghan soldiers. "Sir, do you recognize the man who shot at you?"

I looked closely at the faces for a minute. Two hundred sets of brown eyes, dark complexions, no smiles. "Look. It could be any of twenty of these guys. I don't want to falsely accuse someone. Last thing my guys need are new enemies here in Bahesht."

"Do you think you could identify him in person?"

"Sure. The guy didn't seem right in the head. Crazy eyes."

"Would you be willing to come with us to an ANA camp to help ID the soldier who did this? We will protect you."

Normally we kept distance from the military to maintain our public neutrality, but I wanted to find out if David and Rustin were facing a security threat in town. We decided it was better for just me to go, being that they would be living in Bahesht. Soon I found myself walking in the middle of a team of heavily armed American soldiers in the dark, guided by the flashlights on their rifles, looking for a renegade Afghan soldier. We interviewed two different ANA companies and finally found him!

The next morning I bid farewell to Rustin, David, and Bahesht, and flew to Kabul on the small UNOPS plane. My ears were still ringing from the sound of the gunshots.

October 13, 2015, early evening

I boarded my overbooked Ariana Afghan Airways flight to Dubai with a profound sense of relief. I sat back and closed my eyes, trying to let the cares of Afghanistan fade away, and relishing the fact that I would be reunited with my family in just a couple of hours. *Home free!*

Twenty minutes later, the retired American pilot sitting next to me pointed out that our plane was having trouble gaining altitude. I looked out the window and sure enough we were still circling the city of Kabul, looking up at the mountains of the Hindu Kush. A beautiful sunset was underway. Our pilot got on the intercom and announced that we were experiencing mechanical trouble. He would be attempting an emergency landing at Kabul International Airport. *No! Not Kabul airport again!*

Many of the passengers expressed emotions ranging from mild fear to outright panic. But I was just angry. My experience told me that this would mean several days of waiting at the Kabul airport—a place that I had learned to loathe—until I could manage to get through all the checkpoints and into the terminal, make it into the front half of the mob at check-in, be frisked several times, and hopefully get my violated body into a seat before they all filled up. When Ariana cancelled flights due to weather, mechanical problems, or unexplained last-minute decisions to reroute their planes, they did not schedule replacement flights. The disappointed passengers simply had to wait until more seats opened up (which would often take days), or muscle their way to the front of the mob at check-in the next day, hoping to displace someone else.

The pilot made an excellent landing, and everyone breathed a collective sigh of relief. Everyone except me. I had been too mad to even think about the very real possibility of a crash. I was already plotting ways to use my "foreigner" status to get to the front of the pack the next day. We pulled up to the terminal as the last vestiges of daylight illuminated the fuselage of a parked Ariana 727 fifty yards away. Being that there was higher passenger demand than airplanes in those days, it was rare to see a functioning aircraft parked next to the terminal at Kabul's airport. The sight of the plane didn't give me any hope that evening—the airport's navigational equipment was down, and flights were strictly daylight only.

The door to the cabin opened, but I was surprised that they didn't immediately allow us to disembark. An Ariana official boarded the plane and had a short conference in the cockpit with the flight crew. After five minutes they announced that we should gather our belongings and proceed to the other plane as quickly as possible. Word quickly spread that the other plane had about twenty fewer seats than ours. It was almost a brawl getting off.

Once disembarked, everyone sprinted toward the locked and sleeping 727. By the time two men wheeled the rickety ladder to the door, it was packed with a group of jostling Afghans interspersed with a couple of intrepid foreigners. The ladder rocked back and forth ... *looks like it might collapse under all the weight!*

A larger crowd pushed around the base of the ladder, while several devout Muslims quickly pulled out their prayer rugs on the tarmac and faced Mecca for evening prayers. The pilots made it to the base of the ladder but couldn't make it up due to the mass of humanity insistent on priority boarding. No one was willing to budge. In the meantime, four men and a pick-up truck dashed back and forth between the two aircraft, transporting luggage.

The pilots eventually succeeded in shoving their way up the ladder, unlocked the door, and turned on the plane. Within five minutes most of us had found seats and our plane was taxiing to the end of the runway. *Welcome to Ariana! Where pre-flight checks consist of pulling the dust covers off the engines!* I've never seen such an efficient operation.

As darkness finally set in, we were spiraling up out of Kabul in an airplane that hopefully would make it over the mountains. I stretched back in my seat and decided not to worry. *Whether we make it, or crash into a mountain, at least I won't be spending several more days getting elbowed in crowds at Kabul airport!*

We had a seamless flight to Dubai with a textbook landing. I was part of the fortunate minority who received their bags at Dubai International Airport. I caught a cab to our guesthouse there, a handsome two-story building that looked like a mansion to me. I walked through the lush landscaping up to the front porch. I knocked on the thick, wooden front door and heard a scream of delight inside. "Daddy!" The door opened, and there stood a very pregnant Christine, looking as beautiful as ever. Ellie rushed into my arms.

Top left, Christine and Ellie sent Matthew this note to tell him that they had arrived safely in Kabul. They were enroute to Dubai, where Christine would give birth to the family's newest addition. Top Right, the flight from Bahesht to Kabul on a UN plane. Bottom, Ellie's swing just the way Matthew likes it—with her in it!

Have I not commanded you? Be strong and courageous.
Do not be frightened, and do not be dismayed, for the
LORD your God is with you wherever you go.
Joshua 1:9 (ESV)

Adversity has the effect of eliciting talents which, in
prosperous circumstances, would have lain dormant.
—Horace

Chapter 16

A Winter of Struggle

and Fear

Nov 4, 2005, early morning. Al Zahra
Private Hospital, Sharjah, UAE.

I held little Kurt in my arms and thanked God for the safe arrival
of my son into this world. He waited longer than the doctor had
expected to make his plunge into the world, which gave him a

little more time to develop. I looked down at his little face and felt a burning love, but also another emotion ... *Look at these little feet ... where will they walk one day? And his hands ... what will they accomplish?*

"You did good, sweetheart! We have a son! Maybe he will be a soldier," I told Christine. "Or a pastor!" I knew Kurt would make me proud. He already did.

We spent November and most of December in the United Arab Emirates, where I worked remotely by laptop. Rodney and Sadie bid farewell to Afghanistan, and Dr. Jack and Clay guided our staff and projects in Iskandar. I found more funding so that Rustin and David could expand our quickly growing computer and English classes in Bahesht.

We made a visa run to nearby Oman where I went scuba diving off the Musandam peninsula. Beautiful virgin diving, but our dive boat broke down and we drifted off toward the Strait of Hormuz. Thankfully a dhow rescued us before we drifted into Iranian waters. Christine and I enjoyed hiking with Ellie (and tiny Kurt) along the rims of the "Fjords of Arabia" and exploring old Portuguese forts tucked up in the Hajar Mountains. It was really nice to be in a place for a little while where Christine didn't have to cover her head and I didn't have to worry about security.

We rendezvoused with family for a wonderful Christmas in a stone villa along the deep blue Mediterranean coast of Turkey, and then in January 2006 we began our trip back to Iskandar. I was a little nervous bringing a two-month-old into Afghanistan, but our travel went smoothly until we arrived in Kabul. The city had been hit by a blizzard that continued for several days. We arrived at our NGO's guesthouse to find that its heaters had gas leaks, and most of the occupants were sick from carbon monoxide poisoning. The Americans who normally ran the guesthouse were away on break, and the Afghan staff was not sure how to repair the heaters. This resulted in no heat inside, so temperatures inside our room were sub-freezing. The entire house smelled like propane.

I was angry at the negligence of the Afghan staff. I had experienced this kind of environment before on my own but never with my two-year-old daughter and two-month-old son. That night we did our best to keep our children warm with blankets and body heat, but I stayed awake all night feeling Ellie shiver next to me and listening to little Kurt's breathing getting raspier and turn into grunts as the freezing air irritated his little lungs. It was my darkest night in Afghanistan. It felt as though the devil himself was in the room whispering into my ear: "You fool! What were you thinking—bringing your children to Afghanistan?!" Doubts about God and His calling on my life swirled around inside my mind. *We could get on a plane tomorrow morning for Dubai and be back in America within 48 hours. We could stay with my parents, by the sea, in their warm house until I find a normal job!*

By the next morning, Christine, Ellie, and Kurt were sick, and I was well on the way. But Christine remained steadfast in her faith: "God has called us to this work, Matthew, and He will see us through!"

We spent the next three days trying to catch a flight to Iskandar, waiting inside and outside an airport facility that had no heat. It was below freezing inside. In 2006 airplanes still could not make instrument landings at Kabul International Airport and we were in the middle of a blizzard. Compounding this problem was the fact that many *hadjis* (a Muslim who has made the pilgrimage to Mecca) were returning from Mecca during this time, so the airline would cancel scheduled flights at the very last moment in order to get prioritized hadjis back in country from Saudi Arabia. But they told us on the phone every morning: "Yes, your flight is going to Iskandar today! Come to the airport!"

It was a frustrating time, but Christine was right—God did see us through. He provided a warmer place for us to spend the nights...with extended family! We got an email from Christine's younger sister that her in-laws had just moved to Kabul to work at Cure Hospital, and they welcomed us into their home. The living room heater and hot dinners did much to warm our bodies and souls as we returned shivering each afternoon. And Dr. Rob kept a close eye on Ellie and Kurt's respiratory infections. We will always be grateful for their hospitality.

On day four, we waited with an unhappy mob of passengers for hours outside a barbed wire fence in the freezing cold. Because of the recently ramped-up threat of suicide bombers and vehicle-borne explosives, the airport police would not allow passengers to enter the terminal until check-in began for their designated flight. Flights to Iskandar had been cancelled for four days; everyone knew that only the first quarter of the mob to make it through the doors and to the counter would make the flight. When the call came, it became a madhouse: true survival of the fittest! I tried to shepherd my family through the mass of shoving humanity. It wasn't pretty, but we made it on the plane and safely back home to Iskandar!

It was good to be home at The Museum, but the thick mud walls had become igloo cold during our three-month absence. It took a week to get the rooms back up to a livable temperature of the high 50s F. It took even longer for Ellie, Kurt, and me to fully recover from our walking pneumonia.

Several weeks later I was at home from work for a "riot day" (the Afghan version of a "snow day") sparked by offensive cartoons of the Islamic prophet Muhammad published by a newspaper in Denmark. We heard only a little gunfire but could hear the mob shouting: "Down with Denmark! Down with Holland! Down with America! Down with China!" and down with just about any other non-Islamic country whose name they knew. I was more focused on domestic issues. *There has got to be a more efficient way to heat this house than smelly kerosene and propane! I wonder if anyone here in Iskandar has tried sawdust heaters?* I asked a couple of Afghan neighbors about it, and they had never heard of sawdust heaters (perhaps this should have clued me in). Fazl Ahmad hadn't either but was game to help me try.

The next day we drove all over Iskandar city in my new Ford Ranger on our quest. My mind wandered as I drove: *This could revolutionize Iskandar! A new heat source that everyone can afford!* First we found a sawmill. Yes, they had sawdust, and plenty of it! I did notice a few strange looks (more like bearded smirks) as I filled up the back of my truck with 250 pounds of sawdust. We finally found a guy in a little tin shop in the bazaar who said he could make me a genuine sawdust heater. I ordered two. The next day I eagerly went back to pick up my heaters and brought them home along with about twenty feet of tin ventilation pipe pieces. Fazl Ahmad and I set to work installing the first one in our frigid grand hallway, but then I was called away to the office.

Upon returning home, Fazl Ahmad met me at the gate and said: *"qatsch be kar darem* (we need white plaster)... *dude mekuneh*! (it is smoking!)"* Presumably, he was thinking this could help patch up the ill-fitting exhaust pipes. I walked into The Museum, still a little too proud of my dream to really internalize what he was saying. The inside of the house was so full of smoke that I could hardly see to the end of the grand hallway! To make matters worse, the smoke had a strong metallic tinge... turns out the tinsmith was a true artist and couldn't give me the heaters without first putting on a coat of shiny metal paint!

I approached my prized heater through the smoke with profound disappointment in my heart. *Still, maybe this can work. Maybe less sawdust?* Any residual hope was dashed when I reached out my hand to the side of my heater... it was cold to the touch! There was enough heat on the top of the heater to warm my hand. Christine, Ellie, and Kurt were all in the children's room, bundled up and keeping low to the ground. Needless to say, they were not impressed with my invention! The thing burned for twelve hours—producing much more smoke than heat—before I could get it to stop. Defeated, I gave both sawdust heaters to Fazl Ahmad, who was sure he could get them to work at his place. We gave up trying to heat the grand hallway and moved the large kerosene heater into our living room, where it did its job well. We spent most of the winter in there.

One night a friend from Texas was over for dinner. We were kicking back on toshaks in the living room, listening to country music. Our bodies may have been in cold Afghanistan, but our minds were somewhere in Texas, riding on horses with Willie Nelson, long arms of the law. *TAK! TAK! TAK!* Loud knocking at the gate. "Who would be knocking at the gate this late at night?" I wondered out loud. *TAK!! TAK!! TAK!!* I opened the gate to find a wide-eyed Zelme and Fatima, shaking like leaves. Not from the cold but from fear.

"*Khushamaden*! Welcome, brother and sister! Well, come on in!" I let them into our courtyard and shut the gate. Fatima was crying.

Zelme looked me straight in the eyes. "Fatima's cousins are Muslim extremists. They just came to our house and tried to kill us. We barely escaped. We didn't know where else to come!"

I was about to invite them inside The Museum but then remembered something. "Just wait one moment. I'll be right back!" *I better turn off the country music!*

From the day I met him I noticed that Zelme didn't seem to have the same attitude toward Islam as most of his countrymen. He seemed to be more of an agnostic, with an "all rivers lead to the sea" perspective on spirituality. I appreciated his toleration and open-mindedness but wondered if he really believed in anything beyond this material world. It turned out that he had been carefully watching Christians for many years. Thankfully, he had some good examples: he had translated for American doctors who came to Pakistan to help care for Afghan refugees in squatter camps throughout the late '90s. Many of them were followers of Jesus and had made a real impression on him. In fact, Zelme had come to believe that Jesus must be the Son of God—something Muslims deny—but due to the risks inherent in being an Afghan Christian he wasn't ready to change religions.

Then one night in late summer 2005, Fatima had a dream. She saw a man in shining clothes who she instantly recognized as Jesus (how she knew this, I don't know). She was drawn to Him. Jesus told her that He was the Son of God, and that He would make her heart clean if she would trust in Him. She woke up from her dream and gave her heart to Jesus in the middle of the night on the privacy of her bed. Zelme lay next to her sleeping. He loved her, but she knew that conversion was intolerable in Islam, and that he would likely beat her if he found out about her faith. The next morning she told Zelme about her dream and that she now belonged to Jesus. Zelme's response shocked her. Instead of becoming angry, he broke down in tears. "Today Jesus has come into our house," he said. "We will follow Him together."

When Christine first told me about Zelme and Fatima's new faith I felt conflicted. My heart was thrilled for their spiritual life in Christ, but my mind was fearful for how this might threaten their physical lives. Religion is viewed very differently in Afghanistan than in the West: instead of being a private affair, religion is considered the national identity. The majority of people equate being Afghan with being Muslim. As such, there is no tolerance for other ideas or religions within Afghanistan. Free thought outside the bounds of very tight religious teaching—controlled by the mullahs—is forbidden. Children at a young age are taught exactly *what* to believe; the question of *why* is not tolerated. The religious establishment sanctions violence toward anyone who would dare contradict the teachings of fundamental Islam or convert to another religion. If an Afghan converts to another religion it is considered high treason and the infidel's close relatives bear the responsibility to kill him (or her) or forfeit their family's honor.

My mind raced as I jogged inside The Museum to turn off the country music. *Now you are in a tight spot, Matthew. Getting involved in an Afghan family feud is more dangerous than wading into a land war in Asia! If I bring them into my house, I endanger my family! And where can I turn for help?*

Certainly I could not go to the Afghan police for help. If I brought Zelme and Fatima into my home and offered them protection, I might find myself on the other side of the Afghan law. The fear of Christian proselytization was significant in Afghanistan. The perception was that no Muslims would ever turn toward Christianity of their own free will or moral conscience, but that sneaky foreign Christians might try to lure them over to their side (and make them notches on their belt) by offering them money, jobs, or visas to the West. Of course I found the idea of trying to manipulate someone to my faith repugnant, but providing physical assistance to Zelme and Fatima sure might look suspect. Plus, the police would probably arrest them for being kafirs! *And how can I really protect them from armed relatives who want to kill them?!*

I pulled Christine aside and quickly explained what had happened to Zelme and Fatima. "Right now they are standing outside in our courtyard! This is a complicated situation, Christine. I know we can't just send them packing, but this could put you and the children in danger!"

To her it was clear: "Of course you need to invite them inside, Matthew! They need our help!"

In Afghanistan, when you offer a guest your protection it is to the death. Kind of like it used to be in Texas, I suppose.

We brought Zelme and Fatima into the living room and served them tea and sweets. I texted Dr. Jack; within thirty minutes most of our team had arrived at The Museum. It was late—well after our security-related team curfew—but they just wanted to be with us. If some mad, machine-gun toting relative was going to gun down Zelme and Fatima that night, they were going to first have to come kill a bunch of kharedjis! Those would be high stakes, and I sure hoped the conceptual walls of attacking an American's house were higher than the mud walls of my compound.

We prayed together for a while and read some scriptures about trusting in God during times of trouble. Then we played cards.

Fatima stopped crying and Zelme turned out to be quite the card shark. My teammates finally went home around midnight. We showed Zelme and Fatima to the guest room. I looked at Zelme square in the eyes: "You and Fatima can stay here with us as long as you like." I wanted them to feel safe. "You are under my protection now," I said, with as much Texan swagger as I could manage.

I lay awake most of the night. *'Under my protection now!' Ha! What do I do if a couple nuts with guns come over the wall? Point them to the guest room and ask them to please not hurt my family?! Or do I go gun shopping tomorrow? Tell 'em, 'Over my dead body!' And come out shooting like Dirty Harry?! Can't see that ending well.*

My mind kept running. *Can't let the neighbors find out. If they do, hopefully the value of Afghan hospitality would trump Afghan intolerance for kafirs! Protecting guests is one of their highest priorities. But I dunno. Fazl Ahmad gets here in just a few hours...how do we keep him from discovering they are here? Don't want to put him at risk! What about all our Afghan staff at the office? Should Zelme come to work in the morning and pretend all is normal? How do we get him there?*

I had more questions than answers. I felt the icy grip of fear taking hold of my heart. I prayed, *Lord, I don't know what to do! Please give me wisdom and courage at the moment that I need it most! Please protect all who sleep in my house tonight—Christine, Ellie, little Kurt, and Zelme and Fatima!*

I got out of bed and walked down The Museum's cold, long hallway. *If only these walls could talk! I'm sure you've seen plenty of drama in your days, haven't you? Anyone ever been killed in this hallway?*

I turned left into our living room, now chilly as well, and examined the metal sliding bolts that fastened shut the large wooden doors that opened onto The Museum's front porch. *How long would it take a couple crazed guys to kick you in?*

I looked out through one door's top window. A gibbous moon illuminated the courtyard. I scanned the mud walls for any moving shadows. All was still. The stars shone brightly above it all.

I peeked in the children's room. Ellie and Kurt were sleeping peacefully—Ellie now in her toddler bed, and baby Kurt in the pack and play. They looked warm in their thick fleece pajamas. *Lord, please protect my children! They are Yours!*

I slipped back into bed next to Christine who was sleeping soundly. I pulled out my flashlight and Bible, and found solace meditating on Psalm 46:

God is our refuge and strength,
A very present help in trouble.
Therefore we will not fear though the earth gives way,
Though the mountains be moved into the heart of the sea...
"Be still, and know that I am God.
I will be exalted among the nations,
I will be exalted in the earth!"
The LORD of hosts is with us;
The God of Jacob is our fortress. (Psalm 46:1–2, 10–11, ESV)

The next morning things didn't seem so dire. The warmth of the sun took the bite off the chilly February air. My pansies were recovering from a deep freeze the week before with a few new blooms. Fazl Ahmad gave me the usual morning greeting as we shook hands: "*Shoa Bakhair te Shud?* (Did your night pass safely?)" I gave him the normal response. "It passed safely! Praise be to God!" *Just another morning in Afghanistan. Except that I have two fugitives hiding out in my home, that's all.*

I stopped by the UNHCR (United Nations High Commissioner for Refugees) office to ask about what kind of international assistance might be available to Afghans in the event of religious persecution. Right off the bat I got the sense that I could not trust even the high-level Afghans who worked in the office with the details of Zelme and Fatima's case. "I'd like to speak to your boss, please. Alone." I had to repeat that several times but quickly ended up in an upstairs office with a German named Hans.

"I am very concerned for the safety of a local employee of our NGO. He and his wife have received threats from family members due to their personal religious beliefs. I believe that the family will act on these threats." *Careful with your words, Matt.*

"Yes," he said. "Unfortunate reality here in Afghanistan. They have a long way to develop in terms of human rights." *Excellent English, only faint German accent. This guy has been around.*

I decided to be direct. "Is there anything your office can do to assist them?"

"Well, I'm afraid there is nothing we can do here to help," Hans replied. "You see, our mandate is to assist refugees. If they were from Pakistan, and they had strong documentation of their case demonstrating legitimate religious persecution, then yes, we might be able to help them. But this is their country so they are not refugees."

Then what is your fancy office doing here in Iskandar?! I wanted to ask. *Not a lot of Pakistani or Iranian refugees in Afghanistan!*

"Do they have any recourse with the law? Anywhere to go for help?"

Hans responded with a question. "Are you familiar with the case of Abdul Rahman?"

"Yes. I heard about him being arrested in Kabul for being a Christian. Just a few days ago, I believe. Converted years ago in Pakistan, if I understand the story correctly. The mullahs are kicking up a firestorm, demanding that he be executed."

"That is correct. This is a big problem for Karzai. Afghanistan has signed the International Declaration of Human Rights, which guarantees religious freedom but also subscribes to Sharia law, which demands death for apostasy. The Islamic clerics in this country have a lot of power, and Karzai has to tread carefully here. The timing is unfortunate for your employee. I recommend that they go to a neighboring country where they would legally be refugees. Then they could apply to a UNHCR office to consider their case—if they want asylum."

Back at The Museum that evening, there was a knock at the gate. I had just bid Fazl Ahmad "*Khuda Hafez!*" (God protect you!, i.e., good night). I opened the smaller door to my gate cautiously ... ready to slam it shut. It was Waheed, my landlord's helpful nephew. We had become friends, but I braced myself for whatever he was about to say. "This afternoon some of your neighbors noticed some men in a white Toyota Corolla watching your gate." I swallowed hard. "They looked uneducated, likely from a village. Maybe they were thieves. We ran them off. You have our protection." He shrugged and wished me a good night.

The next few days were stressful, especially for Zelme and Fatima. At one point, in emotional exhaustion, Zelme said, "Tell me what to do, Mr. Matt! I don't know anymore!" I told him that he and Fatima alone could make the decision whether they should stay or flee from their home and country, but we would support them in whatever they decided to do as best we could. He needed to ask God for wisdom.

One day Zelme told the staff that he and Fatima were going on a long trip. Dr. Jack and I drove them to the airport and watched them get on the plane for Kabul. I hoped that perhaps they could stay in Kabul until things blew over with their family in Iskandar, then come home. But they chose to travel to Pakistan, where they applied to the UNHCR for asylum to Europe. Dr. Jack flew to Islamabad to assist them with the paperwork.

At times I have second-guessed my decisions surrounding this event. But then I read 1 John 3:16–18:

By this we know love, that he laid down his life for us, and we ought to lay down our lives for the brothers. But if anyone has the world's goods and sees his brother in need, yet closes his heart against him, how does God's love abide in him? Little children, let us not love in word or talk but in deed and in truth. (1 John 3:16–18, ESV)

Come to think of it, that is exactly what Fatima and Zelme did for us when we knocked on their gate during our time of need in the riots a year and a half earlier.

Part IV

Adapt

Spring, 2006

Dear Family and Friends,

I am very thankful to write that Matthew made it home from his travels today! Thank you for your prayers for him as well as for me and the kids. Even though we missed Daddy very much, it was a good (uneventful!)two weeks. I am still looking forward to sitting down to a long talk with Matthew and hearing about his trip to Bahesht, Kabul, and Kashmir.

It is challenging to write when your husband expresses things so well in emails. However, just so you know I am still here and doing well, I will attempt to paint a picture for you of my life here as a woman. I do not have the exciting stories that Matthew does, and much of my day is spent doing the same things that moms in the West do. I have found a real sense of fulfillment in helping Matthew in his work here and raising our two beautiful children. At the same time I have been blessed with a very close relationship with my Afghan neighbor next door and developing relationships with some other local neighbors. In order to have deep relationships, I have to continue to study and practice language. I can communicate enough to get my points across and understand simple conversations, however I still have a long way to go! Each week I still have two language lessons and then spend personal study time as well. Please pray for motivation and perseverance in continuing to go deep in language and culture.

What is one of my biggest challenges here? I would say not having the same freedoms that I did in America. Now that the temperatures are soaring, it is more of a challenge than ever to put on a thin, long coat over my long sleeve shirt, skirt, and pants. As I cover my head, I process: "Is my head scarf too bright?...I must not attract any attention to myself!...I really need to get a black head scarf instead of this blue one." In comparison to the burqa (which has a mesh that covers even the eyes and nothing but the shoes are seen) that most of the local women still wear, I can't complain about what I have to wear. But having to cover myself so nothing but my hands and face are showing is a continual struggle.

Walking down the street to a little store (which thankfully carries most of what I need), I do my best to avoid looking at any men ... although they are all staring unashamedly at the strange foreign lady. After almost two years I do not miss driving as much as I did at first, although sometimes the desire to get in my Jeep and drive to the mall comes over me. Being that women do not drive in Iskandar, our office provides a driver to take me where I need to go, but if I'm just going down the street I enjoy the independence of walking (as long as the security situation in the city is calm). On most days I do not have a strong desire to get out because of the lack of interesting places to go, the heat, and the stares from men. Other days I'm so stir crazy from being in the house so much that I think of something I need from a store on our street, take the kids, and go walking.

What have been some of my joys? Developing relationships with women here has been something that has kept me going on my down days when I wonder why I am here. We recently went on an all-day picnic with our neighbors. It was such a joy just laughing, eating, and trying to socialize with my limited Dari. I have felt more comfortable when Matthew travels because I deeply trust our Afghan neighbors next door and can call on them for help. I have found joy (OK, most days!) in raising my children here.(But I do miss having zoos, playgrounds, and libraries to take a very social three-year-old to who is always asking "where are we going?") Ellie is involved two mornings a week in an international preschool for NGOs. My ultimate desire is for her to attend a local preschool, but because of security reasons and her standing out a little too much, it doesn't seem this is possible right now. Kurt (6 months now) is healthy and so chubby I had someone question if he was really my baby. Thanks for your prayers for the health and safety of our children.

I must close now as I would like to spend some time with my dear husband and hear more about his trip. Thank you for your friendship over the distance and time (almost two years now).

Much Love,
Christine

Christine, Ellie, and Kurt walking down their alley on a short shopping excursion.

Yesterday I was clever so I wanted to change the world.
Today I am wise so I am changing myself.
—Rumi

Don't judge each day by the harvest you reap,
but by the seeds that you plant.
—Robert Louis Stevenson

Chapter 17
The Story of a Fat-Tailed Sheep

The spring of 2006 brought welcome relief from the cold and tension of winter. Some Taliban moved into our province, resulting in an increased number of suicide bombings in our city. Most of the population just rolled with the punches and we tried to do the same. We walked less and varied our routes as we drove around the city of Iskandar. But everyone was in a better mood with the warmer

weather, driving out to the countryside in droves to enjoy an important part of Afghan culture in spring: picnics. We enjoyed all the
spring green in The Museum's courtyard, punctuated by nearly a
hundred rose bushes blooming in all their glory.

Christine and I decided that it was time to throw a proper
Afghan party to celebrate Kurt's birth. It was a cultural practice
for an Afghan family to kill a goat on the occasion of the birth of a
son and to invite all of the neighbors and relatives to the feast. My
neighbors told me that I should kill a sheep instead since I am a
Christian. "We like lamb better anyway," they assured me.

On a Saturday afternoon in April, Fazl Ahmad and I drove
out to the edge of town—where the shepherds hang out—to buy
a sheep. It was quite a scene ... about fifteen shepherds all trying to
convince me that their sheep was better than the next guy's. Most
of the sheep in Afghanistan are a species called "fat-tailed sheep."
If I was a fat-tailed sheep, I'd really be embarrassed to have my
photo taken unless it was directly from the front. Basically, they
have about ten pounds of fat, resembling a large tumor, hanging
over their rear end. Being that the fat is the favorite part of the lamb
dinner, the way that these guys were trying to convince me that
their sheep were the best was by grabbing these sheep's butts with
both hands and tugging really hard. Add to that picking sheep up
with an uncomfortable grasp right between the rear legs, pulling up
the front lips to show me that they had a good set of teeth, and one
poor sheep's horrific experience of having his master stick his finger
up his anus (not sure what for), and these fat-tailed sheep were an
abused lot.

I felt some sadness in my elective powers that evening. The
sheep I chose would have its throat unceremoniously cut in several days so that we could eat its flesh. I finally chose a large
ram, haggled over its price, and handed over my 7,000 afghanis
($140). It took three of us to manhandle him into the back of
the truck.

"Fazl Ahmad, we forgot to bring rope to tie him up with! How do we keep him in the back of the truck?"

Fazl Ahmad grimaced, but the shepherd came to our rescue. He pulled out a dull blade and grabbed the ram by a horn. Dead sheep don't jump out of trucks.

"Whoa! Stop!" I yelled. The shepherd's knife was at the sheep's throat. "We need him alive! Our dinner isn't until Tuesday night!" The knife withdrew, and I swallowed. *Not sure I'm ready to kill this poor animal. I am too much of a softie!*

Fazl Ahmad found about four feet of cord under a seat. He managed to hog tie the animal, and we began our bumpy journey home.

The last thing that I wanted was for Ellie to get attached to an animal, only to witness or hear about its martyrdom over the dinner mat. I was thinking about how to sneak it into one of our compound's side rooms and to just keep things quiet between now and Tuesday morning, but Christine and Ellie were waiting on The Museum's front porch. Every night Ellie slept with her stuffed lambie so she was giddy with excitement to meet a real lamb. She made immediate friends with "my real live lambie." We had to explain that the sheep would only be staying with us for the next two days, and then would go "bye bye." Fazl Ahmad decided to let the ram dine on our grass for a bit, but it immediately attacked my roses, downing a good bit of an entire bush before Fazl Ahmad and I could tackle the thing. My empathy for the ram evaporated at that moment.

We almost pulled the whole sheep-killing thing off without shattering little Ellie's heart. Fazl Ahmad and I cooked up a plan to do the deed on Monday afternoon while she was taking her nap. His brother, a butcher, came over and killed the sheep, dressed it, and did a great job of cleaning everything up before Ellie came outside after her nap. He took the head home as a prize (for eating, not display), but he thought I might like to keep the horns. When I came home that early evening we let Ellie go outside to play a bit.

A few seconds later we heard crying out in the courtyard. I looked at Christine. "Oh, no! She's fallen!" We rushed outside to find Ellie standing next to the well, pointing at two slightly bloody ram's horns.

"My real lambie!"

"Don't worry, Ellie." Christine explained. "He has gone bye bye. To lambie heaven."

I looked at my wife. *Lamb heaven!*

"Uh, Ellie. Don't cry!" I got down on my knees, eye level with her. "You know how mommy gives you a haircut sometimes. It doesn't hurt, does it?"

Ellie nodded.

"Not really! Well, this lambie just got something like a haircut. Its horns are kind of like hair. See?" I picked up one of the ram's horns. Ellie noticed the tinges of blood. "So this haircut didn't hurt the lambie!" *Because it was already dead!*

I grimaced up at Christine, who just shook her head at me. My three-year-old wasn't buying it.

"Where is my real live lambie?!" Ellie asked through the tears.

There was nothing else to do but hold her and comfort her— and hope she would forgive us.

Dr. Rick Donlon arrived in Iskandar with a small team of doctors he had brought from Memphis. They had spent the past five days staying up at our rustic office in Bahesht while they provided medical training for all the Afghan doctors in the province. Iskandar now looked pretty posh to them and no place more so than The Museum's oasis of a courtyard. On Tuesday morning Dr. Rick rode with me as we picked up large Persian rugs and toshaks from the office and several teammates' homes for use that evening at our fat-tailed sheep roast.

"Matthew, you seem pretty uptight about tonight! Never seen you this way before."

"This is a big deal, Rick. I've got to get it right! Lots of moving parts."

"Just a party, right? Your Afghan friends and neighbors will appreciate that you are respecting their culture."

"Actually, Afghans have a pretty rigid system on how you entertain guests. I've been trying to convince our friends that they can actually bring their wives since the women will all be inside and we men will eat out in the garden. My staff at the office keeps reminding me that we cannot mix the men and women at all, even accidentally. Aziz tells me that if one guy walks into the house while the ladies are in there my reputation will be finished!"

We bounced over some potholes as the last statement sunk in. *A bad reputation with the neighbors is the last thing we need right now! Maybe this whole killing a sheep thing to celebrate Kurt's birth was a mistake!*

Finally Rick spoke up. "How many do you think will show?"

"I dunno. Right now kharedji stock is going down in Iskandar. People don't like us as much as they used to. As security gets worse here, many blame America. There are plenty of conspiracy theories floating around that the CIA is actually in bed with the Taliban! As a pretext to keep American troops around and dominate the region. So when some nut blows himself up and kills school girls, folks are starting to blame America! I think that my Afghan neighbors and staff are loyal, and we have some great local friends here, but they might be nervous being seen going into a foreigner's house!"

"So how many did you invite?"

"We invited fifty. We are preparing enough food for seventy just in case. That is another thing! You run out of food at one of these things and you are a loser for life!"

We pulled into the gate of The Museum's courtyard. Fazl Ahmad had just finished cutting the grass with a reel mower that I had brought back in a suitcase from our last trip out. The beautifully manicured grass soothed our retinas after the drive through the brown city. The roses and flowers were at their spring peak. Fazl Ahmad smiled, basking in the glory of his work. I couldn't help but stare at the garden for a long moment: *This is the nicest yard I've ever had! In Afghanistan, of all places!*

"OK, let's make groupings on the lawn with the rugs and toshaks. Then we can start working on getting the lanterns and Christmas lights up in the trees and the sound system set up."

Hassina and several Afghan ladies from the office worked in a makeshift kitchen that we had set up in one of the courtyard's side rooms to prepare the lamb, while Christine and several other Afghan women busily cooked side dishes in the kitchen inside. Ellie ran from room to room of The Museum, all set up with platters of nuts, dried fruits, and sweets for the ladies to enjoy, then came outside to jump on the toshaks spread out on the grass. I yelled over my shoulder to Rick: "Well, we might only have ten people show up tonight, but we are going to give them a party to remember!"

That night about a hundred people showed up at The Museum to honor God's gift to us of a son. I greeted the men on our front lawn while sporting a new, white shalwar kamis and a navy blue sports coat. Little Kurt wore a small shalwar that matched mine. Dr. Jack turned up in a dressy light blue shalwar kamis and blazer, holding his son Thomas—just a few months older than Kurt—who wore a matching shalwar. All of my team was there in Afghan dress and mixed right in with our upper-class neighbors, several villagers from De Khak, Professor Ibrahim and a small entourage of university professors, Dr. Hakim and physicians from the hospital, and our Afghan staff and their families. Dr. Rick's group might have felt slightly out of place in their Western clothes, but they did a great job connecting with our Afghan friends who spoke English. The ladies navigated the clay sidewalk of the front courtyard, shrouded from the men on the grass by pomegranate bushes and blue burqas, until they reached the safety of The Museum's large, wooden front doors where Christine warmly greeted them.

The first order of business was dinner, and Christine and I were both separately afraid that the lamb would run out. Fazl Ahmad had brought his family but was manning the gate, welcoming guests into the courtyard as they continued to stream in. By now the men were all seated on toshaks around Persian rugs on our front lawn, and my American teammates and I served each grouping of toshaks. Hassina and the office ladies doled up plates in the hot side kitchen, waiting until the last minute to put on their fancy dresses to go in and join the ladies' party inside The Museum. I had to balance personally welcoming each guest and ushering them to a toshak with helping to ferry food out to our waiting guests. If any man had to wait too long for food, he would be dishonored. And if we ran out of lamb for a latecomer, well, that would be the end of the world.

I poked my head in the sweltering side kitchen. "Hassina, how we doing? Are we going to have enough meat?"

She wiped her sweaty brow, looked up for a moment, and managed a smile. "*Enshallah,* Mr. Matthew." *Enshallah* means a lot of things in Afghanistan: "God willing, hopefully, maybe, probably not, I have no clue..." I kicked myself. *Knew I should have bought two sheep!*

But the fat-tailed sheep came through for us and stretched out just enough so that we could feed every guest! The men leaned back on their toshaks, enjoying the cool evening air, the soft lights in the trees, and the stars above. Little Kurt and Thomas were passed around so that each man could hold them and comment on what kind of men they would grow up to be.

I stood up nervously to address my guests. My neighbors had explained to me that normally a mullah would read from the Quran on such occasion. But since I was a follower of Jesus, it would be appropriate for me to read a little from the *Torat* (Old Testament), a book that Muslims also view as sacred.

"Good evening, dear guests, and thank you for coming tonight. It has been almost two years since we came to Afghanistan to serve the poor and sick with our NGO. Jesus taught us that it is better to give than to receive. But I have received a lot more than I expected in Afghanistan. It was difficult leaving my family and close friends in America and coming to a country on the other side of the world. Some people asked me, 'What are you doing? Don't you know it is dangerous over there?!'"

I paused for a moment and scanned the faces of my guests. The lanterns and moonlight provided just enough illumination to see their expressions. A few sideways looks and nods, but I could see they were tracking with me. *OK so far.*

"I could never have expected the friendship and protection that you have provided for my family here in your country. I have learned from you what it means to be hospitable. Many of you have become like family to us. For that I will always be grateful."

They were digging it, but I was not flattering. I meant every word. These people had taken risks to protect us.

"And now God has blessed me with a son! I would like to read to you two verses from the book of Proverbs in the Torat: The first is from Proverbs chapter 9 and says: 'The fear of the LORD is the beginning of wisdom, and the knowledge of the Holy One is insight.' The second is from chapter 22: 'Train up a child in the way he should go; even when he is old he will not depart from it.' My wish for my son is that he would grow up to be one who is wise because He submits to God and truly knows Him. I want to raise him in this way. You have helped me learn to live in Afghanistan; now I ask you to help me as I try to raise my son in Afghanistan."

From what I could see, these Afghan men genuinely appreciated my taking the lower position and asking for their help. They seemed to be thinking: *Now this is a different kind of Christian! One who loves his family, wants to submit to God, and respects our culture!* Hands were placed over hearts, beards nodded, and men pledged their continued welcome and protection to my family.

Now it was time to party, Afghan-style. Men took turns dancing for the crowd to favorite Afghan and Persian tunes. Dr. Jack performed an impressive dance routine, employing his hands along with his feet as he went all in with the loud Persian rhythm. He won over the crowd. I knew there was no way I was going to get out of this part, and that I could not equal Jack's eloquence of Persian movement, so I pre-empted the music style. I threw in a Toby Keith CD into the sound system, and cranked up "Who's Your Daddy?" Ellie and I danced, country-western style, across the lawn through the groupings of toshaks. We were rewarded with smiles and applause, but I still have a lingering suspicion that it was more out of embarrassment for my clumsiness. The next routine was a famous Pashtun folk dance. Twenty men jumped up and danced together in a moving circle, dancing to the hypnotic cadence with their fingers and hands as much as with their feet. I leaned back on a toshak and reflected: *Here we are in Central Asia, dancing the night away with Pashtuns, Tajiks, and Hazaras, educated Afghans with poor villagers and American doctors, Sunnis, Shias and Christians, all brought together at The Museum by little Kurt and a fat-tailed sheep!*

Top, Christine, Ellie, and Kurt celebrating spring in The Museum's beautiful courtyard. Christine and Kurt, Bottom right, in the The Museum, which featured a long cobblestone hallway, one of the family's favorite features. Bottom left, Ellie meets her "real, live lambie" for the first time.

*Jesus answered, "Everyone who drinks this water will be
thirsty again, but whoever drinks the water that I give him
will never thirst. Indeed, the water I give him will become
in him a spring of water welling up to eternal life."*
John 4: 13–14, NIV

Chapter 18

Of Wells and Men

Friday, August 11, 2006

Dear Family,

Thought I'd share another little story with you.

Last week our well dried up, something that usually happens each late summer. Fazl Ahmad wasn't concerned a bit. "No problem, tomorrow we will fix it."

Having a good idea what that would entail, I responded, "But isn't that dangerous?"

"No problem" he said again, with more than a little swagger.

The next day he showed up with his bigger brother and a very unfortunate neighbor. They brought with them a pick, a shovel, a burlap sack, and a cheap plastic rope.

The well in my courtyard could have been dug during the days of Abraham. It is about 50 feet deep, has no ladder down, and only flaky dirt walls. If you somehow ended up at the bottom without a good friend to pull you up, you will be down there for a very long time.

The intrepid neighbor took off his shoes, tucked his tunic into his trousers, rolled up his sleeves, and started tying the rope around his belly.

"Peace be upon you, how are you, are you well, is your health good, how is your family, are you having a good time?" I began the list of Dari greetings.

The wannabe well-diggers responded in kind.

"Isn't this really dangerous?" I jumped right to the point.

They looked at me like Yoda used to look at Luke Skywalker and said something like, "We are masters at what we do. You, on the other hand, are an uncooked young foreigner … Why don't you stop worrying and run along …"

"Be very careful!" I instructed, mostly to alleviate a little guilt for what might happen, and headed inside. I preferred not to watch.

About ten minutes later I heard some commotion outside. The well-descender had just emerged and was doubled over, gasping for air. He looked greener than I've ever seen a live human being look.

"Gas!" Fazl Ahmad explained, with his normal one-word communiqué, designed so that even a not-so-bright foreigner like me could understand.

"There is gas in the water?" … I was pretty confused.

"The well is full of gas. He is sick but will get better soon enough," the older brother explained.

"So ... we cannot dig this well any deeper?" I half stated and questioned, with a mixture of relief that these men would all live another day and profound disappointment that I needed to find another water source.

After a good bit of excited discussion—of which I could only pick out snippets—the older brother turned to me and said, "We need a baadi zarbah. With that he can dig your well."

I had no idea what a baadi zarbah was. After a good bit of questioning, I determined it must be an oxygen mask.

"Are they available here?" I asked, quite intrigued.

"Yes, we can get them at the bazaar for 1000 afghanis." (About $20 USD.)

They can buy oxygen masks as the bazaar??? I wondered. Do they have little oxygen bottles attached or a long air hose? And for only $20? I can't imagine a piece of specialized equipment like that floating around the bazaars of our town, but then again, I've been pretty surprised at what IS available at the bazaar and there must be quite a market for well-diggers.

"Maybe you guys can go look for one and then come back tomorrow to work on it some more," I procrastinated, having learned through experience over here that when in doubt I usually get a better result if I sit on things a bit.

"Nah, we will be back in thirty minutes," Fazl Ahmad's big brother firmly stated.

"But our friend here is really sick!" I pointed with my nose toward the green man who at this point was lying on his back wheezing like a wounded animal.

"He will be better by the time I get back," the big brother promised, with a look that let me know the discussion was over.

With that, I halfheartedly handed him a 1000 afghani bill and he hopped on his motorcycle, off to the bazaar.

Thirty minutes later they were back. I was pretty eager to see what kind of scientific instrument I was the proud new owner of, and found them outside with a small Chinese air blower with a long plastic hose attached. They were feeding the hose down into the well.

"Does the other end somehow attach to his face?" I asked like an ignoramus.

"This will give him enough air to breathe down there" was the unequivocal response I got.

Fazl Ahmad's neighbor—still looking a bit green, but breathing less laboriously—began solemnly tying the rope once again around his belly (this time a little more slowly).

"Please be very careful!" I stammered, once again heading for the refuge of The Museum where I could pretend to somehow not be involved or responsible for what was happening in my courtyard.

Now and then for the next hour or so, I cowardly peeked out the window and watched the air blower at work as the burlap sack kept ascending full of muck. These guys seemed to have it all under control, so I descended into a back room of The Museum and put my mind onto finishing a report that was late.

After an indeterminable amount of time, I heard Fazl Ahmad at my door, sounding pretty upset.

"Cha shuma kherab shud!" which translated in its most sterile form is, "Your well has become spoiled!" He had a wild look in his eye. "The days of your well are over!"

I rushed outside to see our medal-of-honor deserving well-digger once again emerged from the earth and horizontal, making all kinds of painful grimaces and noises. He was trembling more than Ellie's bunny Flopsy did when I pulled a cat off of her back. Fazl Ahmad's big brother was standing nearby and holding his back, complaining about the muscle he pulled while saving his neighbor's life.

"The side of the well caved in on him while he was down there!" Fazl Ahad explained. "The well is full of dirt and the pipe is full of mud ... your well is finished!"

"Do we need to get him to the hospital?!" I asked half panicked, pointing with my face toward the poor man in a medical state of shock.

"Nah, he needs some tea" was the unquestionable response from Big Brother.

"This well is very dangerous!" Fazl Ahmad explained to me. "The next man who tries to dig it out will die!" he said, looking quite wild-eyed. "You will have to dig another one over there."

"Maybe we need to get your friend to a doctor," I persisted, thinking about his health and ruminating about issues of liability and workman's comp in a land blessed with few lawyers.

"He needs to go to his house and eat some bread and sleep on his own toshack." If he is still sick tomorrow, you can buy him some medicine," came the final response from Big Brother.

Thankfully, this story had a happy ending. After a couple of days both well-digger and rope-holder had their health back; they will probably attack many more wells here in Iskandar. Fazl Ahmad hasn't lost his swagger, and incredibly, the next day my well started producing water again. The whole operation (including several purchases of unknown medicine) cost me less than $40, and I have a nifty new breathing apparatus should I decide to do some subterranean well exploration myself.

Love to all of you,
Matthew

The Well in the Collins' courtyard could have been dug during the days of Abraham. It was about 50 feet deep, had no ladder down, and only flaky dirt walls. When the well dried up one summer, three Afghan men took on the task of digging it deeper. Above left, the "well-descender" about to take the plunge. He soon discovered there was natural gas in the well. The big brother, above right, decided the well-descender could continue the job with the aid of a cheap air blower, which hopefully would pump enough air into the well—as long as the electricity didn't cut out.

"These all died in faith, not having received the things promised, but having seen them and greeted them from afar, and having acknowledged that they were strangers and exiles on the earth ... But as it is, they desire a better country, that is, a heavenly one. Therefore God is not ashamed to be called their God, for he has prepared for them a city."
Hebrews 11:13, 16

The noblest question in the world is what good may I do in it?
—Benjamin Franklin

Chapter 19

Fish, Nomads, and

Elephants

As the years 2006 and 2007 passed we expanded our humanitarian work in our part of Afghanistan. Thomas joined Rustin and David in Bahesht in early 2006 and, under Dr. Jack's guidance, started community health projects based out of five district clinics in the province. Our work in the villages grew at an exponential rate; by early 2007 we had trained more than three hundred community health workers to care for patients in their own villages, and they were making a real difference.

Dr. Nurgul, a neonatal physician from Kazakhstan, joined our team. She often worked through the night, combining all of her skills with rudimentary equipment to keep premature babies alive at Iskandar's central hospital, all the while trying to upgrade the capacity of the Afghan medical staff in the neonatal intensive care unit. Meanwhile, Rustin and David continued developing the education project up in Bahesht. Along with a staff of Afghan instructors, they taught English and computer skills to three hundred and fifty students in twenty-two classes each day. Some of these students were from a grotesquely underserved local orphanage. These classes offered hope of a better life through future employment for NGOs, the PRT, or the Afghan government.

My sights were set on our next new project: community development. "Our community health work is great, but it is really a shot-gun approach," I told the team one day, waving my hand over a map of our region of Afghanistan. I couldn't help but smile to myself a little at the Texan-inspired analogy. "We are working in hundreds of villages but just helping with one issue. We need to find several villages where we can go deep with long-term community development. More of a rifle approach! Help them address root issues of poverty and make a lasting difference through not just health, but education, agriculture, and clean water. Catherine, how many villages have you visited that have wells put in by an NGO in the past five years that no longer work?"

"Many. I don't know … maybe half of the wells we drive past are broken. They have expensive steel hand pumps, but the villagers are hard on them. They don't know how to fix them and expect the NGO to come back and repair them when they stop drawing water. The ladies go back to carrying water in buckets from a river.

It is a real health problem, and the broken wells just discourage people!"

"Exactly! The problem is that the village never owned the well! They cost tens of thousands of dollars for the NGO to drill with a rig, then they cap it with an expensive stainless steel hand pump imported from another country. But what if—after health lessons on the importance of clean water—the village was empowered to dig its own wells and assemble its own pumps? Then they would know how to fix them when they break and could do it with minimal expense. The water table is high in most villages from snowmelt in the Hindu Kush. Or they could pipe in water from springs just a couple miles away. We provide the pipe and basic materials, but they do all the work and own it. Better to teach a man how to fish than to feed him fish all of his life!"

"Are you wanting us to get into the water business?' Dr. Jack asked. "There are several big NGOs that do water. I don't see where we have expertise with this on our current team. I'm not saying we shouldn't do it, but shouldn't we focus on our area of proficiency?"

"Clean water is just one example," I responded. "The idea is to build a long-term relationship with villagers where we can empower them through sustainable development. That's our motto. I'm thinking broad-spectrum community development: clean water, latrines, health, literacy, agriculture. Maybe even job skills training. For the past month I've been studying another NGO's community development project. They have been doing this for ten years now but need to wind down the project due to funding cuts. They have offered us their best local staff. I've been out with the team to several of their villages and they really get development!"

We hired a team of Afghan community development experts who were educated in the fields of health, education, engineering, and animal husbandry. More importantly, they had over thirty years of experience working in the villages of Afghanistan, helping villagers learn to help themselves. They chose the first two villages after surveying seventy, carefully assessing their level of poverty, their accessibility, and—most importantly—their willingness to learn to help themselves improve their quality of life instead of simply expecting handouts. These brave Afghan workers then visited every family in the chosen villages, carefully determining their needs and prioritizing the ever-growing list of problems these villagers faced.

I was ready to get going with projects but our Afghan team was patient: before they started project work, they helped the villagers form a male and female village development council in each village comprised of people from every sector of village society. These representative councils met for weeks, prioritizing their own list of their village's greatest problems. Our community development team then compared the two lists, and where the team's biggest assessed needs met the highest ranked village "felt needs," they began their work.

The highest need on both lists was usually health. Instead of just training community health workers, our team members tried to raise the bar of health throughout the village. They trained the village development council and many villagers in a three-month course on basic health and social education. It soon became clear to the villagers that lifestyle change was in order. They discovered that stomach sickness and diarrhea, major killers of children, could be drastically reduced by improving waste disposal and keeping their water sources clean. Many of the family and community latrines simply dumped sewage into the same jewey that brought drinking and bathing water into the village. Instead of constructing latrines for the villagers, our team provided each family with a drawing, two bags of cement, and the PVC pipe for ventilation. They had plenty of rocks and dirt to work with and built the latrines themselves, thus becoming proud *owners* of much cleaner toilet facilities far from their water supply. In this manner, we facilitated the construction of hundreds of latrines.

The village development council also discovered that the reason so many of the women were sick was from smoke inhalation from poorly vented kitchens. Afghan villagers cook on the dirt floor, so the team was careful to keep the plans for clean, well-ventilated kitchens contextualized to their cultural norms for the sake of sustainability. Our team built a "model village kitchen" with cement floor, proper cooking area, and chimney, and it wasn't long before everyone in the village wanted to build one. We helped with the materials, but each family did the work themselves. They took pride in their improved kitchens and showed them off to relatives visiting from other villages.

Agriculture and veterinary training, literacy, micro-enterprise (such as sewing classes for women), and water access were other self-identified needs we helped with in Afghan villages. We did everything possible to help the villagers find the solution for their problems within their own communities. Instead of just bringing in a rig and drilling new wells, we enabled the villagers to dig their own. We provided shovels, cement for well rings, drawings for the steel hand pump, and just enough money for them to go to the nearest metal shop to have the parts made. They constructed the pump, learned how to repair it, and—most importantly—*owned* that well and pump. In other villages, the council decided to dig channels to pipe in clean water from springs. We provided miles of PVC pipe; they did all the labor. I was impressed with one village's plan to build small water collection tanks every several hundred yards so that they could back-trace any potential leak and resultant pollution in their water system. They were learning to plan with sustainability in mind!

At the heart of this community development project was mind-set and lifestyle change. After a year we noticed better health and lifestyle in our villages, but more importantly, increased dignity. Our team provided 1,400 fruit trees for one village to plant. One of the village leaders—rich in livestock—was so impressed by the outcome that he sold a bunch of sheep and bought another 4,000 trees for his village to plant! Our Afghan community development team considered their work in a village successful only if after three years the villagers themselves took the principles they learned and taught them to other nearby villages. I couldn't help but be impressed with these guys: *While teaching a man to fish is good, even better to empower him to teach others to fish as well! Start a movement!*

I like starting projects so this was an exciting time for me. We added local staff and purchased more vehicles. Things at the office got more crowded. Dr. Jack and I moved our offices down into the basement rooms in which Audrie and Catherine had once lived, dodging the dust that poured in the small windows at the top of the wall from Kaka's broom each morning. New projects required more funding and that took a lot more computer work and email communication. But one day our Internet connection died. And, boy, did everyone notice. Panic in the camp! We had all learned to live with dust, IEDs (improvised explosive devices), and brownouts, but take away the Internet and life was just intolerable!

We unplugged and plugged in everything imaginable. We tried to troubleshoot the system several times; Clay got on the phone with the ISP people in England. No explanation why the Internet was down. I was up on the roof one afternoon, messing with the large satellite dish, when I looked down the nose of the dish and noticed a couple of stories that our neighbor had just thrown up on top of his building. The fourth story was directly blocking our satellite signal! We tried to move and recalibrate the dish but couldn't find the bird in the sky. We were already having trouble parking all our vehicles in the office courtyard; now no Internet. I shrugged: *Time to find a new office!*

After several months of looking around, we moved into a new office compound several blocks away in early 2007. The building was nicer and larger, but the real upgrade was the huge amount of land inside the office compound. We could have built a baseball diamond in there! Instead, we built a parking area large enough for a fleet of project vehicles, set up a sand volleyball court, and used the rest of the land to grow various vegetables in a sort of demonstration garden. Our staff loved the hot peppers, and eventually corn, that Clay and Susan grew in the office garden.

Dr. Jack and I took turns visiting the guys up in Bahesht. They made the most of a rustic living environment, sleeping in hammocks strung up near the ceiling of our cold office. They built a crude ladder to get up. "Warmer air up there," Rustin explained. The diet had improved very little over the months. Rice and greasy beans, mostly. On one trip I brought the guys a bag of pistachio nuts. The next morning I overheard Thomas chiding Ruston for throwing away the shells: "There is still good salt to suck on those shells, man!" On the rare occasion that they did eat over at the PRT, they filled their jacket pockets with energy bars and pudding tubes, which they rationed for weeks.

The guys had to navigate the labyrinth of local politics in Bahesht. The existing power structures were tainted by corruption; trying to simply help the poor required walking a tightrope between various tribal and government entities and special interests. Rustin and Thomas sometimes found themselves sitting between shouting men in a government office, but they were great peacemakers.

In the late winter of 2006, our office was robbed by a small group of armed gunmen. Thankfully the guys were visiting Iskandar at the time and were spared the drama, but the bad guys beat up one of our guards and stole a significant amount of cash, some computer monitors, a satellite phone, and Rustin's guitar. When word eventually came about the likely location of the thieves, I was ready to lobby for a military raid, but Rustin wanted to visit their village and teach their chief how to play his old guitar. "Isn't that what Jesus would do?" he asked me.

One early spring day up in Bahesht, my warlord buddy Boss Lord strode into our office and kissed my cheek.

"*Salaam Aleykum! Khushamaden!* (Welcome!)" I exclaimed. "Welcome to our humble office. I was just planning to make a trip out to visit you!"

"We are pleased that you fulfilled your promise to come to our province, Mr. Matthew. Texan!" Boss Lord beamed.

"Please, come to dinner tomorrow night here at our office! It would be an honor to have you as our guest."

I invited him first, and then thought about it. We had plenty of rice and beans, but putting on an appropriate feast for an Afghan feudal lord might be beyond our capacity. It was all hands on deck, and the guys and our office cook pulled it off with aplomb. Boss Lord showed up with a small entourage, including the district police chief. After dinner I pulled out my laptop to show him pictures of us together in his mud castle from last summer when a picture accidentally popped up of Christine in her Supergirl pajamas. Full screen.

The Supergirl pajamas had been a gift from my mother, who envisioned Christine shedding a burqa to reveal: Supergirl! A little strange, perhaps, but I thought it was kind of funny and snapped a photo of "Supergirl" one night. When reproached by Christine, I assured her not to worry—no one would see this but us.

No one but us and Boss Lord, who about choked on his *khofta* (meatloaf) and managed to look the other way as if he had not seen it. Whoops. *Now I've done it! Gonna be in the dog house for a long time over this one!*

One early morning while jogging through the outskirts of Bahesht along the river, I had the rare privilege to witness a spectacular anthropological wonder. A huge caravan of what seemed like a thousand *kuchis* (nomads), at least twice that many camels toting all their worldly goods, and several thousand sheep and goats came walking through town on a singular dirt road. They were obviously heading to a new home somewhere up in the mountains, stirring up the dust in the early morning light. Their caravan stretched for well over a mile. As I ran past countless camels—laden with collapsed, black tents topped by ancient-looking women and led by men who looked as if they had stepped out of the Old Testament—I couldn't help but marvel that these are some of the very few true nomads left on the face of the earth. The kuchis looked back at me as though I was from another planet.

Abraham must have looked like these men, I thought as I continued my jog. *Now there was a true nomad who walked by faith and not by sight! His citizenship was in heaven!* It dawned on me that if I am to be a real follower of Jesus, I am called to be something of a nomad on this earth. I thought of a verse that I had recently read about Abraham and other spiritual nomads, Hebrews 11:16: "But as it is, they desire a better country, that is, a heavenly one. Therefore God is not ashamed to be called their God, for he has prepared for them a city." I smiled at the kuchi men that I jogged past. *I know that I look different, but I am more like you than you may think... I'm a nomad, too!*

Our guys in Bahesht were living as nomads on earth more than I was. I had a family and lived in the fair city of Iskandar in The Museum—basically a mud mansion—and here they were scraping by in one of the most remote and difficult places on the planet, trying to serve the poorest of the poor. They made the most of it, though, playing cricket with local kids down by the airstrip and overcoming strong tribal xenophobia to build friendships with the people of Bahesht. After a year of selfless service that really moved our team's work forward, all three guys returned to the States at the end of 2006—two of them to get married. All three of them made a real difference in Afghanistan.

In the middle of January 2007, I flew up to Bahesht to check up on our Afghan office staff there and to keep the projects going. The office was a lot lonelier at night without Rustin, David, and Thomas around. And colder. We were down to just one large kerosene drip heater working along with a smaller propane heater that ventilated poorly. Our staff had covered the windows with plastic to try to help retain heat inside. I kept the kerosene heater running next to my desk until I couldn't stand the gas headaches and dizziness, then I would switch it off and work and shiver. *How did these guys survive up here last winter?*

After thirty minutes, the remainder of my cup of tea had frozen on my desk. Time to relight the heater!

A blizzard blew through my third night in Bahesht, and the temperatures dropped twenty below zero. Our indoor bathroom at the office (maybe a bad idea of mine) was covered in a sheet of ice, with all plumbing frozen solid, so the only restroom option was the outhouse outside. I bundled up with everything I had and fought the elements to get there and back. When I threw open the office door to return, I was greeted by clouds of kerosene smoke. The winds had shifted and were blowing right into the exhaust pipe for the kerosene heater in my room, forcing all smoke indoors. But the kerosene still dripped and burned. Coughing, I covered my face with my desmal, turned off the heater, and cut the plastic in several of my room's windows to let in some fresh air. Frigid air and snow rushed in. That night I couldn't get warm in my thirty below zero sleeping bag. I was wearing just about every piece of clothing I had brought—now all reeking from the smell of kerosene smoke. I prayed for relief from the storm in the morning. *God, please let it pass and let my plane land tomorrow!*

The storm continued the next day and my flight was cancelled. I endured another night of shivering in my sleeping bag in a room way below freezing. Clay managed to get me a seat on a USAID flight the following day but that was cancelled due to a fuel shortage in Kabul. The morning after, the airplane flew to Bagram air base, fueled up, and tried to get to Bahesht but couldn't land due to low clouds and snow. On the phone, Clay explained that the weather forecast was bad for the next day. Two days later was a maybe for the USAID flight. The next PACTEC flight to Bahesht would be in two weeks. *Two weeks! I don't think I'll survive two more weeks in Bahesht! God, I don't know how You will do it, but please deliver me from this. Help me get home to my family!*

The road trip option—not a good one any time, but especially bad in winter—was starting to look like the way things might turn out.

Cold and dejected, I went over to an Afghan friend's home for lunch. I practically hugged the mud heater in the corner that they kept fueled with dried animal dung. Their room was below freezing as well, but it didn't seem to bother them much. We were eating cold nan when we heard the sound of an airplane!

I jumped up, ran to the office, climbed up a ladder onto the roof, and could just make out the shape of a twin-prop Russian cargo plane taxiing down the snow-covered airstrip. I threw my stuff in our Ranger and drove like crazy to the Bahesht airport. A group of soldiers was offloading cargo. A scruffy Russian in cargo pants and a thick flannel jacket stood next to the aged Antonov, smoking a cigarette.

I ran up to the guy. "Where is your pilot? I need to talk to him!" No time for pleasantries.

"I am the pilot," he responded with a thick Russian accent.

"Look, I need to get out of here. You are not going to Iskandar by any chance?"

"We are going to Kabul."

"Fine." Kabul was the other direction, but I didn't care if they were flying to Moscow. *Anywhere is closer to home right now than freezing Bahesht!* "Could you give me a lift?"

"Do you have money?" For the first time he looked up.

"How much is a ticket to Kabul?" I knew there were no tickets but somehow it felt better to ask.

"How much money do you have?" he asked, like a Russian gangster.

I pulled out a $100 bill from my wallet. It was all I had other than a few smaller bills. *Sure hope he doesn't ask for more! Won't be time to run back to the office safe.*

He took my $100 bill and stuffed it in his pocket. "Climb in the back," he commanded, then stamped out his cigarette and climbed aboard. I joined ten European soldiers in the cargo hold for a low, turbulent flight over the snowy mountains of Afghanistan. A crate of cargo slid back and forth across the fuselage just a few feet away from our legs. But the Russians got us safely to Kabul when no one else could. I was never so happy to step foot in Kabul, a city I normally loathed. I smiled all the way to the guesthouse.

By the summer of 2007 I was starting to feel worn down. The combination of culture shock and declining security was taking its toll. I constantly worried about the safety of my teammates and family. One day I received a call at the office warning of an imminent plot in Iskandar to abduct an American NGO worker. "Get all your people into lockdown at once!" the guy on the phone had warned. We took a head count and had everyone safely indoors within minutes. We could rarely walk anymore, and I asked Christine to let me know whenever she was to go out shopping with one of our office drivers. I'd breathe easy again when she sent me a text that she had made it home. We were all getting tired; Christine, Ellie, Kurt, and I were ready for a vacation.

We flew to Sri Lanka. After an uncomfortable overnight flight from Dubai, we arrived in the Colombo airport's customs hall, which was ornamented by a large statue of the Buddha. It stopped Ellie in her tracks.

"Daddy!" she cried in a loud and earnest four-year-old voice, "is that an idol?!"

"Well, Ellie," I answered softly, "Uh, yes it is. Come along."

Ellie couldn't believe her eyes. We had recently read to her in *The Bible in Pictures for Little Eyes* the story of Solomon bowing before his wives' idols. She knew the picture and that it didn't end well.

"Daddy, do people in this country pray to that idol?!" The decibels had now intensified, and she was pointing right at the Buddha statue.

"Some people might, Ellie." Lots of folks were walking by, plenty of them Buddhists. "We need to keep walking, Little Nut Brown Hare."

Several days later, in the middle of Kandy, we strolled past the imposing Temple of the Tooth, which as its name suggests, reportedly contains Buddha's upper left canine tooth. Battles had been fought for this tooth, for as local legend had it, whoever possessed this tooth controlled the land. We strolled passed an open doorway into the temple, and I felt a tug on my arm.

"Daddy!" Ellie yelled. "Look! Those guys are praying to that idol!!"

Lo and behold, a room full of orange-robed Buddhist monks made prostrations before a large golden statue of the Buddha. I wasn't sure what to say, so just said, "Come along, Ellie."

"Daddy, they are praying to the idol! You have to go in there and warn them that God is going to be angry!"

Later, we got into a taxi. Ellie pointed to the driver and asked, "Daddy, does this guy pray to Jesus or to idols?" Those were the two options.

"Well, I guess you will have to ask him that question, Ellie. But respectfully." It turned out that our driver was a Catholic who prayed to Jesus!

Ellie ended up having a wonderful time in Sri Lanka. She helped bathe elephants in a river at the elephant orphanage. We crashed through the jungle up in Dambulla on the back of an elephant, but Ellie was more impressed by her first pony ride. We took a boat up a river where Ellie got to hold a baby crocodile. I was supervising things, but Christine did not entirely approve. She pet a large python (which I was holding) at the base of Sigiriya rock fortress. We ended up at a nice resort on the beach in Bentota that had its own resident elephant. Ellie helped bathe it every morning, sitting on its side while it lay down in the water and had its hide scraped with a coconut husk. The two became friends.

Christine, Kurt, and I ate lunch one day under swaying palm trees, watching Ellie play with her pet elephant in front of the ocean. She danced in front of him, in her swimsuit, and the elephant swayed in sync with her rhythm.

"Will you look at that, Christine! Look at how Ellie is waving her arm up and down by her face, like it's an elephant trunk..."

"... And the elephant is waving his trunk in sync with her!!" Christine finished my thought.

"That is amazing. They really have a connection!"

"You know, Matthew, God has really blessed our family. Ellie has experienced things most kids only see in movies. She has a rich childhood."

"I know. She thinks it's normal to play with elephants at the beach in Sri Lanka!" I looked up at the sunlight filtering down through the palms. It was a moment of peace and gratitude. *Thank you, God. You have answered my prayers.*

Several weeks later, back at The Museum in Iskandar, I had Dr. Hakim and the Provincial Minister of Health over for dinner. Some of the local doctors out in district clinics were upset with our NGO due to our efforts to stem corruption. This was really more of a diplomatic dinner. I needed these men to keep signing MOUs for our projects. Ellie strode into the room.

"Daddy, do these guys pray to Jesus or pray to idols?"

I cringed inside. Dr. Hakim and his colleague were both Muslims and spoke perfect English.

"Well, Ellie, I guess you will have to ask them that question!"

Ellie looked right at my guests and put her hands on her hips. "Well, do you?"

Both men smiled. Like most Afghans, they viewed all Americans as Christians and respected Christians who really believed in God more than those who were mere naturalists. "It is good that you are teaching your faith to your children," Dr. Hakim politely responded. "We Muslims highly respect the prophet Jesus, you know."

Cement reservoirs, top, designed to test water every few hundred meters for sustainability. Above left, village men dig channels to pipe water for several kilometers from springs to their village. Above right, Afghan girls draw clean water in their village for the first time.

Above, Ellie making friends with elephants in Sri Lanka.

Part V

Overcome

Dear Family and Friends,

Living in a country where there is so much suffering, it is easy for my heart to grow callous to the needs around me. Sometimes I become weary of having a gracious spirit to continue to listen, pray, and love. Yesterday morning while still recovering from my stomach problems, I was particularly struggling with hearing the same story, complaining, and heartache that I hear day after day. It was coming from Shirin, the dear lady who helps me in the house, whose life is truly hard. By late afternoon before she left, she said with tears in her eyes that she really didn't see why her life was worth living. Convicted of my callousness and seeing her deep pain, I reassured her that of course her life was important and that we would be praying for her family all the more.

Her story is just one of so many women here who see their lives as hopeless. Her oldest daughter of six children has a brain disorder (or tumor) that was unable to be diagnosed because of the lack of medical equipment here in Iskandar. The family took their savings, borrowed money, and with some help from us they sent her to Pakistan for an MRI and possible surgery, leaving behind two babies. Despite her increased workload at home in caring for her grandchildren, Shirin had hope that her daughter would come back healed. She talked often of how we were praying for them and how God hears our prayers more than hers. Last week after a long four months of waiting without much word, her daughter came home in worse condition then when she had left, unable to speak or understand, much less able to take care of herself or her family.

This is forcing Shirin to be the caregiver for her daughter's family as well as her own. Suffering from arthritis, cooking and caring for two families now (in addition to her employment during the daytime with us), staying up at night with two sickly granddaughters, and sending her unemployed husband to Kabul for medical treatment for his ear problem are the things that trouble her. I know that she is suffering the most because her daughter did not come back well.

What about her daughter's husband (who is also unemployed)? Can't he take care of his own household, or at least help watch his children? I struggle with the fact that men do not help the women at all here. No matter what the women have on their plate—cleaning, cooking, and raising the children is their sole responsibility. This is even seen as the boys and girls grow up. Boys do not help their moms and are not taught to do "house" chores. This is only for the girls.

"Mother of Ellie, you and the other foreigners are very different. Even when you have a hard day, I do not see you get angry or upset … you are very patient and loving," Shirin said. I responded: "Living in a different country from my family is difficult at times, but my hope is Jesus because He saved me." Some of us will be going to visit her at home next week because she just had a new grandson. We want to use this opportunity to pray for her daughter. I know it would be a miracle, but would you pray for healing for her daughter?

Thank you for your faithful prayers. We are so blessed to have you behind us and do feel your love and support.

Love,

Christine

The wound is the place where the Light enters you.
—Rumi

Chapter 20

A Bouquet of Flowers and a Black Eye

I slowed to stop at the new traffic light at one of Iskandar's main intersections. The Germans had decided to interrupt the organic chaos of Iskandar's major streets by installing traffic lights just a couple months before. *Ethnocentric, ignorant Germans,* I thought to myself. *Trying to import Western order into Afghanistan!* It had actually made things worse. About 70 percent of the vehicles complied with the new stoplights, allowing traffic to pick up to enough speed on the perpendicular roads so that when the 30 percent of trucks came plowing through red lights, accidents became more spectacular and hazardous to the health of those inside.

I glanced in my rearview mirror and saw an Afghan National Police (ANP) truck speeding up. I had little respect for these guys. The abduction threat had become severe in our city over the past few months, and there was no doubt in anyone's minds that the police were right in the middle of it, making money off ransom payments. They were nothing more than corrupt, armed thugs, and I knew exactly what they were going to do—run the light. Not because they were responding to an emergency but simply because they thought they were above the law. And I was going to stop them.

Afghan drivers don't stop; they swerve. When I would stop at an intersection to give the right of way to vehicles coming from other directions, the driver behind me would just swerve around me (into oncoming traffic, if there was any), and either plow into vehicles in the intersection, or, more often than not, slam on his brakes and create a traffic jam. The vehicles behind him would do the same thing, turning it into gridlock that could extend back several city blocks. So I'd sit there fuming for what seemed like an eternity while some horribly underpaid traffic cop would angrily beat on the hoods of trucks with his stick, trying to get them to back up so that he could unclog the jam. (I often thought that if I was a Hindu, I would live in perpetual fear of being reincarnated as an Afghan traffic cop—worst job on the planet.)

I had adapted my driving skills and become quite adept at positioning my truck in such situations that it made it impossible for vehicles behind me to get around me. Stopping is anathema to an Afghan. I would take sinful pleasure as I surreptitiously watched, via my side mirrors, frustration boil into rage as Afghan drivers did their best to slow to a creep without stopping, but finally came to the dreaded full stop. *That'll teach you, barbarians!*

The ANP truck driver blared his horn as he realized he was going to have to stop or crash into the rear bumper of my truck. I just glared at him through my rearview mirror. He was driving the same truck as I was, except that his Ford Ranger was purchased by American taxpayers and had a machine gun mounted in the back. As far as I was concerned, if I could stop at the light, so would he. The driver continued blaring his horn while two guys with AK-47s jumped out of the bed of the truck. One of them punched the side of my truck as he ran up to my window. "This is worth dying for," I mumbled to myself, mired from sanity by culture shock.

"Hey, *bacha*, move your truck... now!" the guy with the gun screamed at me.

"I'll move it when the light turns green!" I yelled back. *OK... turn green, light.*

He winced at the sound of my accent, just now realizing that I was a kharedji. Shooting a foreigner (who might be someone important) came with consequences, putting the odds more in my favor of surviving this encounter. Or so I hoped. The other ANP officer reached the passenger window of my truck and shook his AK-47 menacingly. The guy I was arguing with decided to up the ante, shouldering his Kalishnakov, but not quite pointing the barrel directly at me. Yet.

I raised my cell phone in the air and punched in a few numbers. I'd learned that Afghans often attributed way too much power to an American and his cell phone. They'd seen a few movies and assumed that I could call in an Apache attack helicopter within seconds. By the way I scowled and hung my thumb ominously above the last (random) number, you'd have thought I had command of a Predator drone in the skies above and was about to unleash a Hellfire missile on these poor public servants. Nuclear tipped.

The ANP cops dropped their shoulders and trudged back to their truck. The light was still red, and I was now pleading with it verbally to turn green before these guys changed their minds and filled my truck with lead. When it did, the ANP truck squealed its tires as it accelerated and swerved around me in the middle of the intersection. I glared one more time, thought about flashing them a thumbs up, but then the Holy Spirit cut in with a healthy dose of conviction. I glanced at my own eyes in the rearview mirror: *Did you really come here to force Afghans to follow your traffic rules??*

By the time I reached the gate to our office compound, I was shaking my head in remorse. "Matthew, you are an idiot!" I said out loud. *Willing to lose your life and leave behind your family to win a chest-thumping contest with some Afghans! Certainly wouldn't garnish a "well done" at heaven's gates.*

As Kaka opened the gate, I realized this wasn't the first time. Several years before, Dr. Jack and I had been invited by a Pashtun village (through Dr. Maleki as part of our community health project) to stay the night with them. They had provided us with proper tribal hospitality (protection and a good meal) but included a two-hour sermon on Islam... all in Pashto. Several times I tried to interject that we didn't speak Pashto and would need translation to understand what they were saying, but that was of no matter. It was all posturing for the other tribal leaders. Show them that they could proclaim "the straight path" to these khafir guests of theirs. As we bunked down on toshaks for the night, Dr. Maleki decided to engage in a little Afghan humor.

"We could always sell Mr. Matthew to the Taliban. He is worth $50,000 dollars."

Everyone howled with laughter in the dark, except me.

"Dr. Jack is worth $100,000," I said, in a lame attempt to share the spotlight.

Zelme had come along on this trip. He believed the invitation to be legitimate and that we would be under solid tribal protection, but in an abundance of caution he'd brought along our one-legged, former mujahed-commander/present-day office guard Ghulam just to bolster our ranks. Ghulam decided to join the jocular fray.

"Tonight, when Mr. Matthew is sleeping, I'm going to cut his head off. HAHAHAHA!"

The room had erupted in laughter, but it didn't seem funny to me trying to fall asleep there in the dark on the dirt floor in a

Pashtun village. I'd responded by telling a couple "Mullah Nasrudin" jokes (about an imaginary dumb mullah who is the favorite butt of Afghan jokes) but replaced "Mullah Nasrudin" with "Mullah Ghulam." Back at the ranch, Dr. Jack had confronted me. "I'm not sure what you were trying to achieve by going head to head with a male Afghan." He'd reminded me that the way of the cross was humility … taking the lower position. I had to listen to him because he lived his own advice. He was always making house calls, treating people with such compassion and dignity. The Afghans loved him.

I shook my head and drove through the office gate. "*Salaam Aleykum!*" Kaka roared. I greeted Kaka with less enthusiasm. I feared we would have to let him go soon. Despite repeated warnings, he continued to sell refrigerator-sized loads of unprocessed opium, doing some of his business on his cell phone while at work. He wondered what the big deal was when we confronted him, laughing it all off. Just par for the course in Afghanistan. Neither Clay, Aziz, or I wanted to fire him. We loved him and his family. Little Ellie was a regular visitor to his family during the Eid holiday, sitting happily along with his children around the dastarkhan eating nuts and sweets. Plus, firing employees in Afghanistan never ended well. Ghulam had thrown rocks at our gate and shouted threats for the good part of a morning.

I greeted Aziz, who was in the middle of a dispute with the Ministry of Public Health over funding and bags of rice (they wanted more money; we were concerned about doctors in the clinics taking bags of rice that were intended for patients). My goal was to slip upstairs into my cocoon as quickly as possible. I climbed the stairs and passed the two rooms that housed our community development teams They were vigorously discussing what to do in one village where the locals were demanding that we build them a community center or they would throw us out of their village. We had already invested six months of development work there, but I'd told the team to stick to their guns; we were not a money tree. I picked up the pace to get inside my office before I got sucked into another long, spirited discussion that would lead to no good solution.

I reached the safety of my small office, dropped my backpack on a chair, and tried to switch on the fan next to my desk. I was greeted by the smell of burnt wire. No power; the small Chinese transformer that I had left plugged in had burned out overnight in a power spike. I sat down in my desk chair, which had a slight list, and glanced over at the printer. It had been over a hundred degrees (Fahrenheit) inside my office the afternoon before, so hot that the ink cartridge had melted inside the printer. I had yet to clean it up. Ink stains blotched sheets of paper of a proposal that I had tried to print out the day before.

One friend, who had been serving in Afghanistan for most of a decade, summed up his love-hate feelings toward Afghanistan: "After working here for many years, I feel that Afghanistan has given me a bouquet of flowers with one hand, and a black eye with the other!" At the moment, I was feeling only the black eye. "I hate this place!" I muttered under my breath.

I leaned forward with my elbows on the dusty desk and pushed the palms of my hands into my eye sockets. Darkness was creeping into the recesses of my mind and my heart. *I don't know if we are making any real difference here at all. The more we give, the more people want! They don't appreciate anything we do for them at all. Instead, they accuse us of ulterior motives or of stealing money that was sent for them! I'm sick of the dependency, sick of the corruption!*

I leaned back in my chair and looked over again at the mess of an unfinished proposal covering the left side of my desk, ruined with streams of ink. *I'm sick of proposals!* I never liked office work, but the more projects we did the more time I had to spend on the computer trying to find funding or writing reports. *Maybe it's not too late for a reset.* I leaned my head back in my chair, looked up at a crack in the ceiling, and thought about options for a different career. After a few moments, I settled on becoming a floatplane pilot in

Alaska. *Plenty of adventure and natural beauty, few people to have to deal with, and no Afghans!*

I knew that Dr. Fatima, a veterinarian by training and leader of our community development team, would be walking in the door any moment to ask me if I could consider a compromise on the community center. I rehearsed my arguments. *We don't do buildings! Bad development practice and we don't have the budget for it! It would mean writing up ANOTHER proposal.* Fatima was an Afghan woman of intelligence and dignity, and I had a great deal of respect for her. But she and I had gotten into a spirited discussion a few days before about the effectiveness of women's prayers. She maintained that the Quran taught that a woman's prayer had only half the merit of a man's. "Fatima, that is wrong! God has made men and women both in His image. God does not show prejudice!" But I had been forced to drop it when I realized that (in her mind at least) I was challenging a clear teaching of Islam.

I thought about the plight of women in Afghanistan, from forced dress and demure posture in the cities to the practices of polygamy and child brides in the villages. Our city had a reputation for treating women poorly. The streets were full of lustful stares from men; it wasn't rare for vile comments to be directed toward the women as they walked through the bazaars. Many local women understandably had a chip on their shoulder against men and felt forced to cover head to toe in public for their own protection. I'd recently read about a final act of desperation and protest for some of Iskandar's women: to douse themselves with gasoline and light themselves on fire. Some of our female staff had visited the survivors at the burn hospital.

Out in the villages, things were even worse for the women. I'd asked a group of Afghan physicians once why the majority of the TB burden in their country is female. They thought it was because the village women were tasked with the dirty work, like cooking on a dirt floor using animal dung for fuel. They did the hard work, ate less meat, and gave birth to children on dirt floors. The week before

I'd been out in a village monitoring a community development project. It was sheep-shearing season and the boys were helping the men gather the sheep. It was the job of the little girls to run after the sheep and to scoop up fresh dung with their bare hands.

I let out a long exhale as I thought about the injustice of it all. I hated watching Christine put on her chawder namaz on a sweltering hot day. She did it out of love for the Afghan women she wanted to connect with, but I saw how it dehumanized her. "Someday these men will feel a great deal of shame for the way they treat women!" I fumed to the wall.

Tak! Tak! My door swung open wider from the knocking but it wasn't Dr. Fatima. It was Hassina, our office cook, who carried a metal tray with a thermos of steaming tea and two cups. It was already pushing 90 degrees in my office, and it was barely 9:00 a.m. "*Salaam Aleykum,* Mr. Matthew," Hassina chirped pleasantly in her sing-song voice. "*Khub asten? Chitor asten? Elliejan khubas?*" I returned her greetings with a clenched, plastic smile as I wiped the film of dust off a section of my desk with my desmal. She set the tray down on my desk and filled the first teacup to the brim. The second was for the next guest who would show up in my office wanting something. Hassina was always pleasant; when she did complain about the plight of women she would keep it brief and end it with a smile, saying: "Life is difficult, Mr. Matthew!" Then she would float out of the room.

I looked down at my teacup. Tea was really the saving grace in the practice of Afghan hospitality, the great equalizer, for anyone could afford to give or receive a cup of tea. It was what kept transactions relational, a necessity in a world with little law and order to depend upon. But I was in too foul a mood to smell the roses; I was nursing my black eye. I took a sip out of habit. *I hate Afghan tea! Makes no sense drinking hot tea in the dead of summer with no air conditioning!* I had likely wrecked my kidneys, drinking fifteen glasses a day, because that is what you do in Afghanistan. I spilled a few drops, which congealed together on my desk with the dust to form a small puddle of tea-mud. I drew my first initial on the desk with the tea-mud as I looked out the dusty window at a city that I was feeling bipolar toward at the moment.

The noise of horns, yelling, and general chaos floated through from a distance. I told myself that mine was a righteous anger. After all, I was upset with the oppression of women and the religious fanaticism of the place! But the deeper truth was that my anger was self-serving. I was mad at the general lawlessness of Afghan society.

Afghans have always had a fiercely independent mindset. They believe that "every man is a king" and should first pursue his own honor, opportunities, and interests. They've yet to learn that pursuing the common good will, in the end, benefit each individual. The "get all you can" mindset of a land pirate, combined with a fatalistic disregard for consequences of human decisions, created the chaos out on the street. Barrel-chested men strutted right in front of vehicles, demonstrating remarkable bravery and a lack of concern for the laws of physics.

It wasn't only the men. One day a kid ran in front of my truck. He wasn't chasing a ball or anything; he just wanted to get to the other side of the road. I slammed on the brakes and missed him by a few feet. The large incoming Kamaz truck didn't even bother. It missed him by inches. Heart palpitating, I glanced left over my shoulder to be sure I had seen correctly—that the kid was really alive—and saw a couple of men pat the kid on the back. They were all laughing. I drove to Dr. Jack's place, completely stressed, just to blow off steam. We both knew families whose children had been crushed to death on the streets of Iskandar.

For me, Afghan airports were hairline triggers for culture shock. Afghans were not accustomed to lines; it was every man for himself while going through checkpoints or boarding a plane. It distressed me to watch groups of white-clothed hajjis—just returning from

Saudi Arabia—leading the pack in shoving past women and children (including my own) to get on the plane first. I called them out on it several times: "Excuse me! Why do you men push past women and children?! I thought your religion teaches that we should protect and help the women and children!" Most of my travel experiences were exercises in anger management.

James had a better approach. He let the chaos roll off his soul like water off a duck's back. I was always convicted when I watched him navigate airports. While I was fuming during intrusive pat downs, he was smiling and making conversation with the guards. I'd be squaring up to the crush of humanity in the terminal, ready to fight the mob to claim my seat on the plane. I'd look over and he would be making friends with fellow passengers, networking. Somehow he managed to laugh off the madness of the streets.

We were lifting weights together at The Museum one afternoon. "Matt, listen to this," James said, in between sets.

"This morning I was approaching the intersection near Zayed Khan's house, when this Corolla shot through the intersection. A motorcycle plowed right into him at high speed."

We had both seen this happen plenty of times. I'd just witnessed an old man fly off the back of a motorcycle and roll over the windshield of a taxi. He instinctively tried to stand up and then went back down like a sack of potatoes. Motorcycles had slammed into our vehicles more than once. The first time it happened to me I was pulling into the gate of our office. I'd noticed a motorcycle behind me, but he must have been at least fifty yards back. I put on my blinker and made a normal right turn into the gate. Then I heard the sound of an accelerating engine, followed by squealing brakes and a serious skid, and glanced right just in time to see and hear an airborne body fly into the side of the Big Land Cruiser like a rag doll. The guy thought he could pass me on the right, somehow squeezing in between my front bumper and the gate! Miraculously, he jumped up, ran around to my door, and instinctively raised his fists to fight. When he realized that I was a foreigner, he lowered his fists and suddenly his neck and back began to hurt. The crowd that soon encircled me decided that the accident had been my fault until I settled it with a five hundred afghani bill (about $10 USD). James had better motorcycle-collision stories, which he could tell with a hearty laugh.

"Well, here is what happened, Matt. This guy is lying on the asphalt, hurting big time, when three guys jump out of the Corolla and start beating on him. They whaled on him for a while until they realized that he was seriously injured. Then they picked him up, stuffed him in their Corolla, and drove him to the hospital!" James laughed. "Will you get that?!"

I pushed the barbell off my chest, not sure whether to laugh or to cry.

It wasn't just out on the street. Culture shock penetrated my office and work. Afghans felt that if the law inconvenienced you, you followed it only if you had no other choice. The nature of much of our work—medicine, education, water projects—required precision. There wasn't much precision in Afghanistan where people were resourceful but used to "winging it." When combined with the intrinsic optimistic spirit that "it will all work out," many details were left undone and numbers fudged in reports. A particularly careful eye had to be kept on the finances. Plagiarism was common at the university, bribery a key ingredient of government bureaucracy, and taxation a new and mostly unenforceable concept. In his novel *The Kite Runner*, Afghan-American Khalid Husseini explained that "Afghans cherish custom but abhor rules."[6]

This was getting in the way of *my* chi; violating *my* cultural values in the areas of truth, justice, and the American way ... how stuff should be done! I realized that I—Matthew Collins, cross-cultural expert and professor of anthropology (at an Afghan university)—was

---

6 Kahlid Husseini, *The Kite Runner* (New York: Riverhead Books, 2003), p. 45.

ethnocentric. Despite my efforts to follow my own advice on cross-ing cultures and adjusting my cultural expectations, I hadn't shaken my belief that the Afghans should follow my concepts of law and order. Yes, I was ethnocentric and I was plenty ticked off.

I looked down at my tea-mud initial on my desk, quickly evap-orating in the dry heat. *Road raging with a technical! Not too bright.* "You've become an angry man, Matthew," I said to the desk. "You may hide it well most of the time, but it burns under the surface."

In many ways, I had become more Afghan during my three years in Iskandar. Much more aggressive. And angry. Or, perhaps, the anger had been in there all along, carefully managed by my con-trolled environment. But when culture shock shook things up the anger boiled over. My brother-in-law, Douglas, called culture shock "alternative sanctification," whatever that meant exactly. I consid-ered the irony: here I had endeavored to see things through Afghan lenses so that I could make a real difference in people's lives. I tried to become more Afghan. But this Afghan anger was now keeping me from making a difference in Afghanistan. *I hope I'm doing more good here than harm.* I could feel my heart beating faster, my pulse quickening. *I feel like I might explode. Maybe I should get some help?*

"What is wrong with you, Matthew?" I asked my initial, barely discernible on the desk.

Clay stuck his head in my office. *Did he hear me talking to myself?*

"Morning, Matthew. Just wanted to let you know that Aziz and I are taking Mr. Ferooz to get some new eyeglasses. Should only take about an hour."

My first thought was: *What a waste of time! We have an NGO to run here. Don't you have more important things to tend to, like the stinking report for the Ministry of Economy?*

"Sounds good," I said. "Hope you find him some cool glasses."

Clay closed the door behind him as he left. A few weeks before we'd been in here trying to figure out how on earth we could conform our reporting of project spending to the new rules the Afghan Ministry of

Economy were imposing on us. They wanted everything now reported according to their Islamic lunar calendar. But our accounting system and project cycles—like the rest of the world—were all set up according to the Gregorian calendar. Our donors required it.

"Clay, this is just their next step in trying to fleece us. They put on the squeeze, hoping to find some discrepancy they can use as a pretext to steal money." The MOE had already told us that our project vehicles and capital assets really belonged to them. Their view was that anything that had been donated to help Afghanistan by the international community belonged to the Afghan government. As soon as the project ended we'd have to turn them over. Our donors begged to differ. "You think the other NGOs will comply with this, Clay?"

"They don't really have a choice," Clay replied. "Neither do we. It's their country. They are the government."

I'd fumed about corruption, ingratitude, and biting the hands that feed you.

Clay had looked at me and said: "You know, Matthew, Susan and I were talking last night and we are a little concerned for you. You seem pretty stressed."

"Clay, I'm fine."

He'd persisted. "You don't really get out as much these days, either in Iskandar or out in the villages. It seems like you are always working here at the office."

I'd been defensive. Where was I supposed to go? None of us could walk around the city anymore due to the elevated abduction threats. The day I'd taken away the women's freedom to walk (they already couldn't drive) I'd parked the motorcycle in one of The Museum's side rooms. I hated computer work but expanding our projects only added to the administrative load. But Clay was right and I knew it. The office had become my cocoon, my place to withdraw from Afghan culture. A clear sign of culture shock.

"Matthew, you need to get out and smell the roses some. Go hang out at the fort or take Ellie to the blue glass shop," he had said.

I looked up at my map by the door of our region of Afghanistan, full of pins marking villages where we were doing projects. I was so focused on the big picture that I was finally able to drive past lame beggars sitting in the dirt on my way to the office without feeling the pangs of guilt. But Clay still cared for each individual person. A few months before, we had flown one of our project staff in Bahesht down to Iskandar due a medical emergency. This guy had been fleecing our NGO—cooking books and extensively using his assigned project vehicle for personal use—but he was so slick I couldn't find a smoking gun. I'd reluctantly agreed to fly him down to have his heart palpitations checked out. When he'd arrived at the office, Clay had put his arm around him and prayed for healing in the name of Jesus. About a year later I learned that at that very moment, he felt "electricity" come from Clay's hand and his heart was healed.

I knew he had days of culture shock, but Clay—like James and Dr. Jack—loved Afghans. And they loved him. The more I thought about Clay caring about the little things, like Mr. Ferooz's glasses, the more clearly I saw grace piercing the darkness. And I saw my hero Jesus.

Now *there* was an extreme culture-crosser! He left the glory of heaven to live with us on our speck of dust planet. And to be abused by the people He came to teach, love, and save. Talk about culture shock. Verses that St. Paul wrote to new Christians in a city called Philippi came to mind:

> Have this mind among yourselves, which is yours in Christ Jesus, who, though he was in the form of God, did not count equality with God a thing to be grasped, but made himself nothing, taking the form of a servant, being born in the likeness of men. And being found in human form, he humbled himself by becoming obedient to the point of death, even death on a cross. (Philippians 2:5–8, ESV)

I looked down at my desk. My own initial drawn with the tea mud had evaporated, leaving a slightly discernible trace on the dusty desktop. Without really thinking about its significance, I traced a cross in the dust in its place.

Now, there is a contested symbol! The Muslims looked at the cross and saw Western imperialism, heresy, or their own eschatological prophesies of Jesus returning to break the cross and unify the world under Islam. The Europeans looked at the cross as a piece of their own history, for many something restrictive or even oppressive that they've evolved beyond. If they really thought about the cross, my fellow Americans might resent its implications regarding the pursuit of power and prosperity, or simply shrug and syncretize it with naturalistic materialism. Or they might just wear it around their neck as a cool piece of jewelry. I looked at the cross in the dust on my desk and saw my only hope. Jesus. My Savior.

But I also saw my own depravity. *God, I am a hypocrite!* I was mad at corrupt Afghans, but there was corruption and self-serving in my own heart. I talked about making a difference while resenting the people I had come to serve. I wanted altruism without sacrifice, the kind that makes you feel good about yourself and look good to others, where you don't have to give up much. I liked helping others on my own terms with no personal suffering. Afghanistan wasn't going to give that to me.

But Jesus showed us costly grace, the kind that hurts. He loved His enemies and taught me to do the same. He crossed cultures all right, contextualizing His message of the kingdom into stories about shepherds and farmers. He demonstrated grace, touching lepers and healing blind people. Then He sacrificed Himself for the sins of the world on the cross. Not just for the world. But for me. For my sins. I whispered the words in my office in Iskandar that St. Paul had written to believers in Rome. "But God shows his love for us in that while we were still sinners, Christ died for us" (Romans 5:8, ESV). I wasn't worthy of His love, but love me He did. I teared up at the thought.

I traced the cross again in the dust, bigger this time. I whispered to myself: "The answer is love!" People saw me as a man of faith. I tried to keep my stuff together, but fear and sometimes doubt crept in underneath, chipping away at the foundations of my faith. I'd started asking God why He allowed so much evil in Afghanistan. I believed He was sovereign and loving but that was difficult to square with all the suffering that I saw. I knew suffering was tied to the sinful actions of mankind—those cause and effect relationships were easy to trace—but couldn't God have set the whole thing up better or intervene by changing wicked men's hearts? Stopping their oppression? Why didn't He? I knew He did, but why didn't He do it more? Why allow a place like Afghanistan, where the strong oppress the weak, to exist?

St. Augustine found the answer in God's love.[7] Sure God could have given human breath to clay puppets or robots, but He desired a relationship of love with His creatures that necessitated human wills that could reject Him and do evil. At the cross, God not only redeemed sinful humans, He entered into our experience and suffered with us. Through faith I had been given the ultimate prize: a relationship with Him. And He had called me to be His hands and feet of healing in this broken world.

I sat before the cross and wept. I was unworthy: a fearful and angry sinner but forgiven. Righteous in God's eyes because of Christ's death and resurrection.[8] I prayed through my tears. *God,*

---

7   To investigate St. Augustine of Hippo's complete theodicy (answer to the problem of evil), read his *Confessions*, translated by John K. Ryan, New York: Image Books, 1960. Deitrich Bonhoffer and C.S. Lewis also wrote much on the subject: Dietrich Bonhoeffer, *Creation and Fall: A Theological Exposition of Genesis 1–3*, Translated by Douglas Stephen Bax (Minneapolis: Fortress Press, 1997), and C.S. Lewis, *The Problem of Pain, 1940 Signature Classics Ed.*, (HarperCollins Publishers: London, 2002). God be with you on your quest!

8   "For our sake he made him to be sin who knew no sin, so that in him we might become the righteousness of God" (2 Corinthians 5:21, ESV).

help me to love Afghans. To love them as you do. To see them through Your eyes. To follow after Christ by serving them with humility. Help me to die to self so that I can truly overcome culture shock. Through the power of the cross.

⌢

A few days later I took four-year-old Ellie to the blue glass shop to buy a present for one of her friends. Ellie walked in wearing a beautiful blue dress, her purse slung over her shoulder like a little fashionista. The owner—my friend Sultan Ahmed—was beside himself to win her affection. He took her by the hand to view his finest blue glass and asked her to pick out a specimen. She chose a small goblet. When she pulled out her savings of twenty-three afghanis, he refused to take even one. He painstakingly wrapped up her little goblet in newspaper and then invited me to have some tea. When Ellie piped up and asked me if she could have some, too, he wouldn't allow me to say no.

Sultan Ahmed then unwrapped her little goblet, cleaned it with his tunic, and poured her a little cup of tea. While we waited for it to cool, Ellie noticed a small container of Iskandari rock candy. She asked me if she could have some. Sultan said yes. I told her she could have a small piece; he handed her a huge slab of candy. Ellie then asked if the tea had sugar in it. I told her to drink the tea Afghan-style (with a small piece of candy in her mouth to sweeten the tea), but Sultan proudly held up a large jar of sugar that he kept for situations like this. He asked Ellie to come sit next to him and then grabbed a *dutar* (the Afghan version of a guitar) and proceeded to play for her. Ellie sat next to Sultan Ahmed happily sipping her tea, while this 65-year-old Afghan man serenaded her with all of his might. Before we left, he produced a small silver necklace and, with shaky hands, fastened it around her neck.

As we drove back home to The Museum I noticed an old man gently helping his elderly wife across the street. I glanced into several shops and saw boys assisting their fathers, carefully counting out change for their customers and solemnly producing the purchased goods. *How about that?* I mused. *In America, ten-year-olds complain about not having the latest PlayStation!* A group of kids engaged in a spirited kite battle on a street corner. Just before we turned into our *kutche*, I saw something that you don't see every day on the streets of Iskandar: a father teaching his son to ride a bike.

I sensed God's grace sweeping into my heart, renewing in me a love for these people. I could start to smell the roses again. Love is a wonderful feeling. But ultimately it is a choice that we make. A commitment. And it covers a multitude of sins.

Top Right, a beautiful village girl helping with the sheep. Top Left, a neighbor-hood burqa shop in Iskandar city. Bottom, Matthew enjoying an early spring day in the village.

Part VI

Love

Dear Family and Friends,

I find it's an encouragement to stop and relect on the high-lights when the drudgery of the day in and day out of life takes over. Since you encourage me so faithfully, I wanted to let you know what these things are.

Parties for Afghan women here are all the same ... loud music, dancing (of course there are no men around!),lots of tea and candy, and pretty much sitting for hours. There is not the concept of including a program in a wedding or engage-ment party (again only for women). So I was a little nervous when I decided to invite our Afghan friends to a bridal shower I hosted for Catherine, who will be returning to America soon to get married. We made it very clear to everyone that this was going to be an "American party," but we still had the green and black tea (instead of punch), and all the desserts, nuts, and candy dishes set on carpets outside. (Buffet style does not work well as Afghans are not used to that.) There were almost thirty ladies in attendance, the majority being our Afghan friends. To start, we had a lively game with teams making their "bride" a dress out of toilet paper, which I can guarantee none of them had played before. They all loved it. We then had a time of sharing with Catherine. The married foreigners among the group gave advice to the bride-to-be and some of the Afghans encouraged her by sharing special memories and what they appreciated about her.

Even though we always miss our home country especially around the holidays, the real meaning of the celebration is clearer because there is no distraction by commercialism. This Easter we joined some other Christian foreigners (who are working for various NGOs in Iskandar) and went outside the city to the top of a hillside. Overlooking other hills, barely green with small blades of grass, we held a morning Easter service. In the distance shepherds tended their flocks of sheep. After a picnic lunch we returned home feeling much of the Easter joy in a land that looks very much like the land of Jesus in His day, but where virtually no one has ever heard of this holiday. Later that afternoon we had some friends over, and Ellie and Kurt proceeded on an egg and candy hunt in our lovely front courtyard.

After almost two years of what feels like "little nothings" (many visits, tea, small talk), I feel like my friendship reached a new level of trust with my best Afghan friend (my next-door neighbor). While Matthew was at an evening wedding with her husband, Ellie, Kurt, and I had dinner with her. She cried for most of the evening, sharing with me a burden that had been on her heart for a long time. I felt very inadequate with advice but assured her of my love and prayers. It burdens my heart to see her suffering, but I am thankful that she values our friendship enough to be vulnerable with me.

May God bless you in all your activities this week, but pause to reflect upon the highlights that He brings into your lives!

With Love,
Christine

Twenty years from now you will be more disappointed by the things that
you didn't do than by the ones you did do. So throw off the bowlines.
Sail away from safe harbor. Catch the trade winds in your sails.
Explore. Dream. Discover.
—Mark Twain

Chapter 21

Happy Fourth of July from Afghanistan!

July 4, 2007

This month marked the third anniversary of our lives in Afghanistan. Living in a very different country on the other side of the world made us more thankful for our own country, so we decided to pull out the stops and have a proper Fourth of July celebration.

We invited all of our American friends in Iskandar to The Museum to celebrate our nation's birthday. Christine made it known that in order to prepare, we needed as much patriotic paraphernalia as could be found to decorate the place; she amassed a stockpile from the Americans in town. We decided to make the focal point of our celebration outside in our front courtyard. Despite strong cultural Afghan norms against looking into a neighbor's courtyard, some of the women in the houses around us just couldn't help themselves when something exciting took place at our house. As we began preparations, I noticed several pairs of eyes peeking out from neighboring second-story windows and even the top of a roof. *Tonight, we will give them an eyeful!*

I proudly hung two, six-foot American flags from The Museum's front porch, and—American tunes playing from strategically placed speakers—got to work with all the other decorations.

Meanwhile, a nervous Fazl Ahmad stoked a large fire on a grill that we had borrowed for the occasion, unsure of what foolishness we had planned for the evening and likely worried about any consequences. Christine had given food assignments to all of our guests, and by the time they started arriving I was cooking up marinated chicken on the grill. We were quickly becoming the talk of the neighborhood, but for once we didn't mind. Musicians ranging from the Beach Boys to Alan Jackson belted out songs reminding us of home. I turned the music up.

By the time all of our guests had arrived more than thirty Americans sat on blankets on our lawn enjoying potato salad, grilled chicken, apple pie, and other foods you don't find in Afghanistan every day. Fazl Ahmad was in a state of minor shock over the sin all around him: women with their heads uncovered, sitting next to men, even talking and laughing with them! He retreated into the safety of his guard shack. Eventually I went over and let him go home early.

It was a good thing that I did, being that after dinner Tiffany got us all going with three-legged races, egg tosses, and other games. Catherine won the squatting contest; she had a lot of practice from all her time in Afghan villages. It didn't take long for the water balloon toss to devolve into a free-for-all water balloon fight. (At this point, more than a few voyeuristic, wide-eyed neighbors were starting to think that the mullahs might just be correct in warning them of the sinful wiles of the West.) Children joined in the fun with their own relay races, and for a couple of hours we all forgot that we were so very far away from home.

After dark the sparklers came out. It had been three months since the last drop of rain had fallen and I was a little concerned that we might end up burning down the neighborhood. *Wouldn't that be a legacy? American burns down ancient city of Iskandar during night of debauchery!*

Before long I joined the fray. Ellie and Kurt had the time of their lives, tearing through the courtyard with sparklers. One guest pulled me aside and showed me a couple of Roman candles.

"Where did you get those?" I asked with surprise. I had never seen fireworks in Afghanistan.

"Joseph gave them to us this afternoon. He wished us a happy Fourth and told us he hoped we had a good time at the party tonight."

About a year earlier rumors started flying around Iskandar that an Afghan named Joseph was going to open up a small store selling mostly foreign goods. I didn't believe it at first, but when his store opened I walked in and saw a thick, mid-40s Afghan man sporting a beard and dressed in traditional shalwar kamis.

I put my hand over my heart and said, *"Salaam Aleykum."*

"Hey man, what's up?" he replied, sounding a little bit like a gangster from LA.

"You speak good English," I replied, surprised by the accent.

"Yeah, man, I lived in the Bay area for 15 years. Sure do miss McDonald's and watching NFL. Who do you think is going to win the Super Bowl this year?"

The Europeans in town called him California Joe. The contents of Joseph's store were as impressive as his use of American slang:

he had Gatorade, Dr Pepper, cereal, Pringles, Spanish olives, mozzarella cheese, and oatmeal lining his shelves, much of which must have "fallen off a truck" while headed to an American base. I read somewhere that the US government spent $12 to produce, package, and ship one MRE to Afghanistan. Joseph sold them for a buck a piece. He changed our lives and waistlines in Iskandar.

But now I experienced a pang of guilt. *Shoot! Slipped my mind to invite Joseph!* He was very much an Afghan but also an American citizen.

"Do you think we could shoot one off?" my intrepid friend persisted.

Fireworks are not a good idea in Afghanistan. For starters, everything is bone dry in July. It wouldn't take much for a couple of numb-brained foreigners to burn down part of the city, something that would be spoken of for generations. It also was not really conducive toward trying to maintain low-visibility, something we normally did as an important security protocol. Thirty Americans in one compound in Afghanistan, loudly enjoying themselves, already wasn't the brightest idea; shooting off fireworks might qualify us for entry into the Darwin Awards should the evening turn tragic. Russian helicopters used to flee from the Roman candles fired by mujahedeen, thinking that they were Stinger missiles. How might an armed Predator drone, piloted by some guy in a dark building in Arizona, respond to this strange heat signature?

"We are going to need some sand and water," I replied.

A group of Americans never enjoyed a singular Roman candle so much. I was rewarded with "ooohs" and "aaahs" worthy of a professional fireworks display.

"Daddy, it's beautiful!" Ellie exclaimed.

"Matthew, is this a good idea?" Christine whispered in my ear.

"Uh...No!" I responded.

I winced at each shot, half expecting my roof to catch fire any moment or a Hellfire missile to come streaking down from the dark skies above. The little balls of fire flew much higher than I remembered. I counted them down in my mind, but after ten shots they kept firing even higher. *What kind of Roman candle does Joseph have here? Bad idea, Matt!*

"That's it!" I exclaimed as soon as I was convinced the tube was empty. "Nothing more to see here…move back to the front yard, everyone!" I hadn't noticed any fires yet but was expecting to hear rightfully angry neighbors banging on my gate at any moment.

The knocking came about five minutes later. I hurried to the gate before any of our guests could get there, took a deep breath, and opened it. Instead of an incensed, barrel-chested neighbor, a thin young man on a bicycle greeted me with extensive salutations. Then he sheepishly asked if Dr. Jack was around. The very Joseph that I had forgotten to invite required his services and it was most important!

Dr. Jack was alarmed by this news. Earlier that day he had made a house call for two of Joseph's sick children. Jack looked at me. "This could be bad. His son was really sick. He might have gone downhill!" Jack's vehicle was blocked in so he set off on foot, never a safe prospect in Afghanistan. "I've got to run. This is an emergency!" he called out over his shoulder.

Twenty minutes later, an out-of-breath Dr. Jack returned to our compound. He was carrying an armload of Roman candles.

"What happened? Are Joseph's kids OK?" I asked.

"Yeah, they are fine," he responded. "Joseph saw our little fireworks display and wanted to give us these."

My cell phone rang. "Salaam. Hello?"

"Matthew!" Strong German accent. "Zhis is Bernhard."

"Hi, Bernhard." My German friend.

"Iz Dr. Jack doing OK?"

"Yeah, sure! He is actually right here with me now at my place."

"OK." Bernhard sounded relieved. "I zvas just driving by and svought I saw him running through the shadows along the road! Which would be svery dangerous!"

"Uh, well, he is here right now, and everything is fine. Thank you."

"Huh! Maybe it zvas just my imagination!"

We Americans are a unique breed. And a blessed group of people. We grew to love our Afghan friends, neighbors, and colleagues. But living abroad helped us better understand what a privilege it is to call *the Land of the Free and the Home of the Brave* "home."

⌒

Several months later, my family was enjoying dinner at a restaurant on the top floor of Iskandar's tallest building. I got a call from Dr. Jack. He wanted me to go up on the roof and look in the direction of his house.

Ellie and I climbed the stairs to the roof. "Look, Daddy, it's beautiful!" a giddy Ellie exclaimed. At that moment from his rooftop, Dr. Jack put on a fireworks show for us and the rest of the skyward gazing city of Iskandar.

Happy Fourth of July from Afghanistan! The Collins family hosted a July 4 party for the American community in Iskandar.

So now faith, hope, and love abide, these three;
but the greatest of these is love.
1 Corinthians 13:3

Chapter 22

A Kite fluttered in the Breeze

November 5, 2007, 7:30 a.m.

It had been three years, three months, and ten days since Christine, Ellie, and I arrived in Afghanistan as a family to begin our new lives. Kurt turned two the day before; in a few minutes we would begin a long trip back to America. It was time to take a break from Afghanistan for a while and to spend some time with our families. Yesterday we had said goodbye to our team, local colleagues and friends. Bags were packed; we were ready to go. I walked around the courtyard of The Museum, pondering our time in this place. I sat down on a stone bench that I had built under an almond tree.

God, You have been faithful. All my fears about something happening to Ellie and not a hair on her head was harmed! Thank you! Indeed, Christine and I were so pleased at the sweet, adventurous child Ellie was growing up to be. She was so alive! *And you have blessed us with a son!*

I thought about our time in Afghanistan. Several questions came to mind. Had the benefits of our lives and work here outweighed the hardships, the greatest being the distance from our family and loved ones? Had we really made an impact on the lives of the people we came to serve? If something happened that prevented us from returning, would the work we had begun continue, or would it effectively die the day that my team pulled out? The bottom line question I was asking myself was: *Are we really making a difference here?*

A variety of answers came to mind, not all of which I liked.

Would our dedicated Afghan staff of health workers, teachers, and community development specialists be able to keep all of the humanitarian work going if we left and the funds dried up? Hundreds of Afghan community health workers had been trained in the districts, and village life had dramatically improved in some places, but most of our projects had not reached the level of self-sustainability that I would have liked. We had trained thousands of Afghans in subjects ranging from literacy to birthing skills, computers to cultural anthropology, but how many of them would go on to make a real difference in the future of their own country?

I wondered if all of the foreign NGOs pulled out of Afghanistan tomorrow, would the country really be better off than it was six years ago? Or would it simply implode? If the international community suddenly vanished from Afghanistan, could the country stand on its own, or would the Taliban move right back in and victimize our neighbors and friends?

Are we really making a difference? I asked myself again. I looked up at the peaceful morning sky and watched a solitary kite flutter in the cool breeze. It seemed to whisper: "There is still hope in this land."

I saw the face of Fariba, a bright twelve-year-old girl who had been cured of TB. I thought of the many young women like her, once sentenced to death by this cruel disease but now given a new lease on life through the careful application of modern medicine in their own villages. I remembered the smiles on the faces of dozens of orphans as they played on the playground that Rustin built for them next to Iskandar's orphanage. The look of hope on a creased face as an old man carried a fifty-pound sack of rice on his back to his hungry family at home. I smiled at the thought of village school-children sitting cross-legged on carpeted floors (instead of in mud). And the pride of the village elder as he gave me a tour of the newly constructed kitchens that families in his village had built.

I pictured the tears of relief on a young father's face after Dr. Nurgul had saved his baby's life at Iskandar Hospital's NICU. And the glimmer of pride in the eyes of young professionals in Bahesht as they received their certificates of completion for a course we taught them in leadership development. I remembered the dignity and poise of the young women at the university as they wrote papers about their ideas and dreams for the future.

I thought of Rauf, an orderly at the hospital in Bahesht who enrolled in our English and computer classes at the very beginning of our work in his town. After a year, he was designing spreadsheets that I could barely keep up with. A master at logistics, he was now running our community health program in Bahesht. His future seemed bright. A difference had certainly been made in his life.

I considered our personal sacrifices and realized that they paled in comparison to the deep, inner fulfillment that comes from a life of service and purpose. I thought of the team that had become family. I respected and loved each one of them; these were friend-ships that would transcend this lifetime. I thought of my incred-ible wife, Christine, whose quiet strength and faith helped me to never give up.

I realized I wasn't the same man I had been when I came to this country three years before. The fires of culture shock had revealed much to me about my own personal weaknesses, especially my sins of fear and anger. I had learned to overcome through my *faith* in Jesus. As a family, we had learned the value of *endurance*. And above all, the eternal truth: *love* covers a multitude of sins.

Clay's horn honked on the other side of the gate. Suddenly I realized that it wasn't just about making a difference; it was about loving these people. *I do love this place! I love these people! We are coming back!* I embraced Fazl Ahmad and loaded up the family in Clay's truck. I looked back at The Museum and bid her farewell as Fazl Ahmad closed the gate. *Thank you for keeping us. I hope to see you again!*

Top, taking food to internally displaced people in Bahesht. Bottom, modes of transportion.

Top, Ellie and Kurt with a furry friend in early spring. Bottom, the Collins family enjoying a summer morning in The Museum's back garden.

Author's Note

This book has been years in the making, but it would never have seen print without the help of some special people: I'd like to thank Gwyn for the enduring encouragement to publish this, giving up precious hours of sleep during his deployment in Afghanistan to read chapter after chapter, assuring me that if this story makes it to print, others will follow. Catherine, Tiffany, and Bob, thank you for reading through the manuscript and providing helpful feedback, and Jana, thanks for the beautiful cover. Special gratitude is due to my editor, Sheryl Martin Hash, for not only turning my writing into something readable but going up and beyond to include all the photos. I'm grateful to Janet Grant, my agent at Books and Such, for believing in this project early on and investing the time in a new author. And Virginia Smith, thank you for your help in shepherding this project to completion. Even though she lived it, my incredible wife Christine never tired of reading this manuscript and making helpful suggestions (and keeping the Texan from stretching the fish too much). Sweetheart, you are the wind beneath my wings.

My team in Afghanistan owns my highest respect, gratitude, and love. They risked their lives to serve (and some continue to do so) the poorest of the poor without any thought of human recognition. To help protect them, along with brave Afghan aid workers we served alongside, I've changed the names of almost all people, including myself and my family, and most locations (with the exception of places I visited early on, like Faizabad and Mazar, as well as

Kabul) within the book. I've written about some of my teammates in this book; it was an honor to serve with all of them. They demonstrated God's grace through their lives ... my hope is that as a result, others will be inspired to make a difference with theirs.

A number of donors, government and private, supported our humanitarian projects, but one that stood above the rest is Baptist Global Response. As such, the majority of proceeds from this book will support the humanitarian efforts of BGR in disaster response and community development around the world. To learn more about BGR's excellent work, visit their website at: www.gobgr.org.

Ultimately, my prayer is that this book points glory towards the One to whom it is due ... my Lord, Savior, and Hero, Jesus Christ. Thank you for taking care of my family in Afghanistan.

Made in the USA
Columbia, SC
30 October 2017